IMAGES
of America

THE NORTHERN LITCHFIELD HILLS

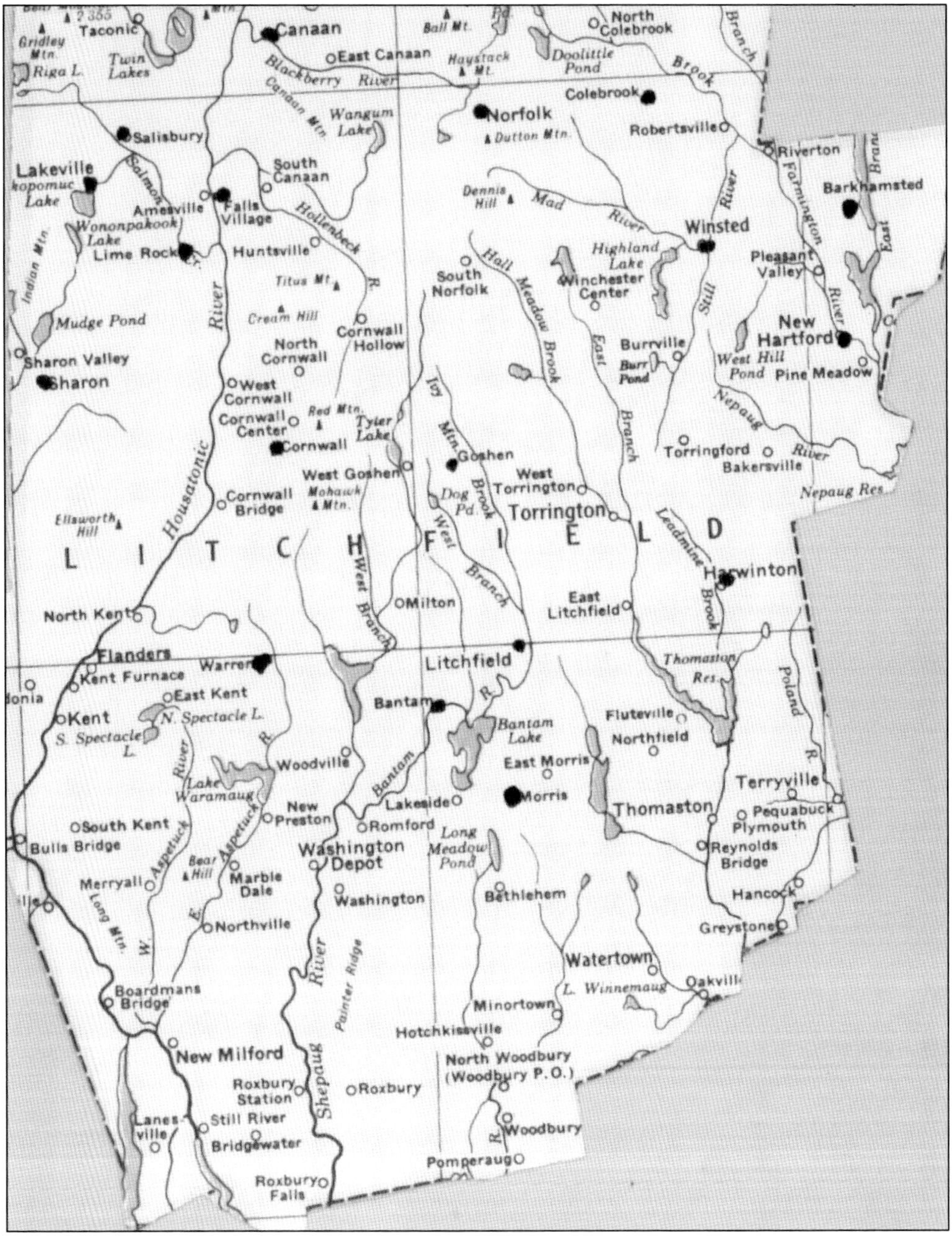

This map represents the area of the Litchfield Hills that the author has attempted to represent in this book. Not all areas are equally represented, although it is recognized that each community has its own historical significance and value.

IMAGES
of America

THE NORTHERN LITCHFIELD HILLS

Betsy McDermott Fecto

ARCADIA
PUBLISHING

ISBN 978-0-7385-8953-4

Published by Arcadia Publishing
Charleston, South Carolina

Printed in the United States of America

For all general information contact Arcadia Publishing at:
Telephone 843-853-2070
Fax 843-853-0044
E-mail sales@arcadiapublishing.com
For customer service and orders:
Toll-Free 1-888-313-2665

Visit us on the Internet at www.arcadiapublishing.com

I dedicate this book to my daughter, Sarah.
May she, too, realize her dreams.

Contents

YEAR	Torrington	Litchfield	Harwinton	Goshen	Winchester	N.Hartford
1790	-	-	1367	-	-	-
1800	1417	4285	1481	1493	1371	1753
1810	1449	4610	1718	1641	1466	1507
1820	1651	4456	1500	1586	1601	1685
1840	1707	4038	1516	1734	1766	1766
1850	1916	3953	1201	1529	1667	1703
1860	2278	3200	1175	1457	2179	2758
1870	2893	3113	1044	1381	3513	3078
1880	3327	3410	1044	1223	4096	3302
1890	6048	3304	1016	1093	5142	3160
1900	12453	3214	943	972	6183	3424
1910	16840	3005	835	835	7763	2144
1920	22055	3180	1213	675	8679	1781
1930	26040	3574	1440	675	9019	1834
1940	26986	4029	2020	683	8674	1836
1950	27820	4964	949	778	8482	2395
1960	30045	6246	1288	1288	10469	3033

Note the gradual but steady decline in the population of the Litchfield area between 1820 and 1870, and the many fluctuations in the population of the Litchfield Hills area throughout the years. One could speculate as to the cause(s) of these shifts. Did farms suffer from droughts? Businesses collapse? Were areas impacted by the Industrial Revolution or other economic issues? There were natural disasters: hurricanes (1938) and floods (1955), as well as other disasters, took many lives. Were some of the more "mysterious" reductions or gains in population due to epidemics, widespread "witchery," or supernatural occurrences? Did war impact the fluctuations of population? Some possible answers and explanations lie between the pages of this book. Perhaps you will come up with your own theory by the end.

Introduction

The Litchfield Hills occupy the northwestern corner of the state of Connecticut. Ironically, this region is often referred to as the "unspoiled" portion of Connecticut because of its rolling hills, acres of farmland, quaint historic villages, and panoramic views. In actuality, during the eighteenth century, the Litchfield Hills area was, like much of New England, quite industrial. The hillsides, now green, were stripped bare of trees. The Mast Swamp area (of what is now considered Torrington) once had an abundance of tall pines, but they were cut down during the early years of the settlement to build masts for ships.

The settlement of Litchfield began in 1719, and it was formally established as a town in 1721. As early as the 1730s, smoke from the furnaces and forges, particularly in the Salisbury area, polluted the air. Kent, and other areas rich in iron ore deposits, began to manufacture such items as nails, cooking pots, and firearms.

In 1751, Litchfield became known as the "county seat." The years between 1784 and 1834 were termed the "golden age" of Litchfield. It was viewed as an active and growing urban center, and local merchants made a fortune in trade with China.

In 1872, when Litchfield became accessible by railroad, it became known as a summer resort. Between the years of 1876 and 1916, many homes were remodeled from the Victorian style to the Colonial style. In 1915, which became known as the Colonial Revival era, sidewalks were made, garbage collection was arranged on a regular basis, and a clock was placed in the courthouse tower.

During this same time period, Litchfield continued to have the smells and noise of a manufacturing town. At one time there were eighteen running saw, grain, and paper mills, as well as forges, manufacturers of hardware, and tanneries. In fact, Litchfield was renowned for its books and shoes.

As the mills began to shut down, people invested in farm land. One of the more notable farms that has existed for decades was, until quite recently, owned the Webster family. Known as Arethusa Farm, it was bought from the Webster family by the Guernseys. The Websters are direct descendants of Noah Webster.

Many interesting and significant people have connections to the communities in the Litchfield Hills area. Torrington was the birthplace of John Brown, an abolitionist who planned a slave revolt. He and his followers captured a government arsenal at Harper's Ferry in Virginia, and waited to be joined by slaves. To Brown's demise, no slaves arrived; he and his supporters were captured and Brown was hung for murder and treason. Though considered a hero by some, others scorn his actions. Ethan Allen, born in Litchfield, was a revolutionary leader of the Green Mountain Boys. Winsted introduced William L. Gilbert, a famous clockmaker. Picturesque Sharon flourished as a manufacturing center during the eighteenth century, thanks in part to inventors Benjamin and Andrew Hotchkiss, who designed exploding shells and machine guns, among other arms. Salisbury sent many of its men off to wars, and several became renowned war heroes. Other prominent citizens of the area include Benjamin Tallmadge, Judge Tapping Reeve, and members of the Beecher family. The first law school in the nation was opened here, and graduates of that school include two vice-presidents, seventeen U.S. Senators, and three justices of the Supreme Court. The list of prominent citizens, events, and landmarks is remarkably long and shows how much the Litchfield Hills area has contributed, and continues to contribute, to the maintenance and flavor of New England.

There are also many who did not make the history books but who played a significant part in the area's history. Some of the unsung heroes of more recent times include war veterans such as "Pete" Radocy, who saved a battleship (and perhaps two) during World War II. Frank Treadway, along with many others, is credited with saving lives during the Flood of 1955. There are families who maintained family-owned businesses during times when small businesses struggled for survival. Musicians, artists, poets . . . they all have played a part in the life of the area. It takes a great sense of pride and loyalty to maintain the Yankee spirit and values in modern day life. The Litchfield Hills area, in many respects, has succeeded in doing so. There are so many to be proud of, so many to be commemorated, so many to receive acknowledgment for their contributions, no matter how small they may seem to some. This book is an effort to bring forth a sense of unity among the residents of the Litchfield Hills—the legendary and the ordinary.

One

A Time for Birth, A Time for Death

"Mr. Sperry and his son, Egbert traveled from their home in what was then known as Wolcottville to New York by train. While there, Mr. Sperry decided that he would purchase a load of watermelons. He asked that young Egbert travel in the baggage car to keep watch over the melons. Just before the train reached the Thomaston Railroad Station, the train met with a washout and only the baggage car, with young Egbert in it, went into the water. Egbert was drowned while no other car on the train or individual was harmed."

(From Memories of Wolcottville by Charles Johnson, with the permission of the Torrington Historical Society.)

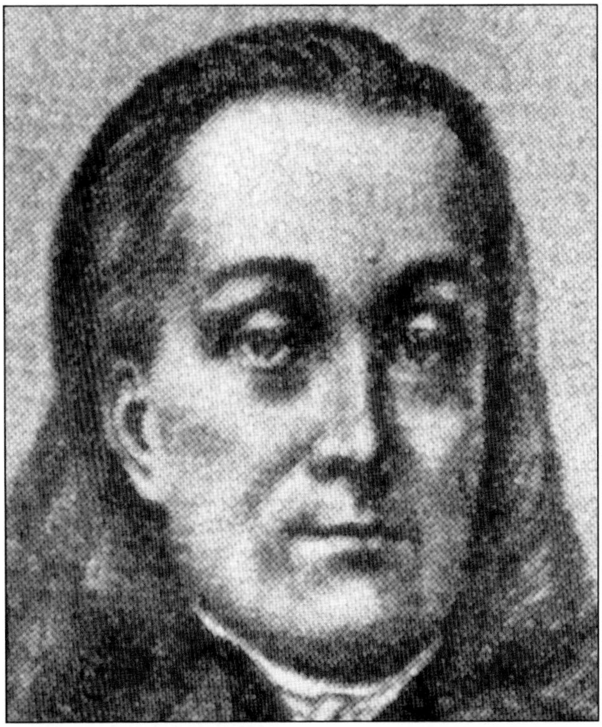

Judge Tapping Reeve established the first law school in the U.S. in 1784. Reeve was later partnered by Judge James Gould. The wife of a local attorney came to Reeve complaining of her husband's cruelty. The unnamed attorney was arrested, brought before Judge Reeve, and found guilty. An immediate divorce was granted. The once-prominent attorney turned into a "drunkard and beggar." Reeve had made one of our nation's first statements regarding the unacceptability of wife-beating during a time when there was growing intolerance toward slavery.

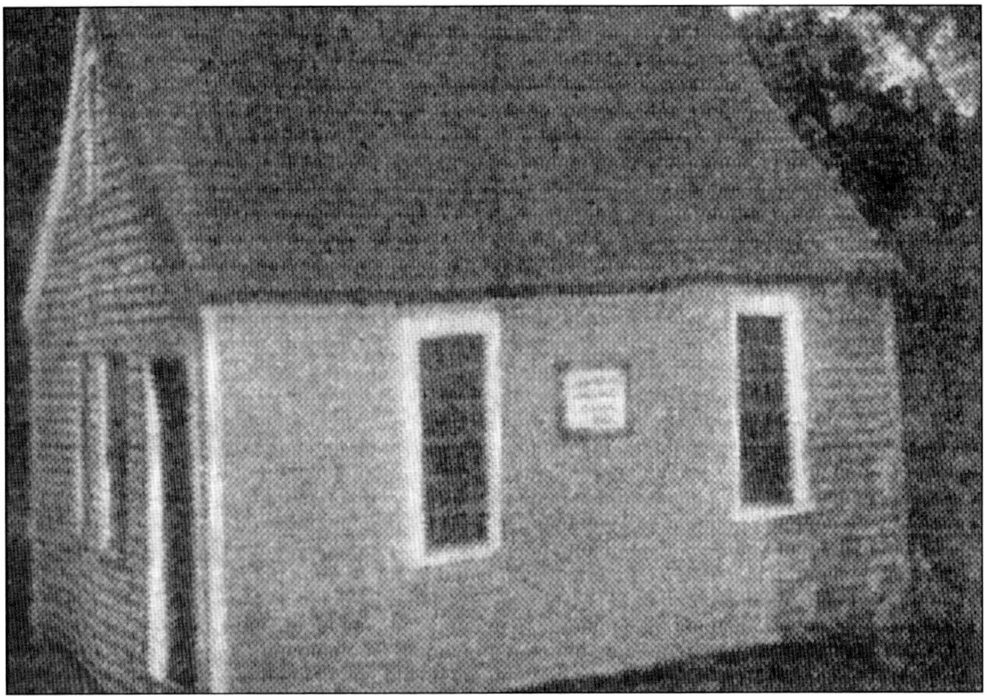

The first law school in the U.S. was established in Litchfield. The school operated for over sixty years, graduating over 1,500 students, including two of our nation's vice-presidents and over one hundred members of Congress. The school was restored in 1976 to enable it to continue as a museum. The original structure was built in 1782.

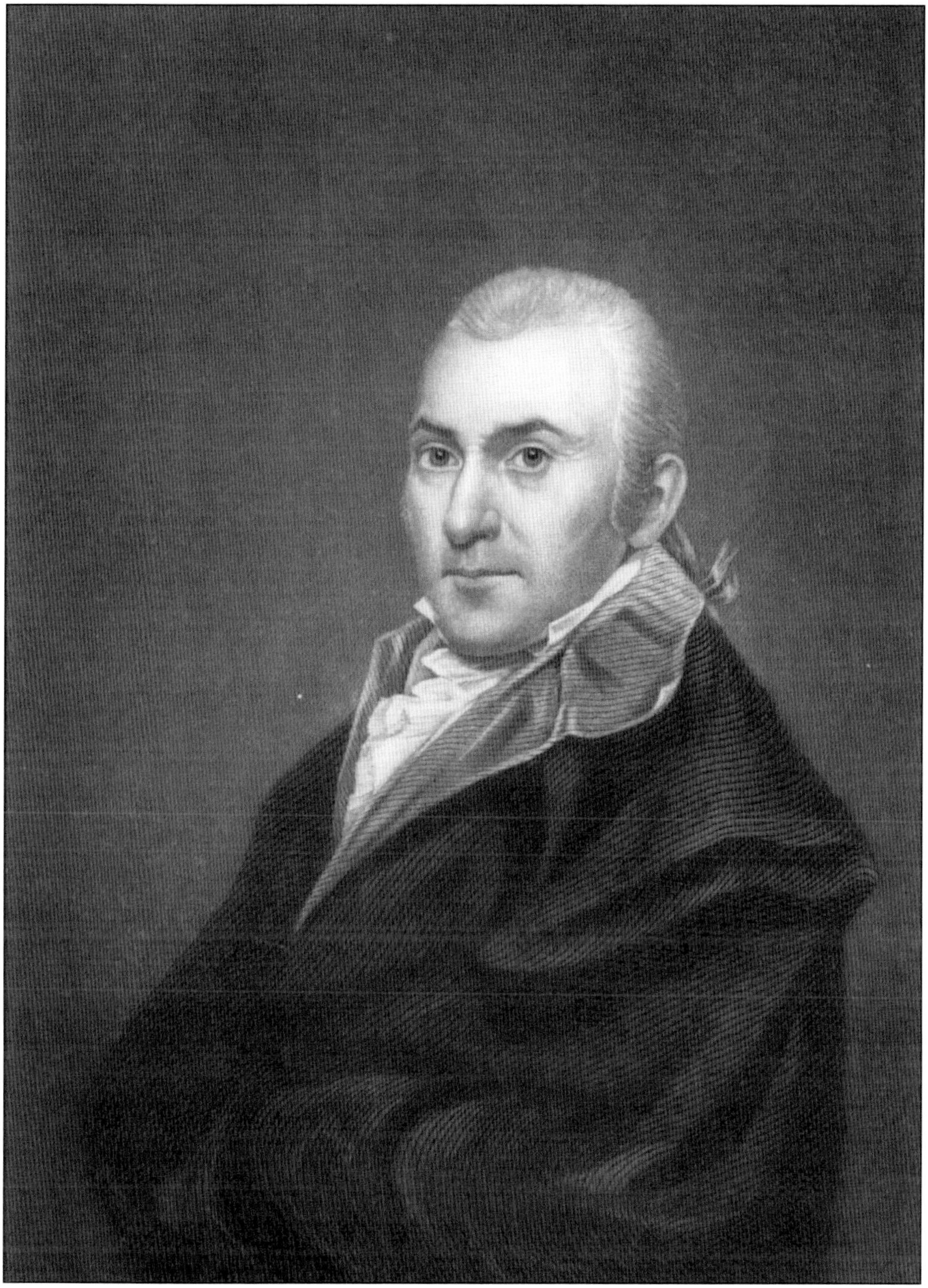

James Gould was a Yale graduate who settled in Litchfield and was an associate of Judge Gould. Judge Gould conducted the first law school from 1798 until 1820. He was also the judge of the Superior Court from 1816 to 1819.

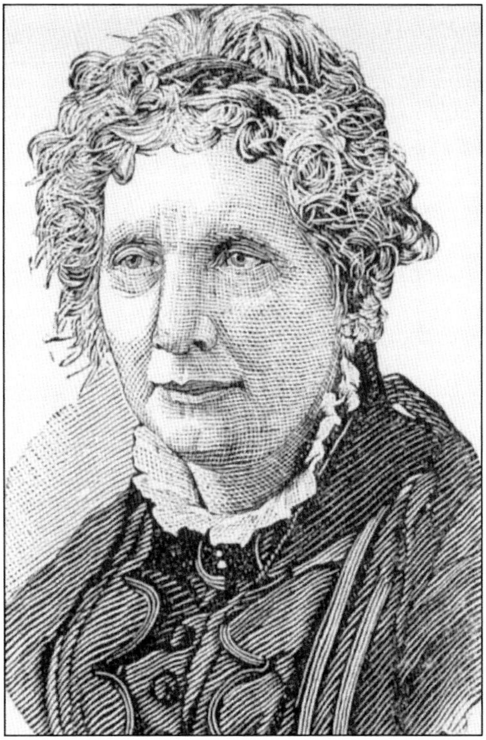

Harriet Beecher Stowe (1811–1896) was also born in Litchfield. Her claim to fame was her book *Uncle Tom's Cabin*. It is said that when Harriet met Lincoln in Washington, he loomed above Hattie (who was barely 5 feet tall), stating "so you are the little lady that started this great Civil War." Many believe that no book has had a more direct and powerful influence on history as Stowe's novel.

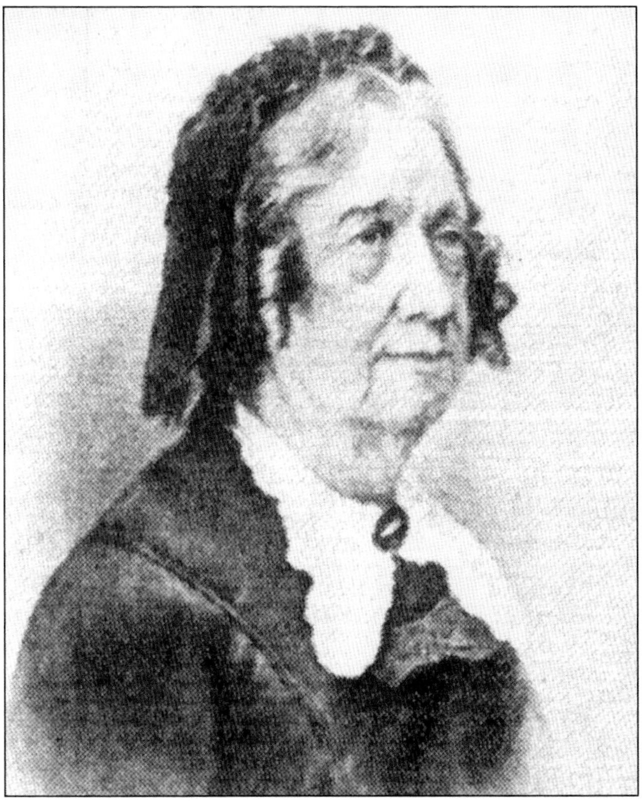

Catherine Beecher (1800–1878) was Lyman Beecher's eldest daughter. Catherine became noted for her work on behalf of the higher education of women. She attended the Sarah Pierce Academy in Litchfield and later opened academies for women across the nation. Oddly enough, although Catherine was a strong advocate for women, she did oppose their right to vote.

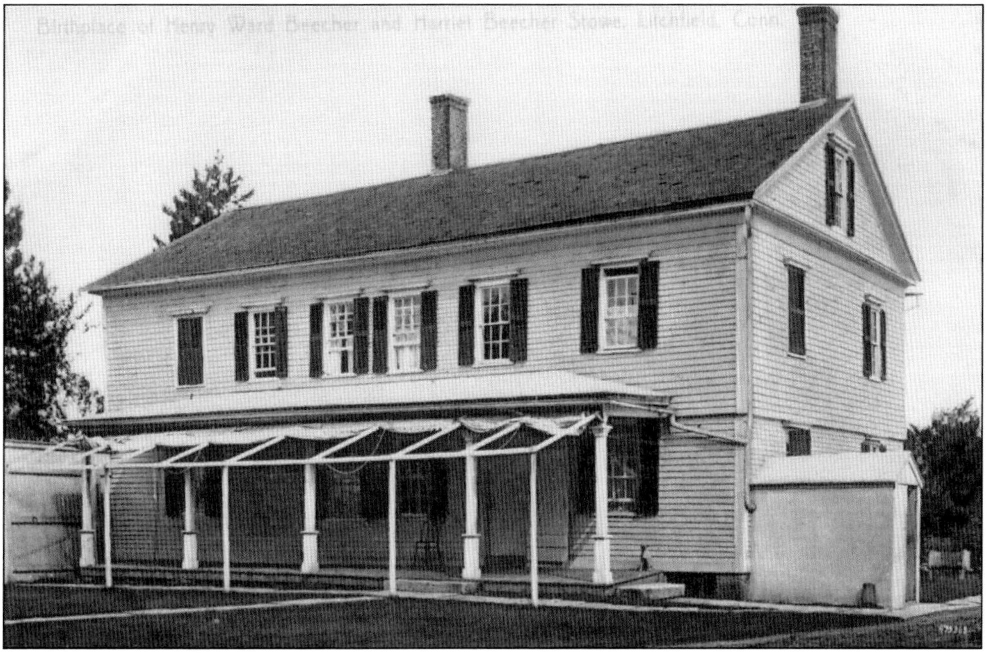

The homestead of Lyman Beecher and his family was located in Litchfield. The Beecher family has been described as one of our nation's most brilliant. Family members achieved their fame as writers, preachers, and educators. They all descended from an Englishman who had settled in 1638 in New Haven. Lyman Beecher was born in New Haven in 1775. He was viewed as a heretic by Ohio Presbyterians because of his ideas about excessive drinking, Catholicism, and religious tolerance.

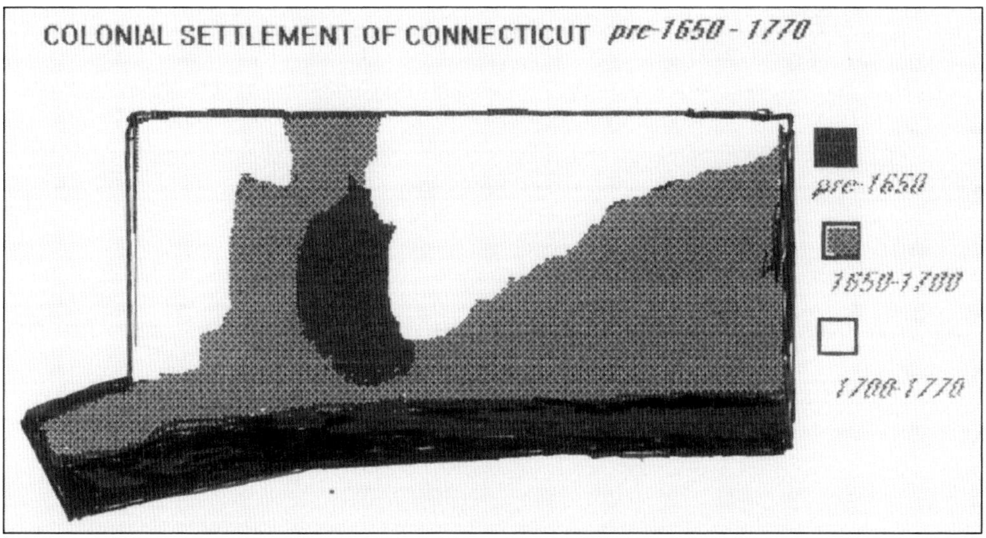

This map shows when the different areas of Connecticut were settled. Note that the Litchfield Hills area was not settled until the 1700s, whereas other areas of the state were settled before 1650.

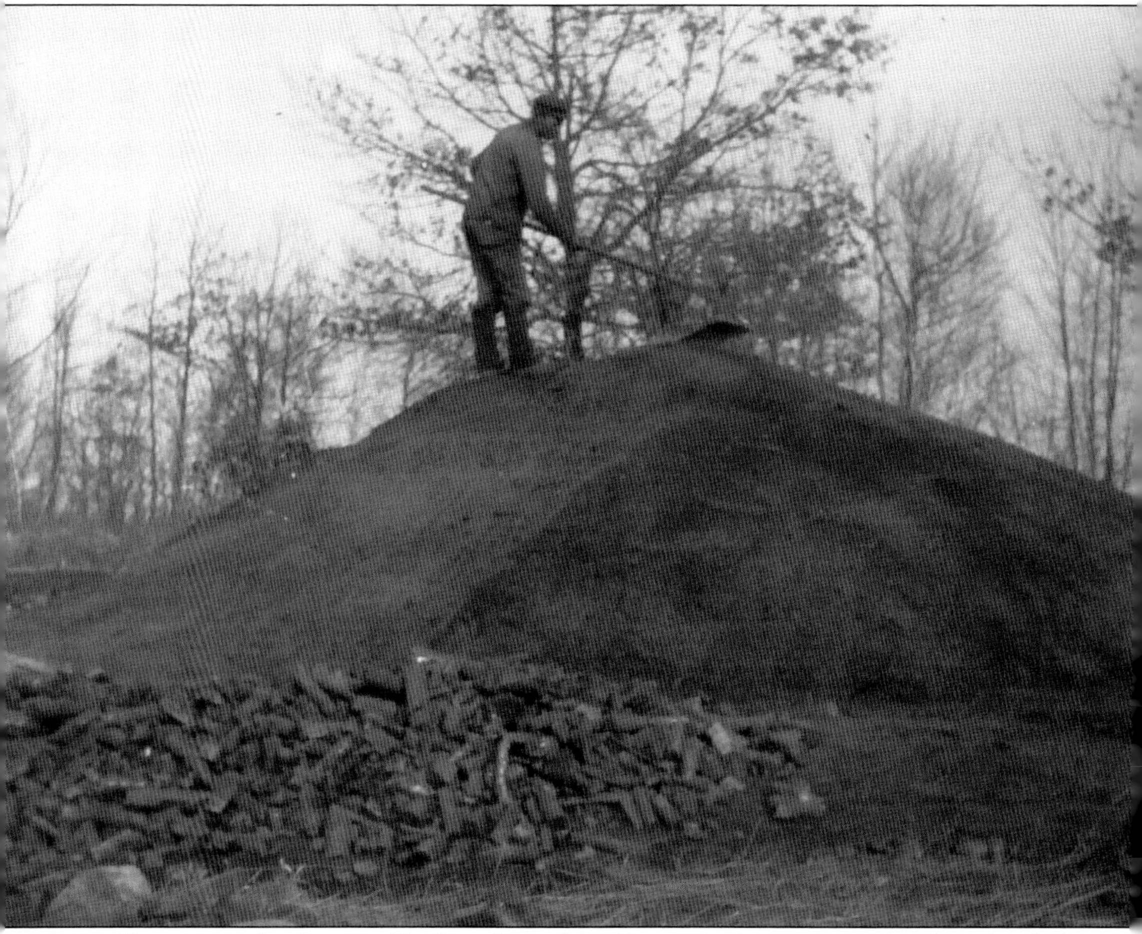

The process of making coal back in the early 1920s involved covering a pile of wood with dirt and charcoal dust. This photograph was taken on Hogan's Farm and the fellow on the peak is Pat Hogan. Though the Hogan family was in the cider-making business, they also made coal to sell. (Courtesy of Alice Szczesniak.)

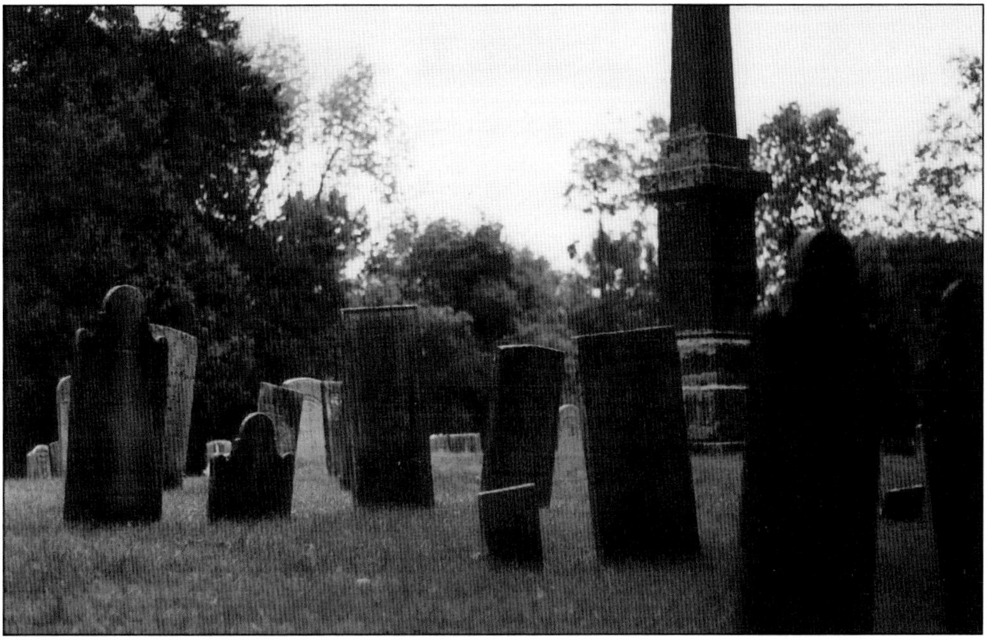

The Flanders cemetery, located in Kent Hollow, offers a unique sense of the area's history. Ancestors of Sherman Green moved into the area in 1745. The family owned several farms, including one on Arrowhead Point, which is now a state park. Members of the Green family were both farmers and traders. Elisha Green is buried in the Kent Hollow cemetery, while William Green is buried in the Warren cemetery. (Courtesy of Katherine Hubbard.)

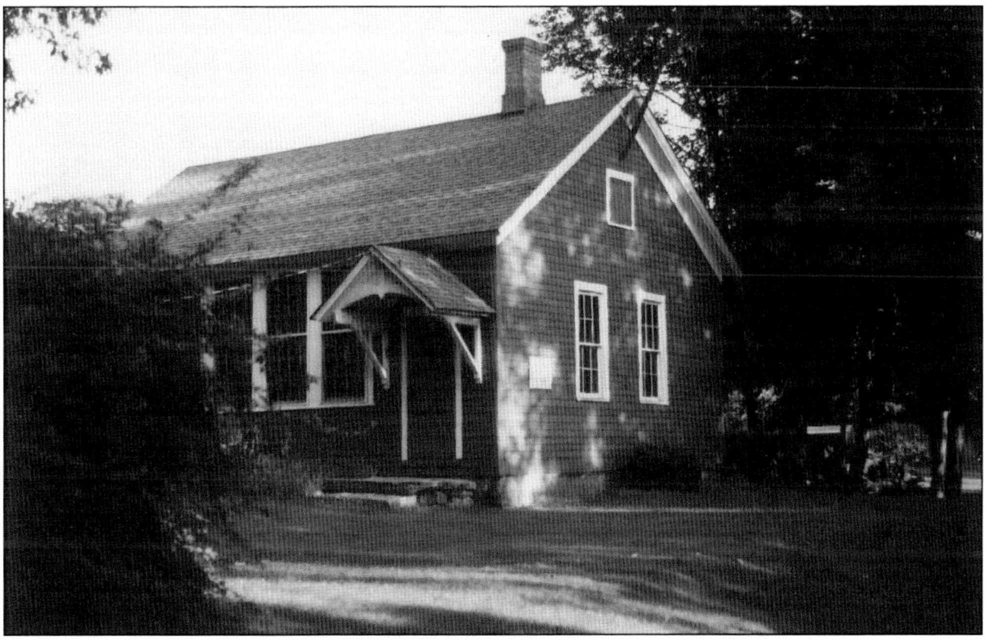

This is a one-room schoolhouse that stands in Kent Hollow. Sherman Green's great-grandfather once held the deed to the schoolhouse, and he left it to his son Gerald. Upon returning home after World War I, Gerald liquidated the estate, leaving the school to the town of Kent. (Courtesy of Katherine Hubbard.)

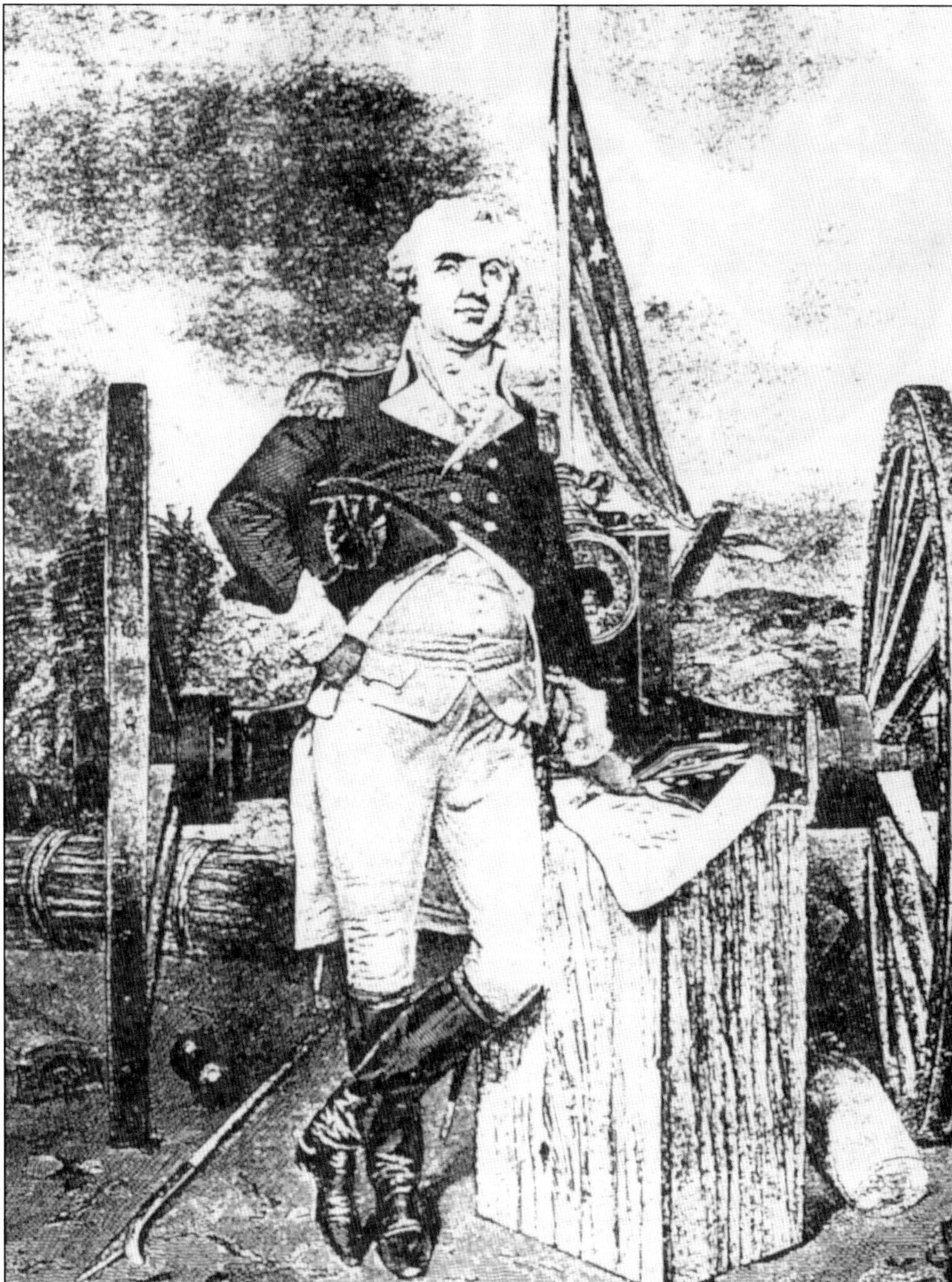

Henry Knox was born in 1775 and was the owner of many bookshops in Salisbury. Henry kept himself well-educated, especially in regards to artillery, military tactics, and gunnery. When he was informed of the massacre in Lexington, Massachusetts, he and his wife Lucy decided to join the rebels. They entered the area as citizens but within the lining of Lucy's petticoat was sewn Henry's militia sword. They were allowed to enter Fort Ticonderoga on December 5. Knox proved his skills immediately and quickly rose in the ranks to be a major and then a general. He served his country as the chief of artillery until the end of the war.

Some Northerners viewed Brown as a martyr, while many Southerners viewed him as a cold-blooded murderer whose actions caused the death of his own three sons. Few would deny that his goal was a noble one but that his actions were often cruel and ruthless. Brown was hung in 1859 for treason, murder, inciting insurrection, and conspiracy.

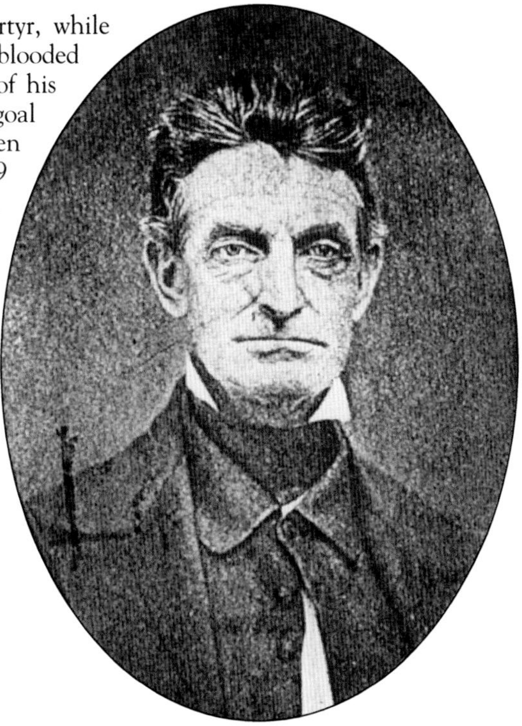

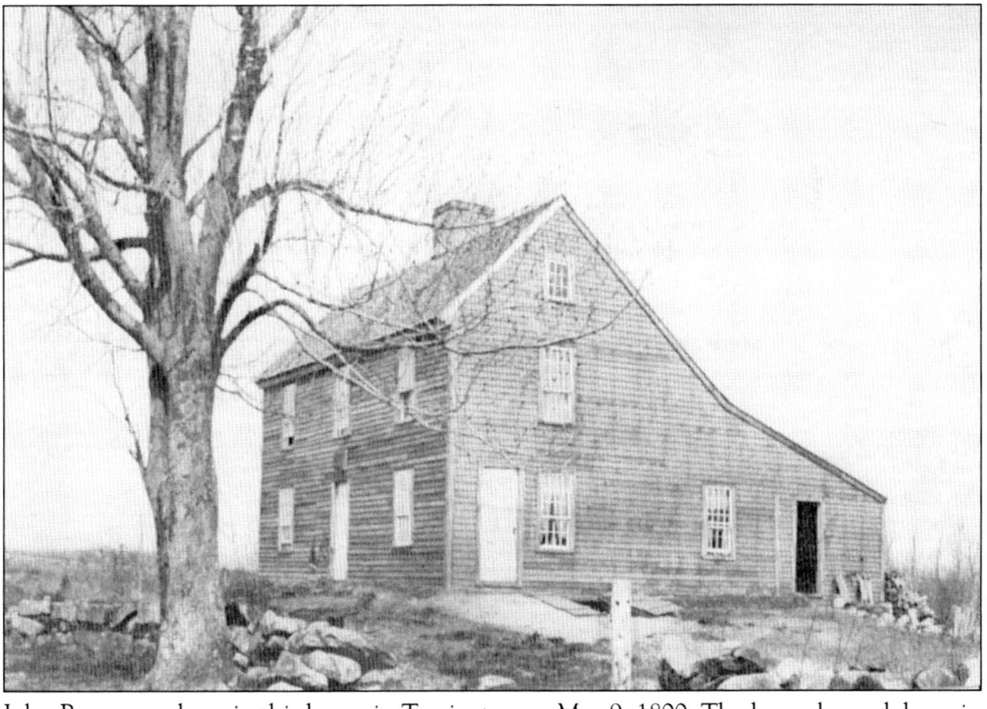

John Brown was born in this house in Torrington on May 9, 1800. The house burned down in 1918. There are many who take no pride in the fact that Brown was born in Torrington. He is commemorated in a song verse "John Brown's body lay a 'mouldrin in the ground," which it did after he met his doom at the gallows on December 2, 1859.

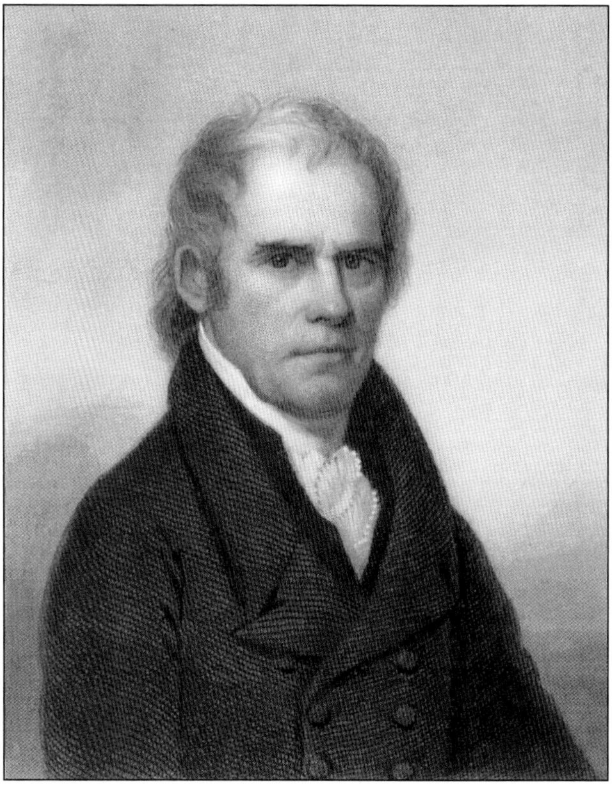

Julius Deming, one of Litchfield's eminent merchants, opened his business in 1781. Deming, who also held prominent political offices, was best known as an astute proprietor, and was one of the few merchants who flew to London and imported goods directly from that city. He also imported goods from China and was a local manufacturer of paper and iron.

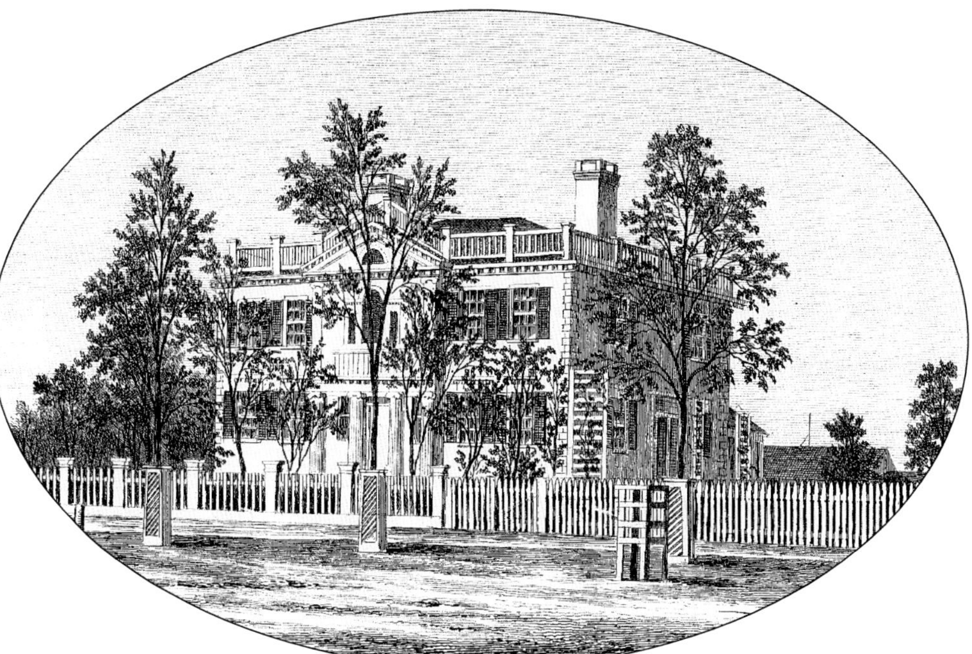

This is a sketch of Julius Deming's residence in Litchfield. The home was built in 1793 and is among the finest examples of Federal architecture in Connecticut.

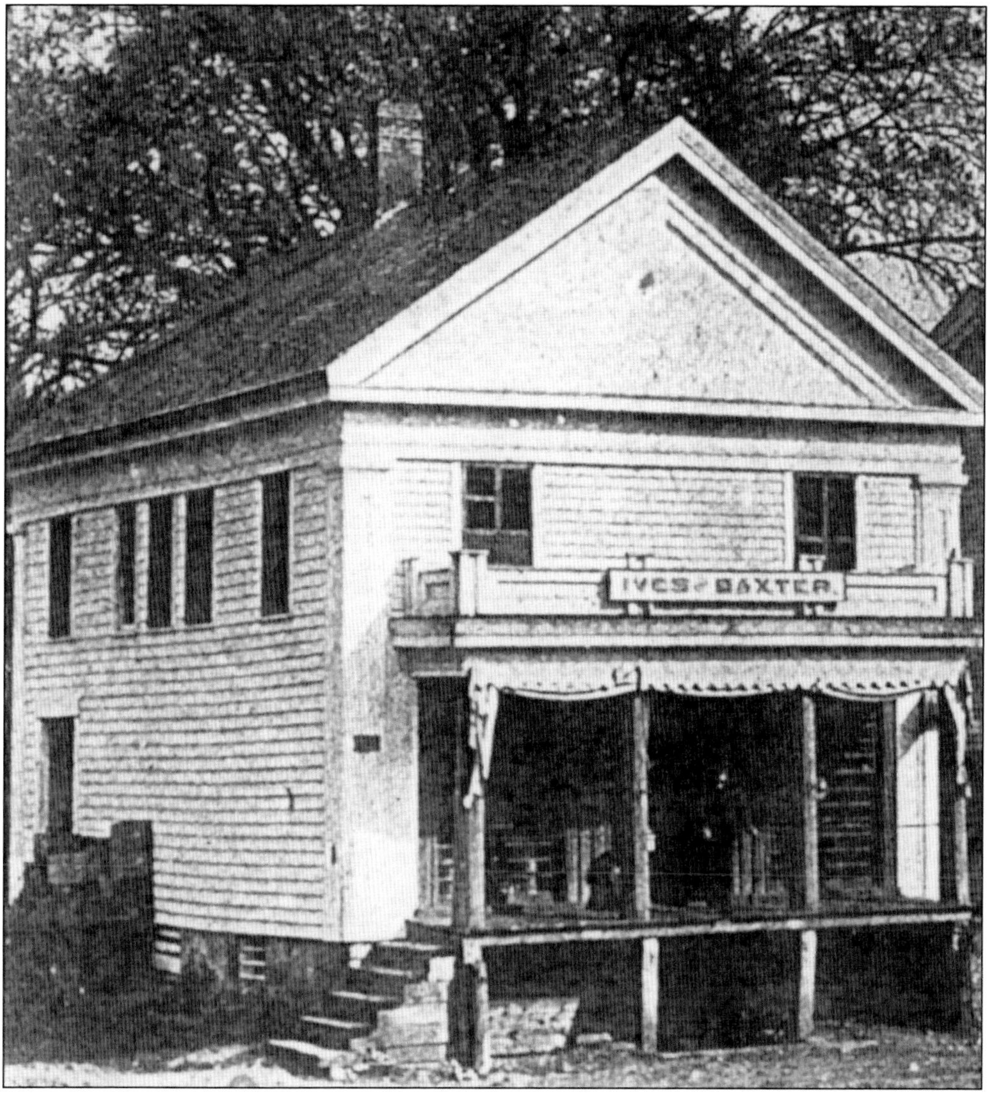

This general store was once a busy place in what was known as Colebrook River, or "the town that disappeared." The late 1930s and early 1940s was a time of war, deprivation, and confusion. The nation was focused on one man: Adolf Hitler. The sky overhead Colebrook River was filled with squadrons of fighter-bombers from a nearby air force base. Through a series of actions that took place over several years, many of the homes were sold to the water district. Townspeople were distraught and initially refused to sell, but eventually there was only one family left that refused to move. When that family finally did move, the town of Colebrook River was flooded over as a reservoir. Folks who once lived in Colebrook River, some of whom still live upon the banks, hold fond memories of their quiet little town. Some are still angry at the water district for their actions in forcing (convincing, bribing) residents to move on and sell their property.

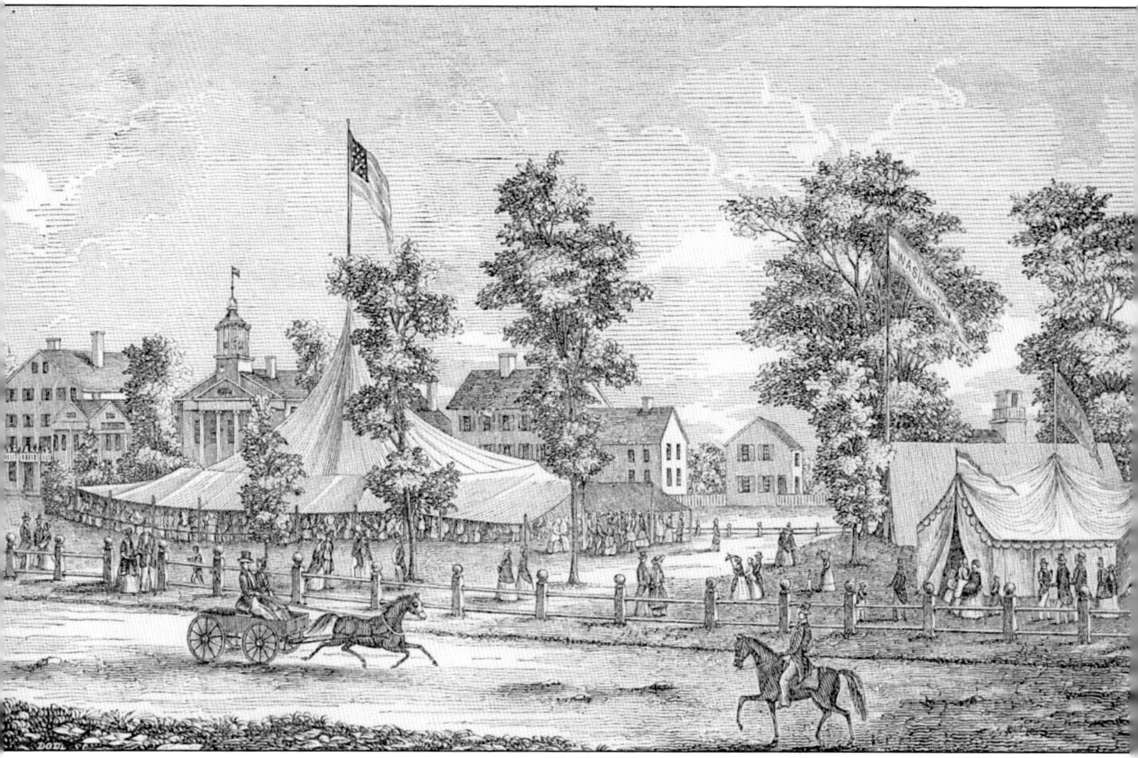

This is a sketch of the Litchfield Centennial Celebration of 1851. The bicentennial celebration was held in 1971. Locals dressed in the attire of preceding centuries and the Litchfield Green was filled with booths and tradesmen.

Two

A Time to Plant, A Time to Reap

"TAKEN UP by the Subscriber, in a suffering condition
TWO SWINE (one spotted and one white)
with rings in their noses. The owner is requested to prove property,
pay charges and take them."
Anson Rogers of Cornwall, December 28, 1828

"A dark bay Mare, a few white hairs in the forehead,
no shoes on, supposed to be 15 to 18 years old—broke into an enclosure
in the east part of South Farms. Its owner is requested to come forward,
prove property and take the Mare."
Andrew A. French, January 22, 1830

(As printed in the Litchfield Enquirer.)

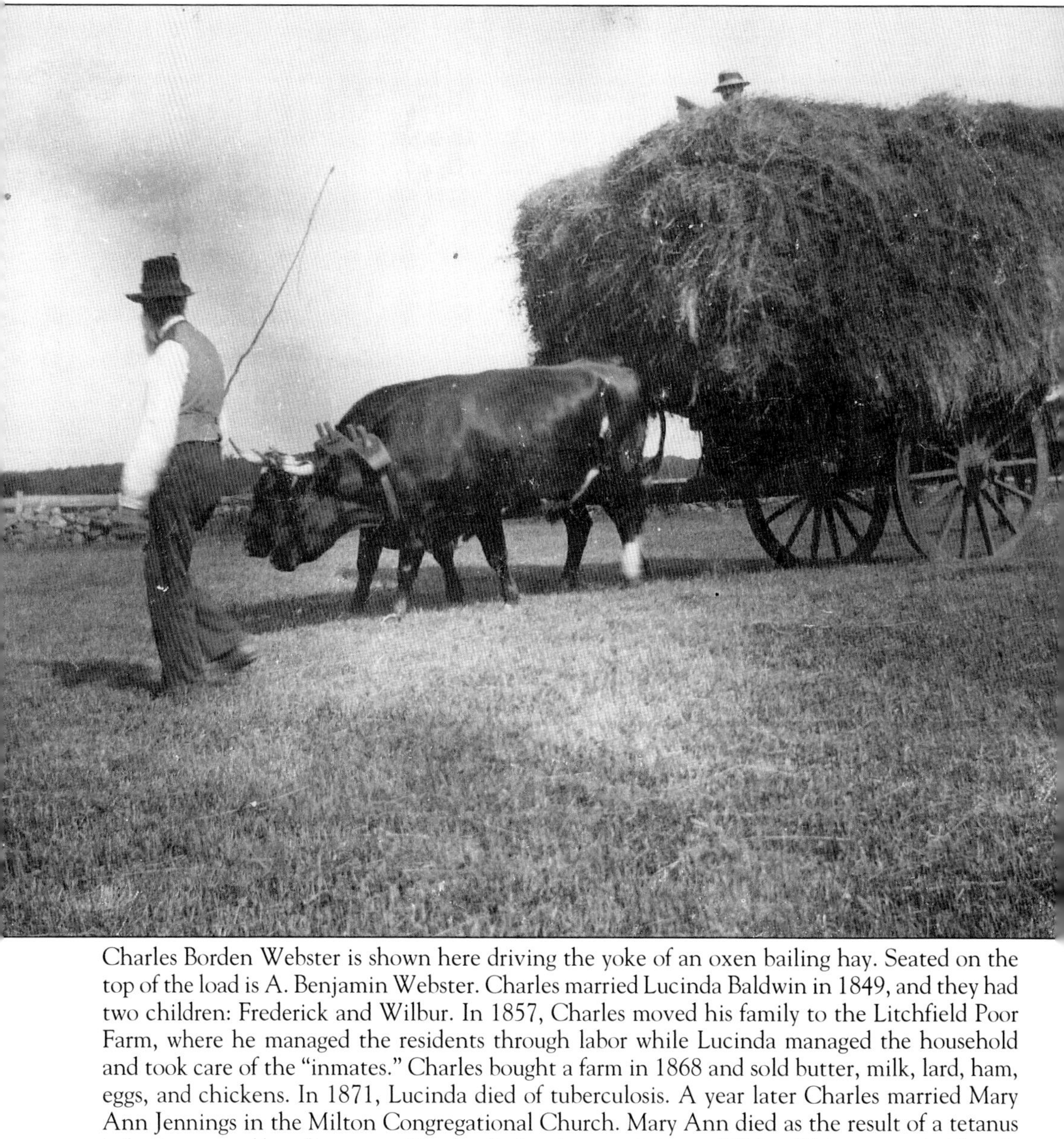

Charles Borden Webster is shown here driving the yoke of an oxen bailing hay. Seated on the top of the load is A. Benjamin Webster. Charles married Lucinda Baldwin in 1849, and they had two children: Frederick and Wilbur. In 1857, Charles moved his family to the Litchfield Poor Farm, where he managed the residents through labor while Lucinda managed the household and took care of the "inmates." Charles bought a farm in 1868 and sold butter, milk, lard, ham, eggs, and chickens. In 1871, Lucinda died of tuberculosis. A year later Charles married Mary Ann Jennings in the Milton Congregational Church. Mary Ann died as the result of a tetanus infection caused by a finger cut. Charles died at the age of ninety. Wilbur Webster married Jennie Wooster, a teacher, and they had three children: Ernest, Benjamin, and Charlotte. Wilbur became interested in cattle and eventually bred purebred Guernsey cows. Wilbur suffered from periods of "depression" and on the morning of April 5, 1930, he took his own life.

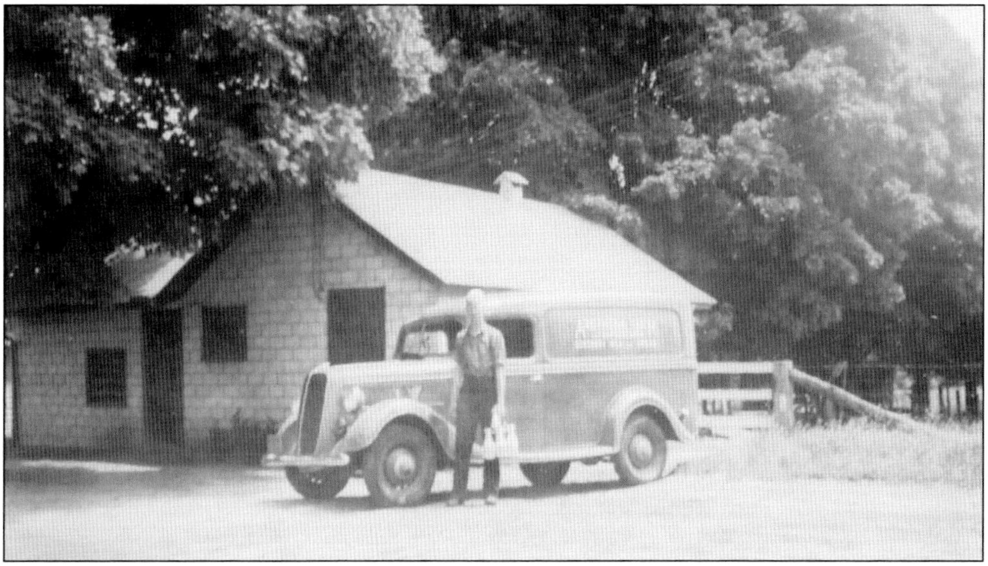

Wilbur Webster is shown here by one of the Arethusa Farms delivery trucks. For thirty-five years his brother, Art Webster, delivered dairy products weekly to four hundred customers. Many left sentimental notes with their orders. The notes were carefully saved in a scrapbook by his wife Lillian, the family historian. Over the years Frank Clock left many humorous notes, but when Art retired, the note read: "We are sorry about your bad news (for us). Frank is in bed crying." His retirement was viewed as "the end of an era." Milk would now be purchased at grocery stores and carried out in plastic jugs.

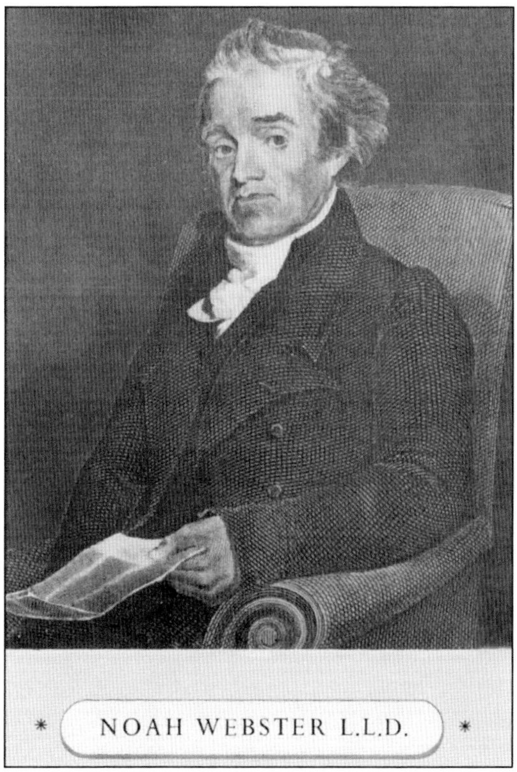

Noah Webster, a member of the Litchfield Webster family, is best known for the dictionary he compiled and for his early writings about epidemics. Educated at Yale, Webster began writing the American Dictionary of the English Language in 1807. It took until 1825 to complete the work and it was not published until 1828. Webster included over 12,000 words and between 30,000 to 40,000 definitions that had not appeared in any earlier dictionary. He was one of the founders of Amherst College and died on May 28, 1843.

White Flower Farm

White Flower Farm is a business that has continuously "blossomed" since its conception back in 1939. William Harris and his wife, Jane Grant, purchased 5 acres of land and a small barn on Esthers Road. They were both writers from New York City and renovated the barn that stood there as a "getaway" or "summer residence." During their stays, which became more and more frequent, not only did they discover that they could write just as well in Litchfield as they could in the city, but they also became fascinated with gardening and selected unusual breeds of plants from nurseries across the United States and abroad. Sixty more acres of land were added. Jane Grant passed away in 1973 and in 1977 Harris sold the nursery to Elliot Wadsworth II. When Harris died in 1981, he left a legacy of excellence.

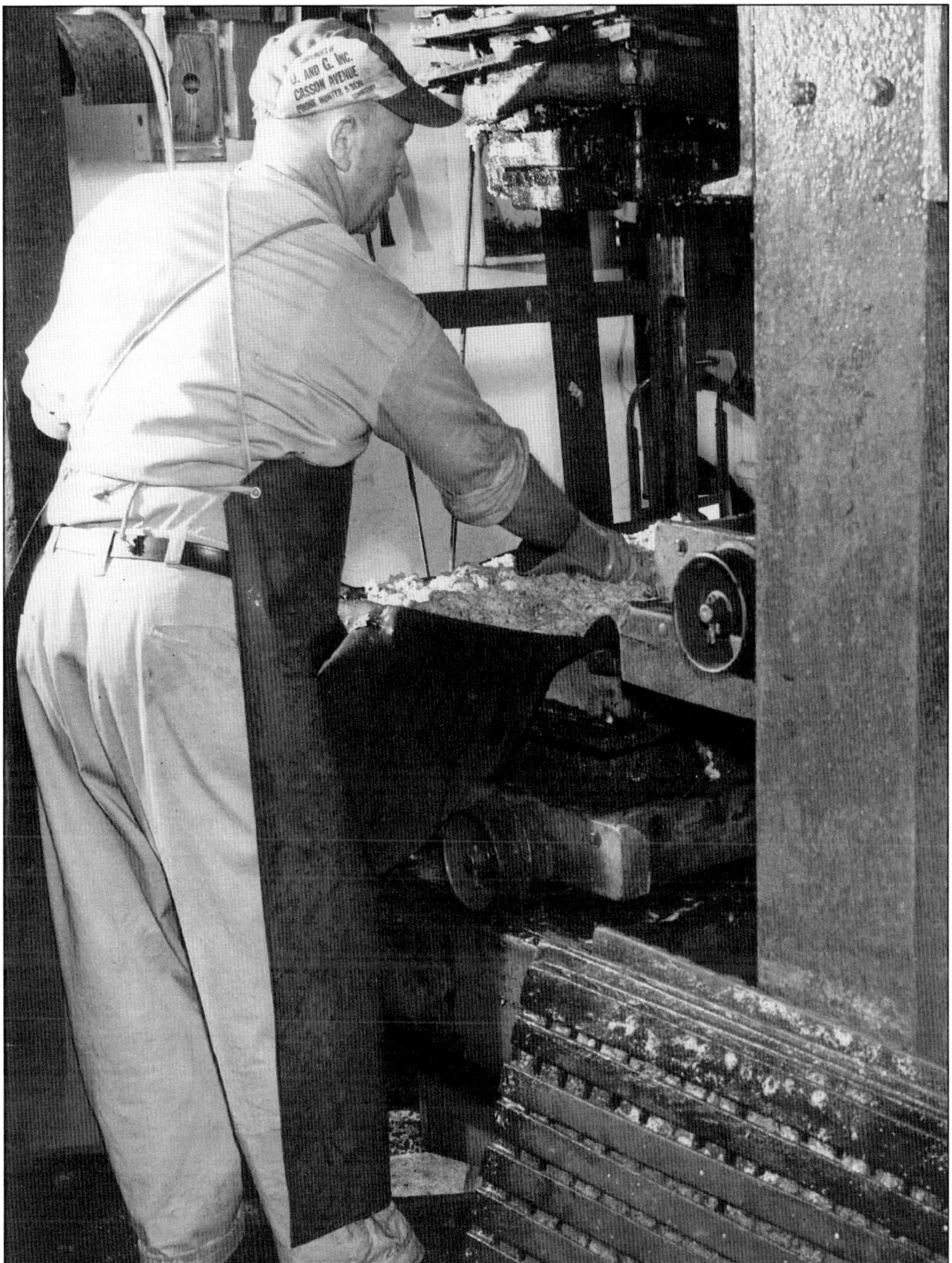

Morris Hogan is shown here in the process of making cider at the Hogan Cider Mill just outside of Harwinton. Morris died recently, leaving his personal belongings to a long-time friend and employee, Alice Szczesniak. Patrick Hogan and his son Richard built the Hogan Cider Mill in 1909. In 1912, Morris Hogan (the baby of the family) overtook its operation and the mill continues to run to this day. Much of the information in this caption was offered by Wendall Gunn, who worked for the Hogan Cider Mill for over fifty years. (Courtesy of Alice Szczesniak.)

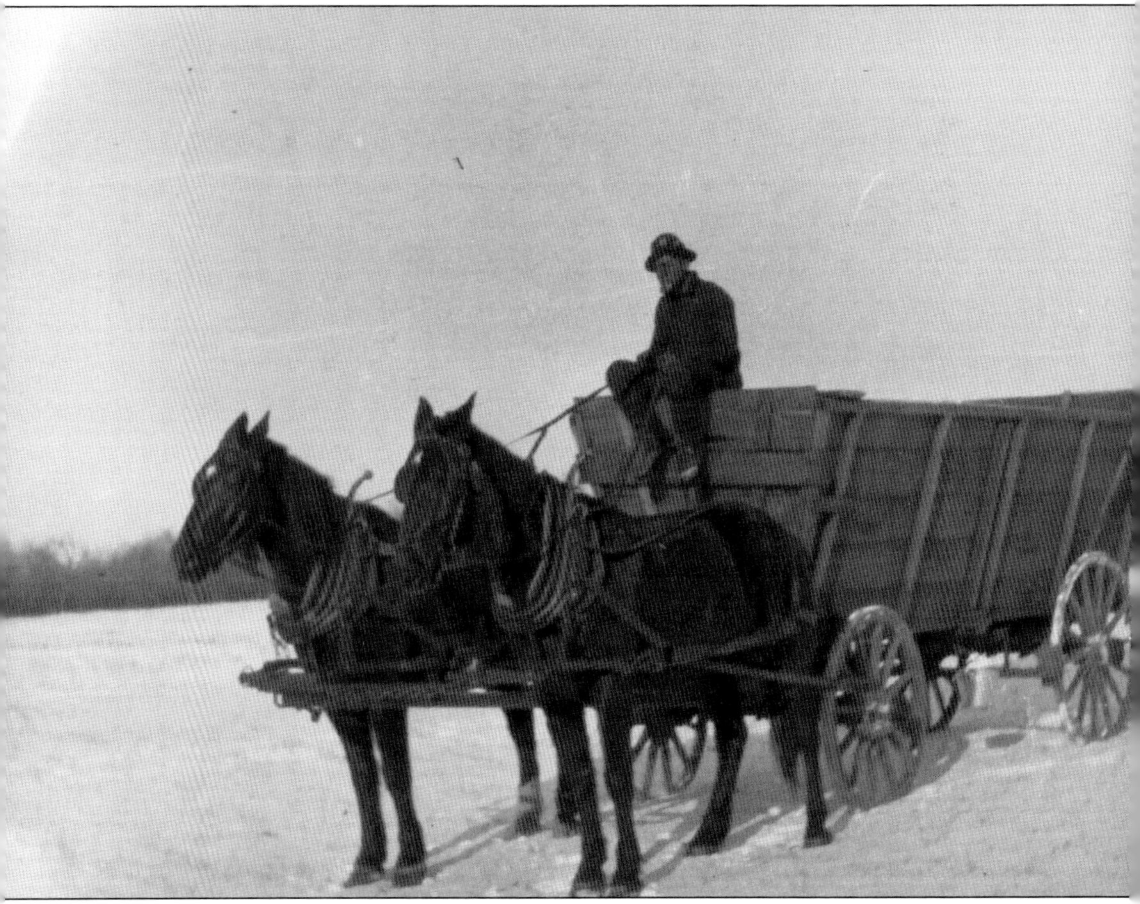

This charcoal wagon was used on Hogan's Farm, which sat on the border between Harwinton and Burlington. The photograph was taken in the early 1920s and was contributed by Alice Szczesniak of Harwinton, who worked for the Hogan family for many years and who has contributed numerous photographs to the preservation of local history.

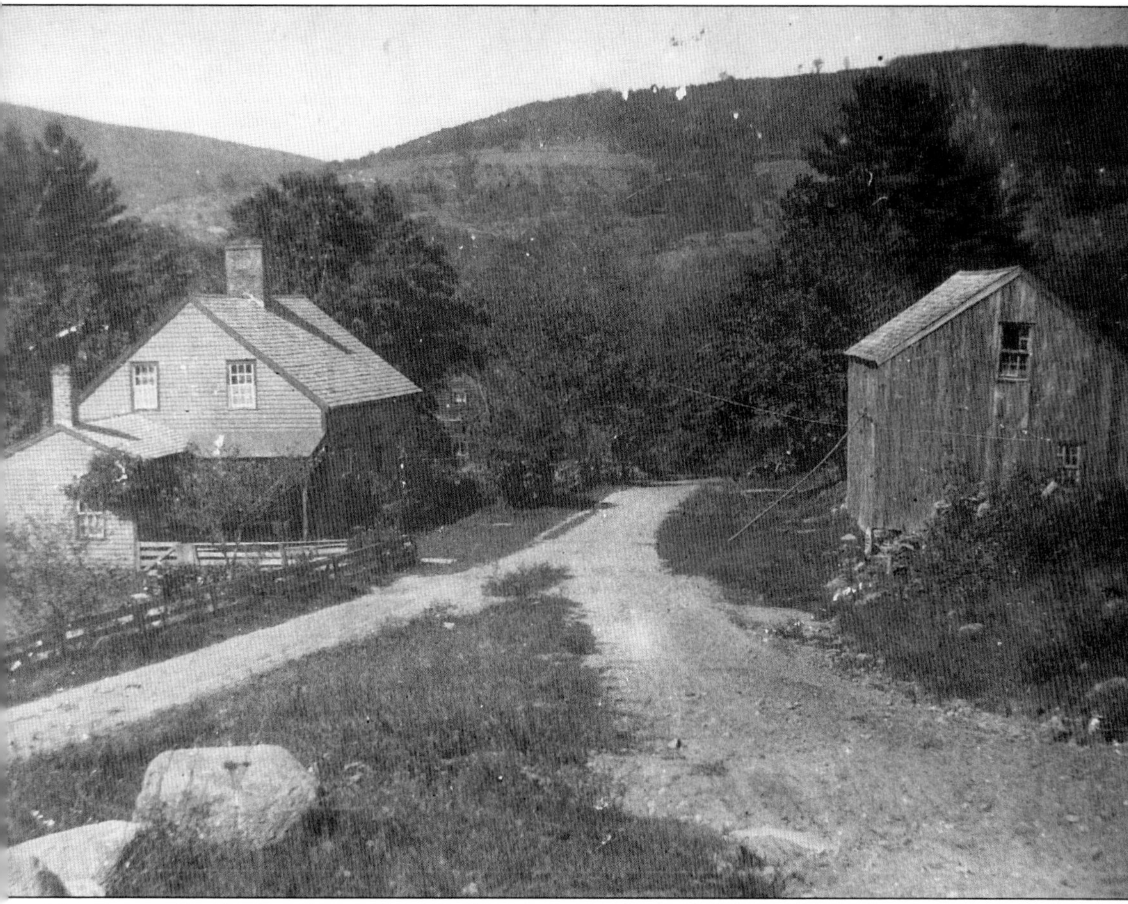

This beautiful photograph of Flora Richard Brown's homestead and barn, located in the Puffingham section of Cornwall Bridge, was taken in 1910. Alice Szczesniak and her family lived there for many years. During World War II Alice and her sister moved to the Hogan Farm and became "farmeretts." She was only fifteen at the time. She met her husband, Waldy, at the farm when he returned from serving with the Marines. (Courtesy of Alice Szczesniak.)

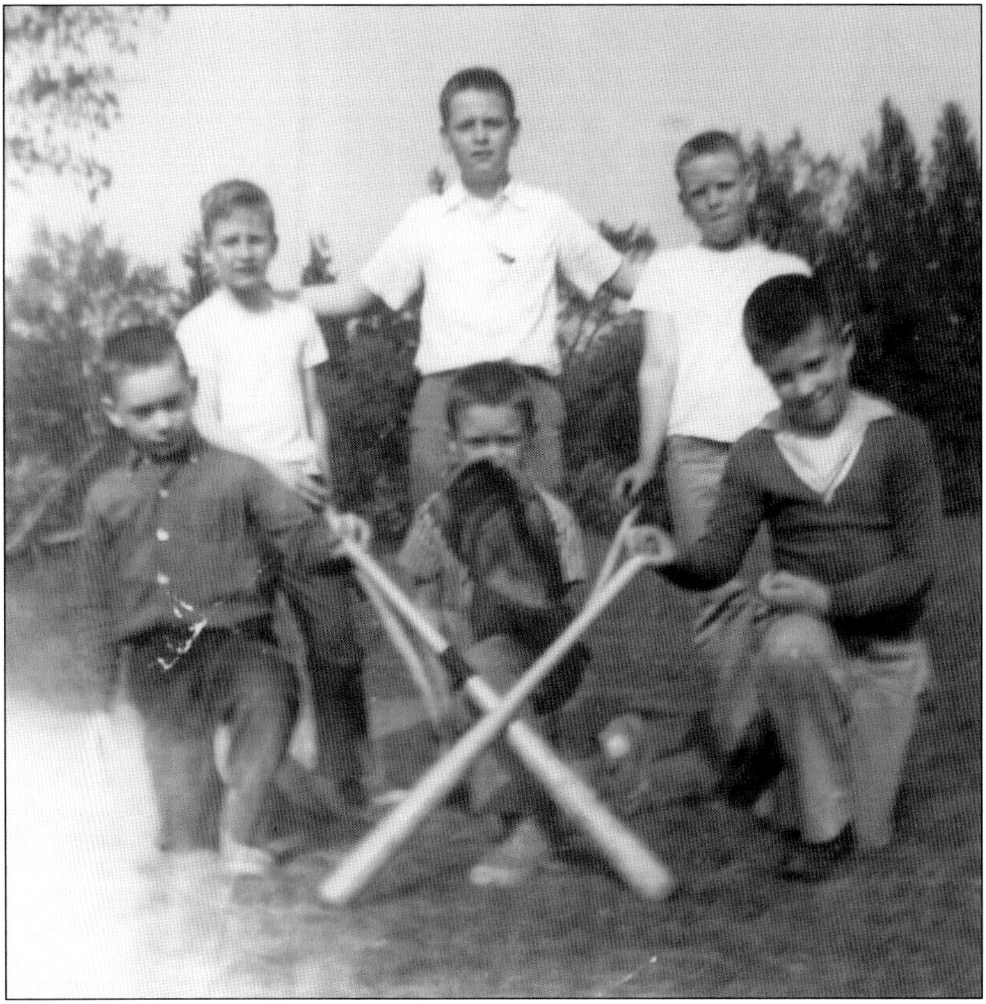

In the late 1950s, the children of East Street, Litchfield, formed a baseball team. Not all the parties are identifiable, but the following are known: (front row, from left to right) Eddie Kelly, Paul Rutkowski (perhaps—it is hard to tell with the mask), and John Torrant (a guess); (back row) Greg McDermott, an "unknown," and perhaps a member of the Dwan family (Billy?). The games were played in a lot behind the McDermott home. The grass and weeds in the lot grew very high, and the team grew tired of carrying the bases way out into the field. One of these young masterminds, who has not stepped forward, decided that burning bases in the field would be much easier. All agreed and they promptly set the entire field ablaze.

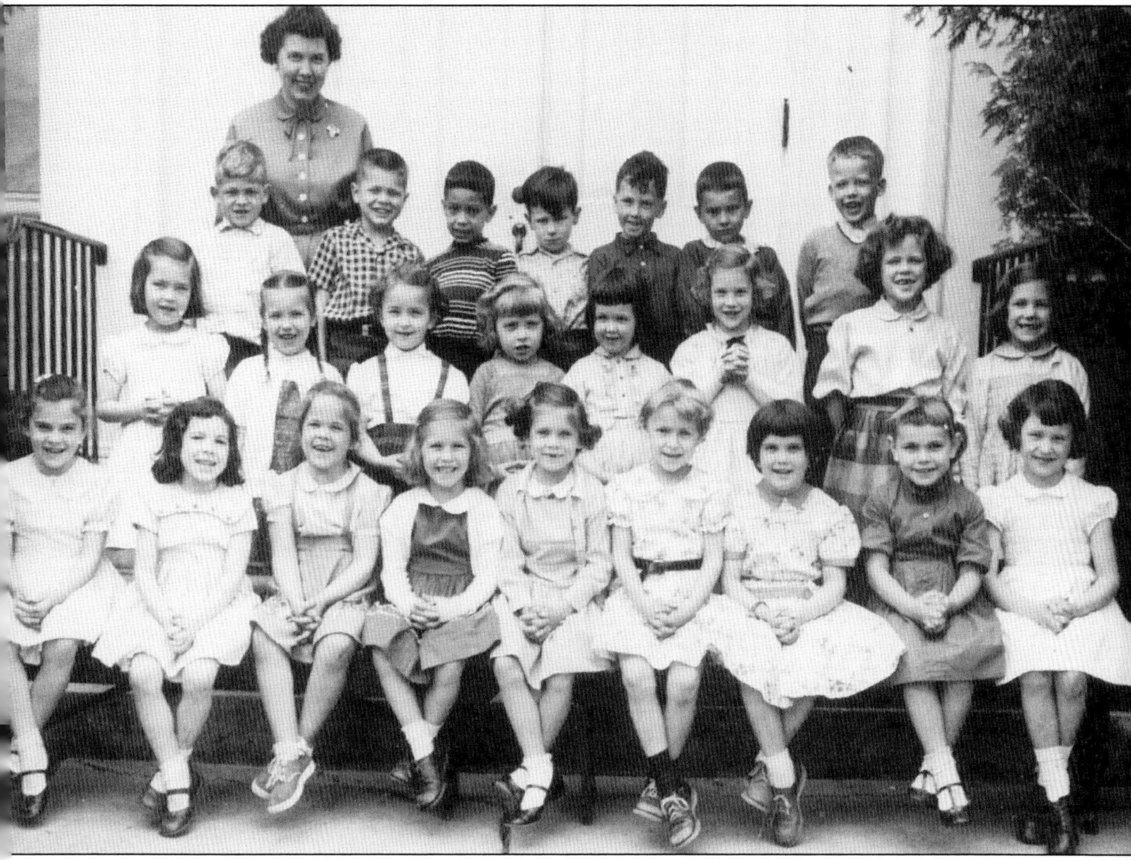

Mrs. Korns' kindergarten class at the Center School in Litchfield was photographed in 1957. These fine young ones grew to be Litchfield High School's Class of 1970. During the early years of the Vietnam struggle, students were instructed in how to defend themselves should a bomb ever be dropped over the area. Just as "fire drills" are held in schools today, students were led to the basement and told to line the walls, squat, and cover their heads. It was a frightening time for all and a difficult concept for the children to understand.

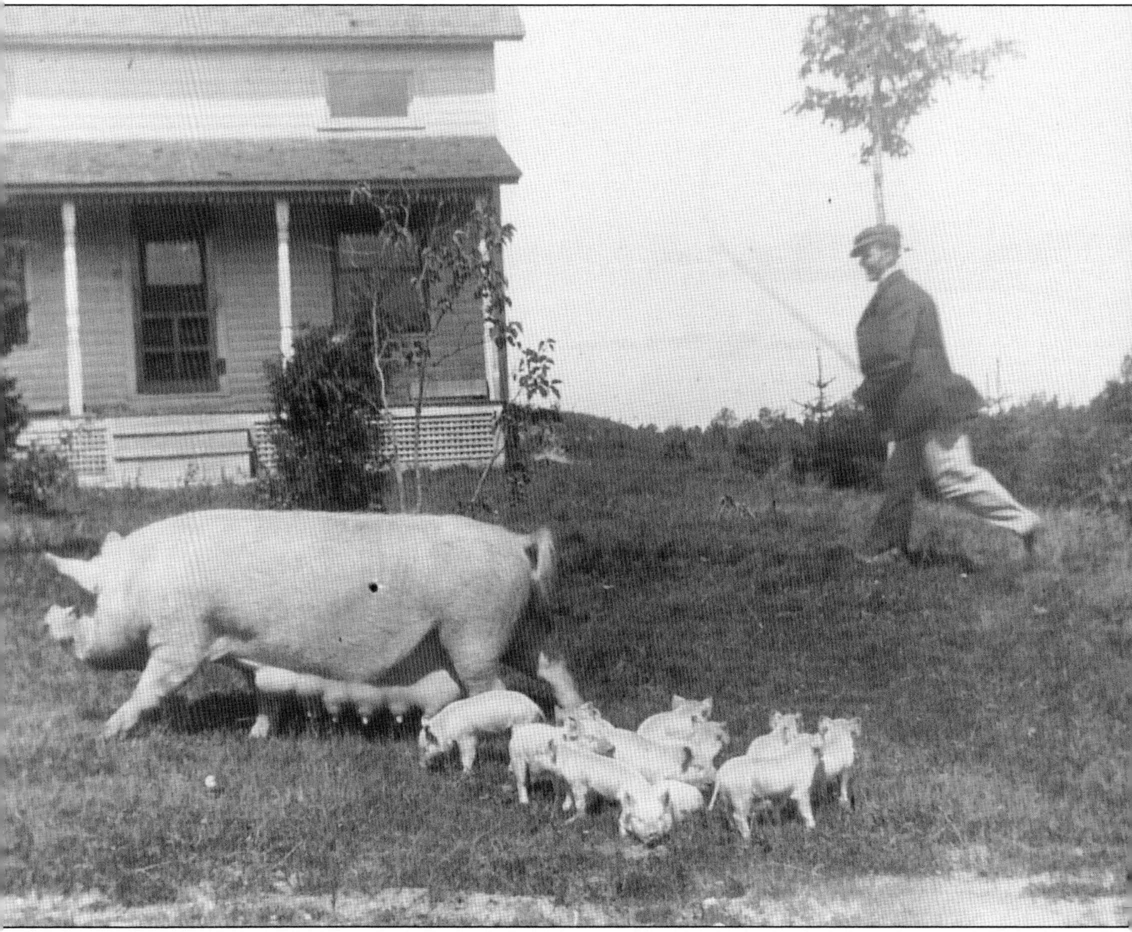

A mother pig and her piglets trot across the lawn of the old Hogan residence in Burlington during the early 1920s.

Gail Borden of Burrville obtained a patent for his process of condensing milk. The process provided greater nourishment to many, ranging from soldiers in the armed forces to infants. The Borden Condensed Milk Co. was organized in 1863.

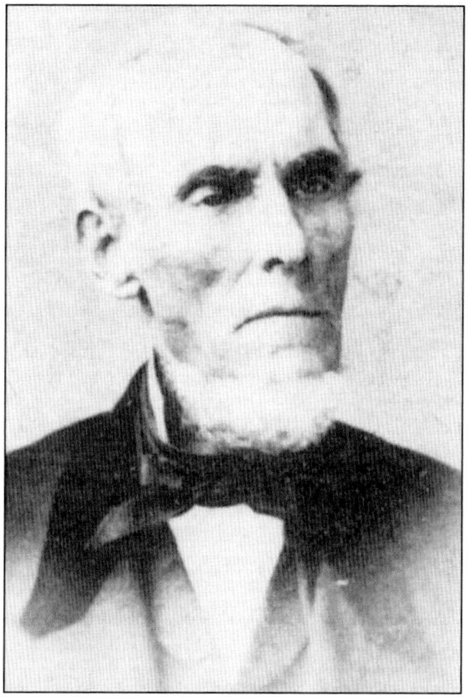

Ed Richards (the father of Flora Richards Brown) is shown here working on his "sugar house" in Warren about 1940. Richards was a farmer, carpenter, and stoneworker. A sugar house is where maple syrup or maple sugar is made; some people referred to them as "sap" houses. (Courtesy of Alice Szczesniak.)

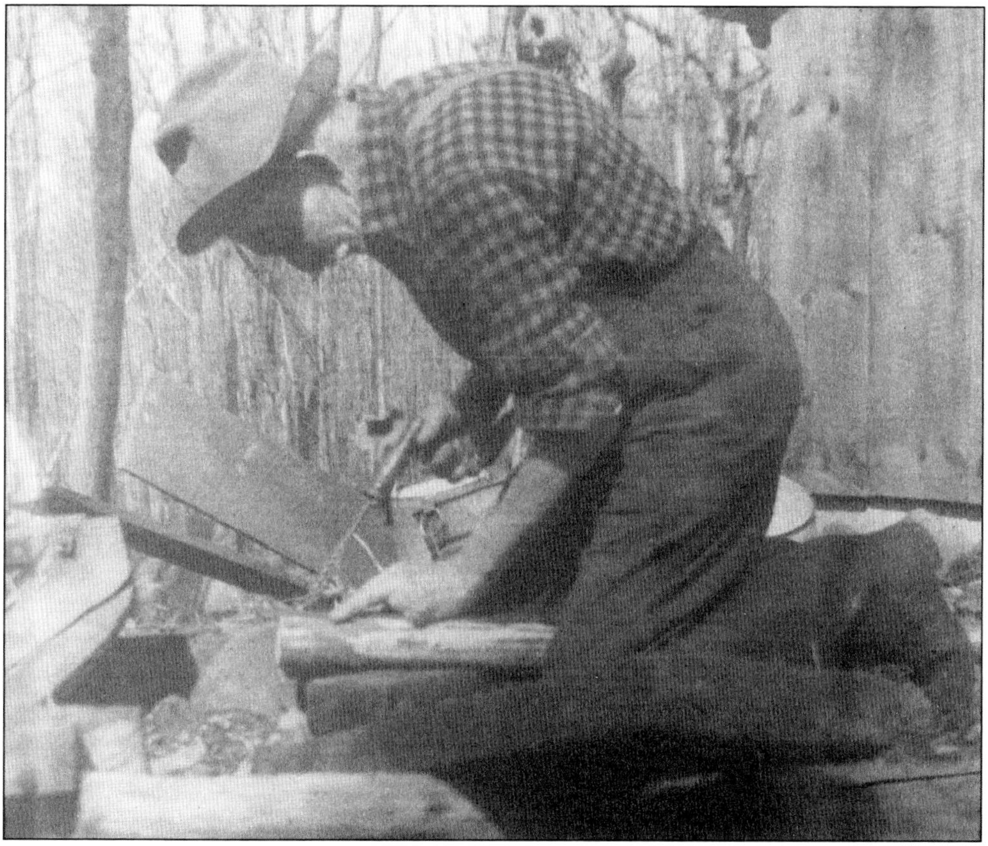

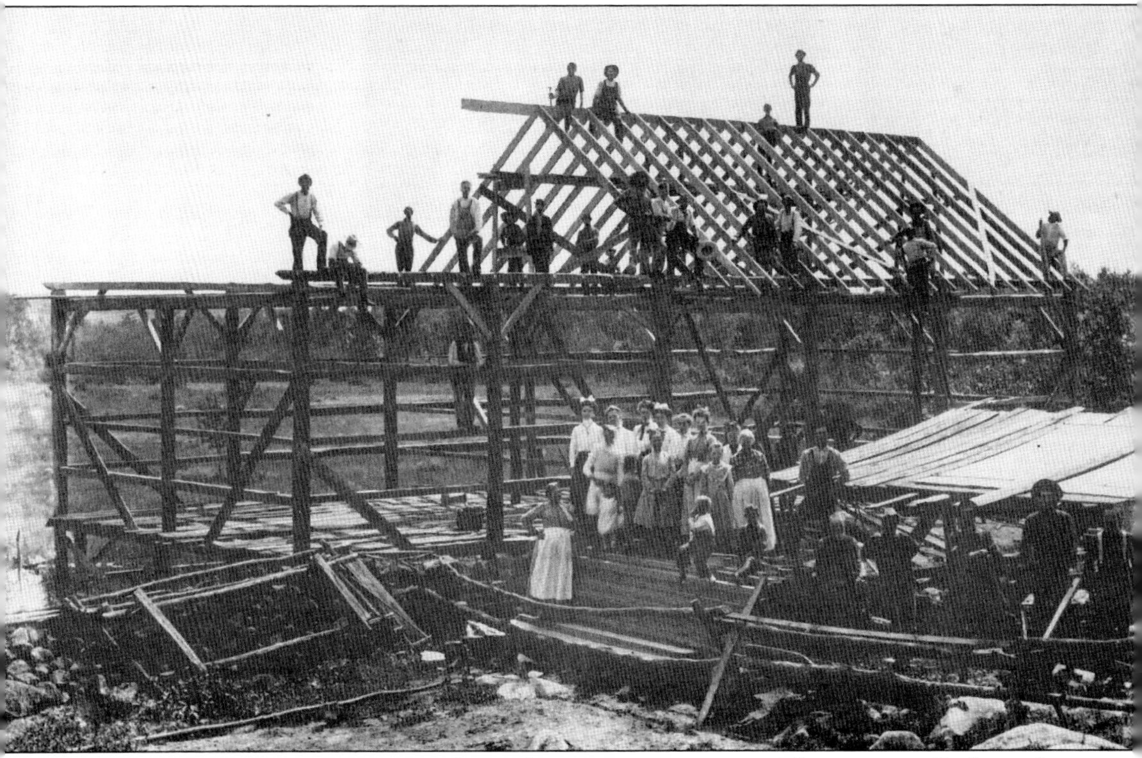

Barnraisings were common in the early nineteenth century. This one, in Goshen, shows approximately forty-five people—friends, family, neighbors, and passersby—as they help to build a barn in this agricultural area. Barnraisings symbolized a unity of purpose, respect for the farm way of life, and "neighborliness."

Three

A Time to Laugh, A Time to Weep

Dr. Rush and his anti-dyspeptic, or sour stomach, pills were touted as an infallible cure for indigestion:

*"The inventor of these pills was one
of the most eminent practitioners of medicine in the United States
and used them successfully in his practice for many years.
They are not got up as a nostrum to delude the credulous,
but are recommended on the basis of truth and experience.
In order that they may become extensively useful
and within the reach of all,
they are offered at the very low price of fifty cents per box."*

Doc. S.L. Childs
East Street, Litchfield (early 1800s)
(As printed in an advertisement from an old edition of the Litchfield Enquirer.)

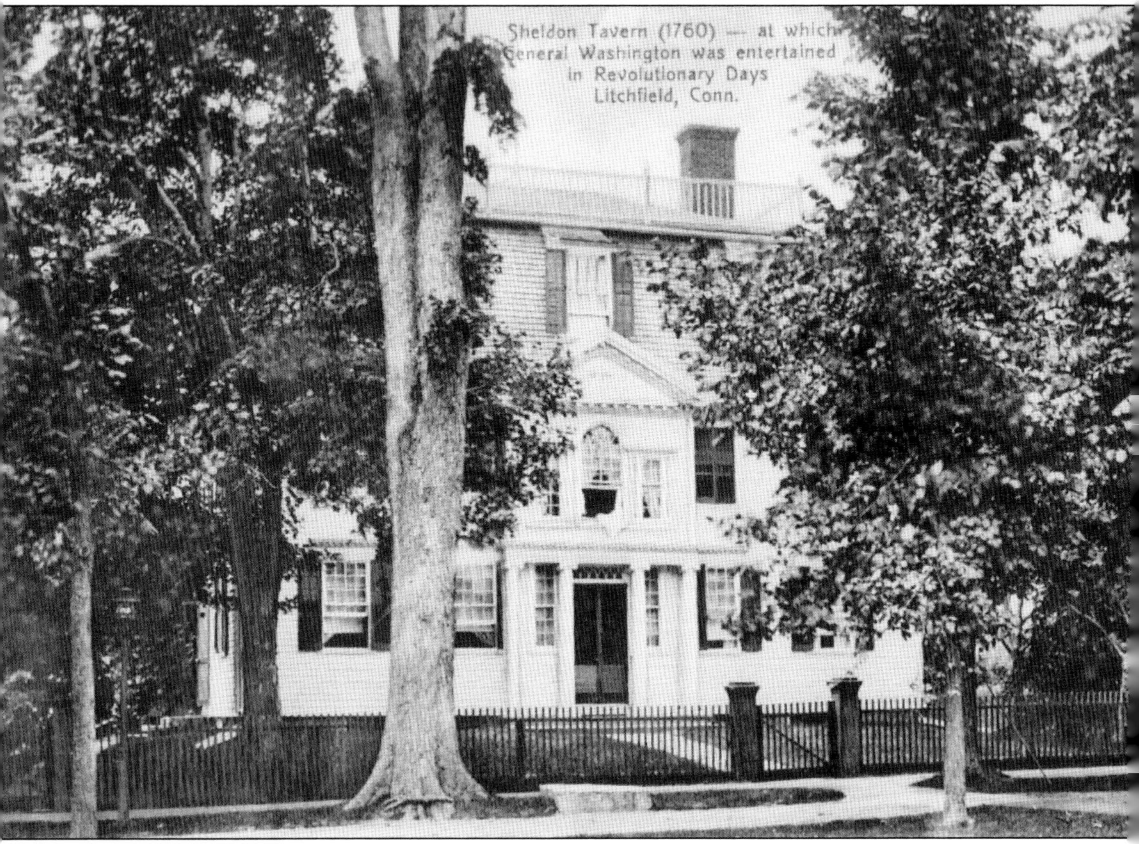

The Sheldon Tavern was built in Litchfield in 1760 by Elisha Sheldon. It is well known that George Washington was entertained here as he traveled from battle site to battle site during the Revolutionary War. Although the building only housed a tavern for a few years before being renovated into a private residence, it maintained its name. The home was remodeled in 1795 by owner Uriah Tracy. Tracy held a number of political positions including state senator from 1796 until his death in 1807. His home became the property of his son-in-law, James Gould, who was a partner in the Litchfield Law School.

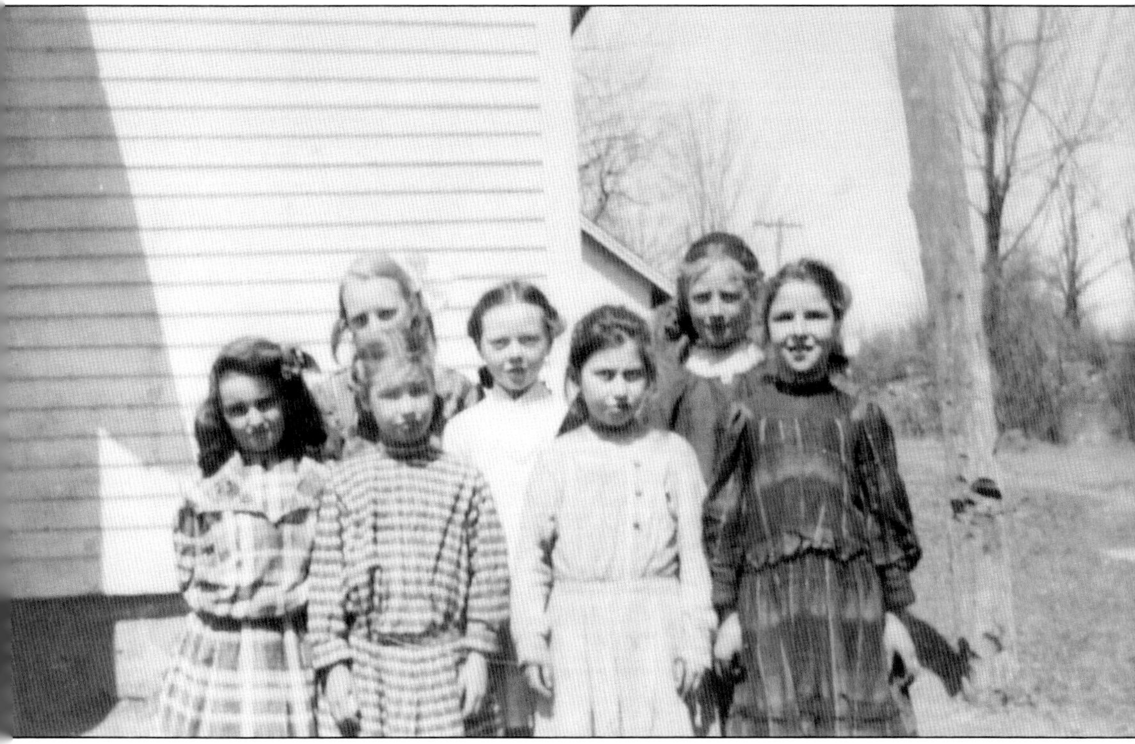

The fifth-grade class of North Canton (*c.* 1910) was composed of only seven children. From left to right are: (front row) Edna Miller, Nellie Sweeton (Humphrey), Annie Smith (Schmidt?), and Mary Rich (Jensen); (back row) Alta Root, Gertrude Vining, and Lillian Drake. The photograph and information were contributed by Eunice Sweeton.

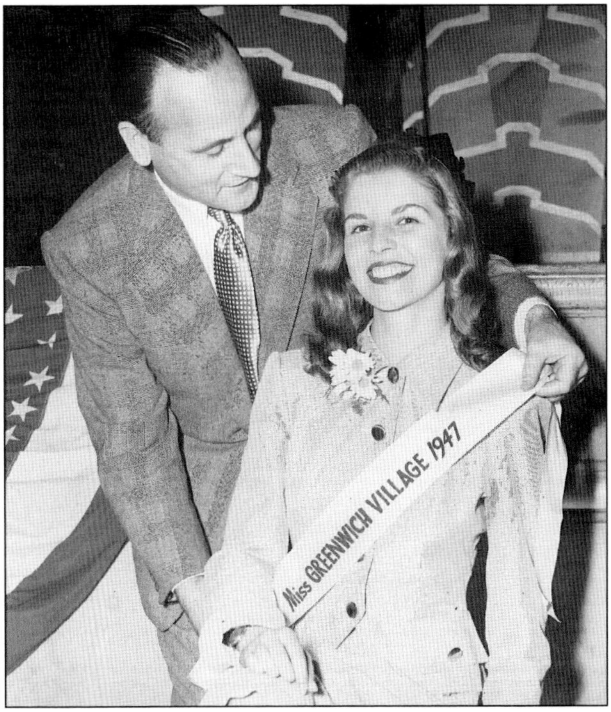

Nancy Reinhart Charleton was Miss Greenwich Village of 1947. Nancy, a resident of Cornwall Bridge, became well known as a journalist and businesswoman.

Nancy Charleton is shown again a little bit older but no less than sensational in her beauty. Nancy led a varied life, and was successful in almost all of her endeavors. Her beauty did not take away from her professionalism as a journalist and businesswoman.

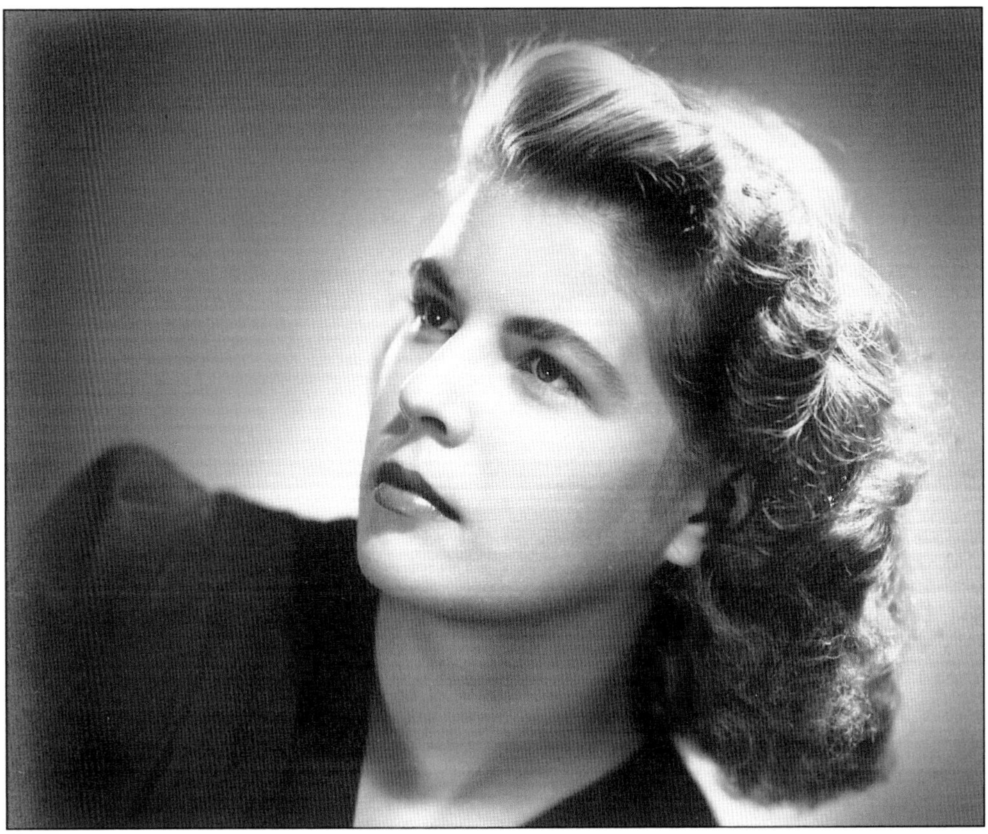

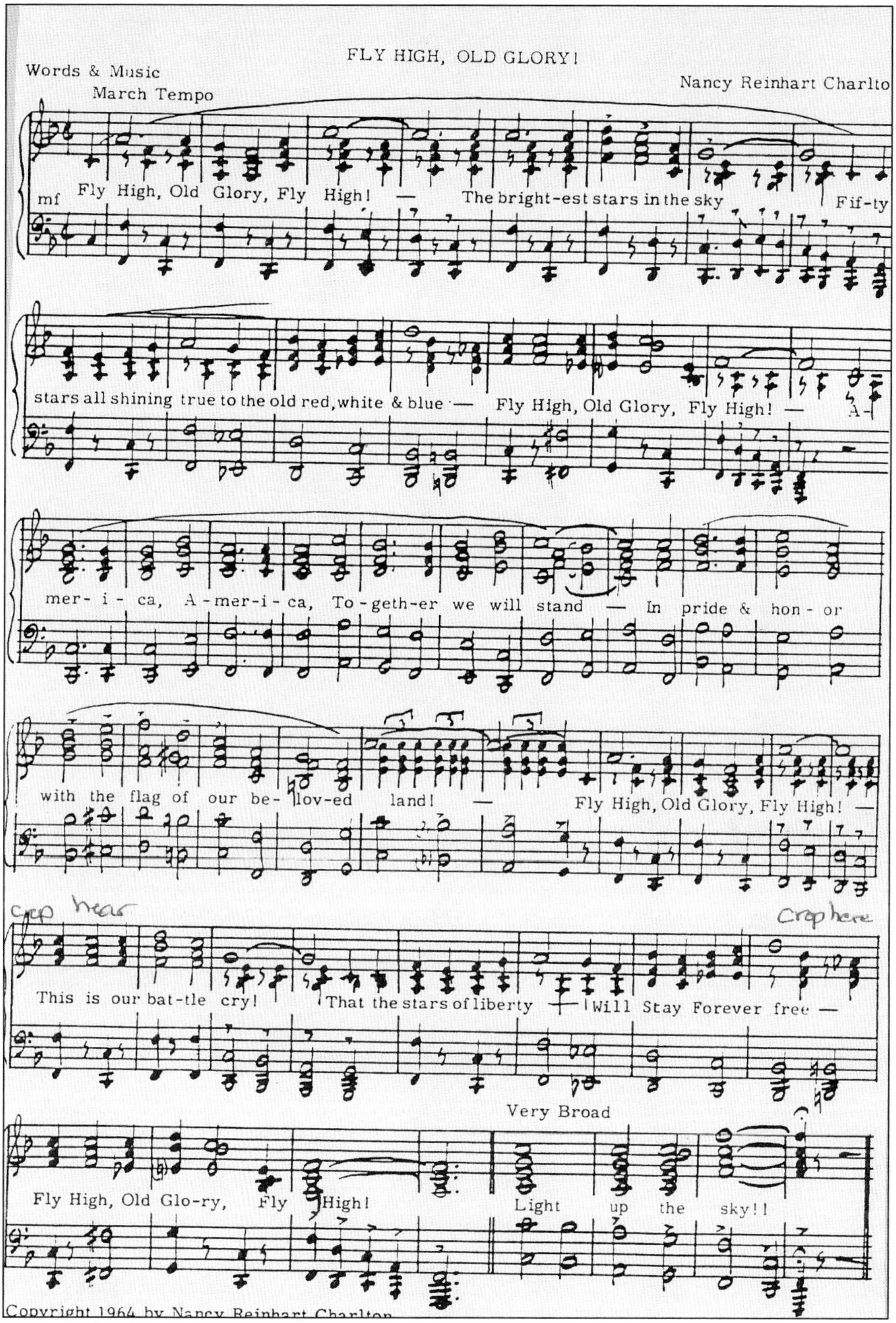

Nancy Charleton wrote "Fly High, Old Glory," which was highly recognized but never published. Beverly Sills thought the song showed great talent but informed Nancy that "patriotism is dead."

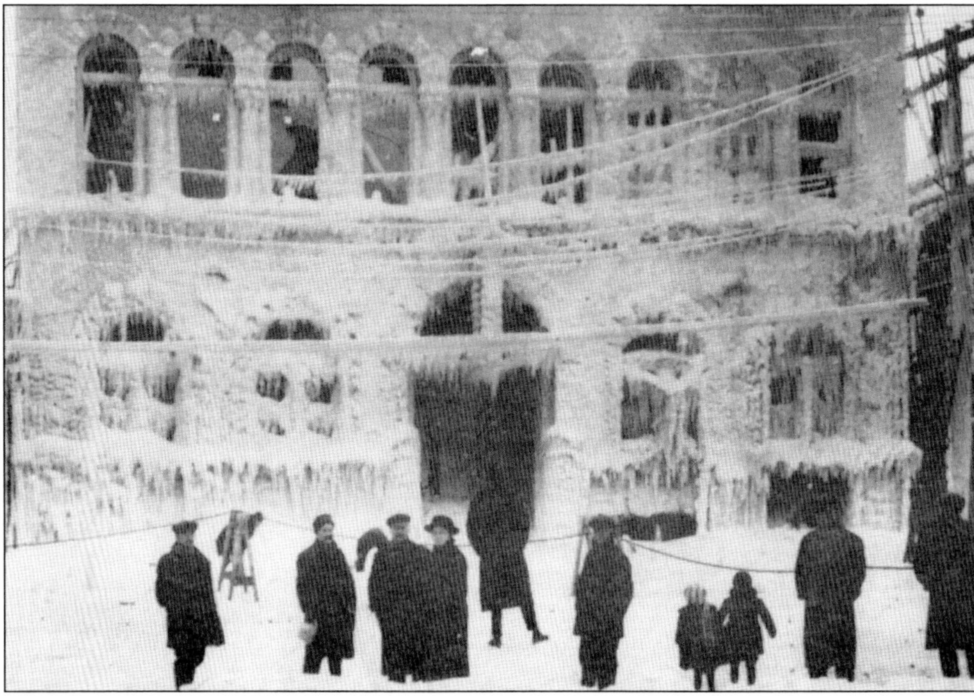

When the Strand Theater burned it was one of Torrington's three movie theaters. The Palace Theater is no longer in operation, leaving only the Warner Theater to compete with modern-day movie theaters.

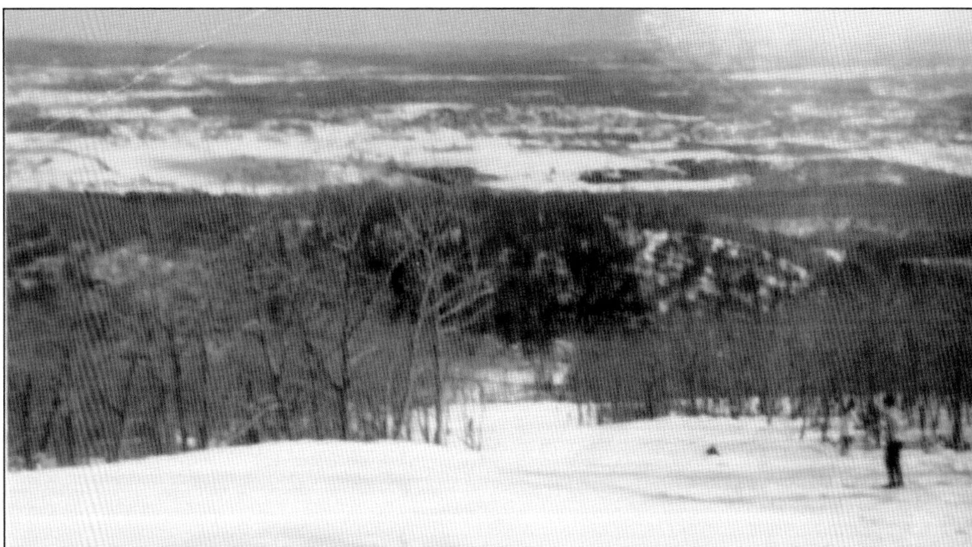

Mohawk Mountain, the Nutmeg State's first ski area, was due to open in 1948 when a ferocious winter storm dumped tons of snow on untested slopes. The first two seasons were Mohawk's snowiest. The third season became known as "the winter that didn't snow." Undaunted, Walt Schoenknecht created the first artificial snow ever made, saving the season. No historical photographs of the area are available as they were "blown away" during the tornadoes that struck the area in the late 1980s.

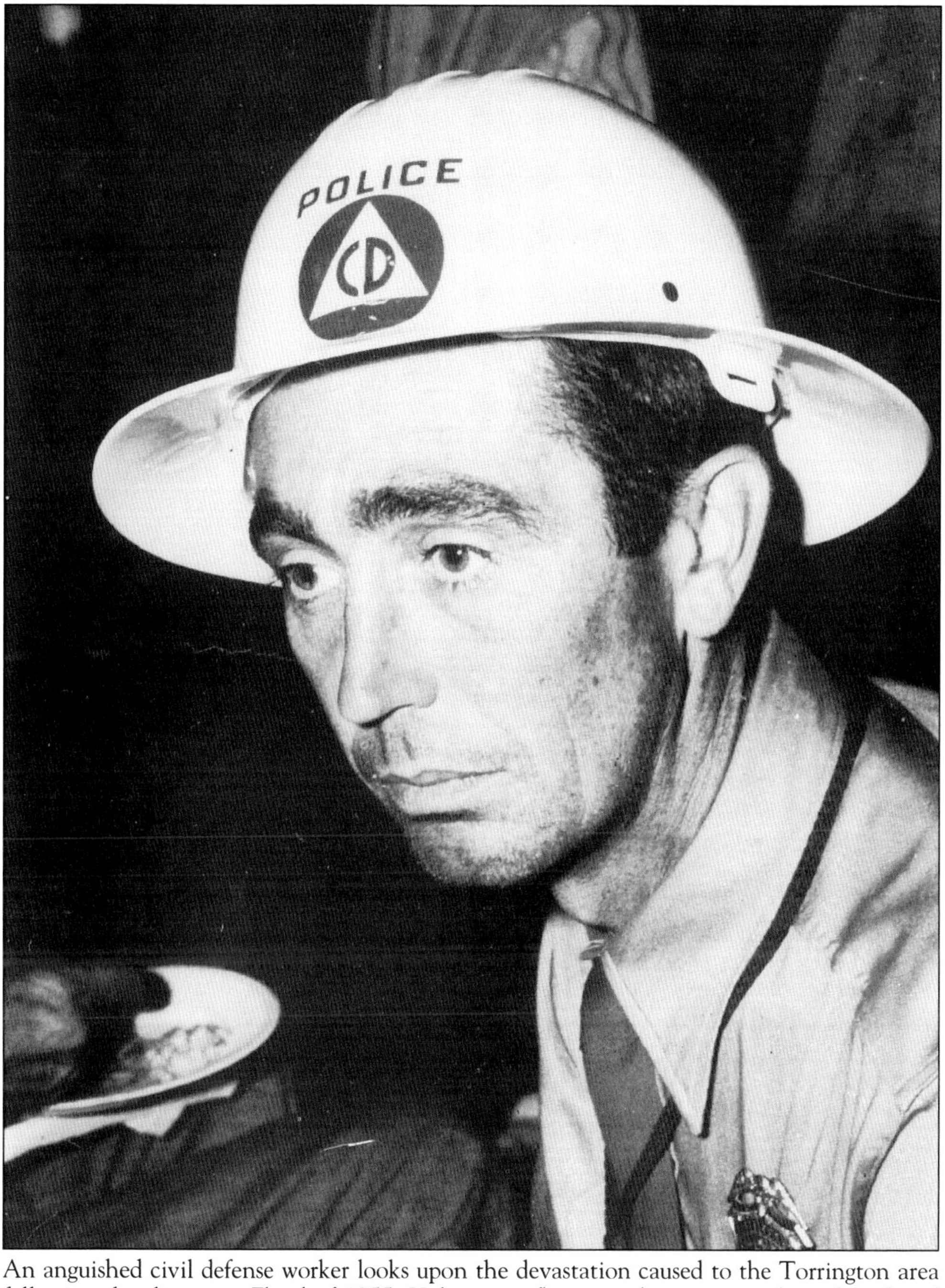

An anguished civil defense worker looks upon the devastation caused to the Torrington area following the disastrous Flood of 1955. Helicopters flew in volunteers, supplies of food and clean water, and medical supplies for the injured and ill. Typhoid inoculations were given to protect the citizens of all of the towns severely impacted by this storm, which was a result of Hurricane Connie.

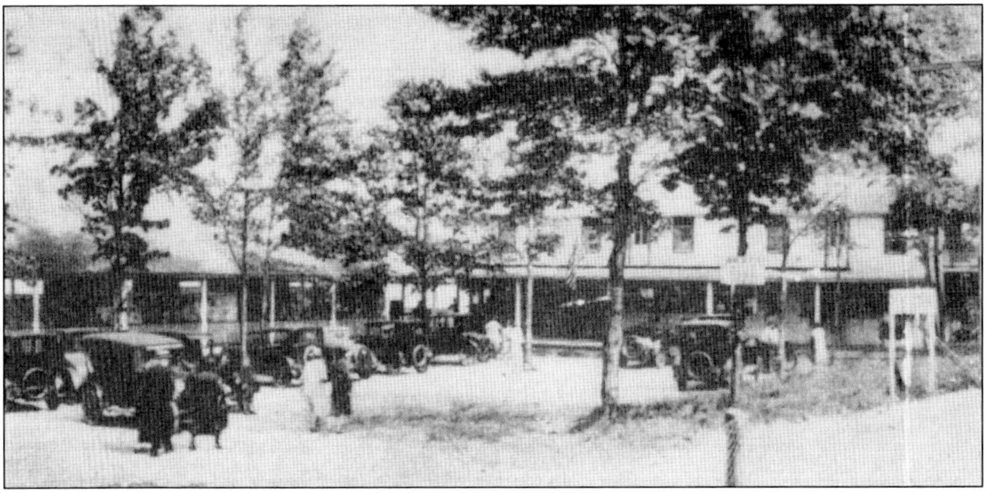

The Music Box Casino was located on Bantam Lake in Morris. The Music Box later became Beverly's—a well-known dance club that featured such artists as Chubby Checkers. When the building became too unsafe to use for public recreation it became a boat launch.

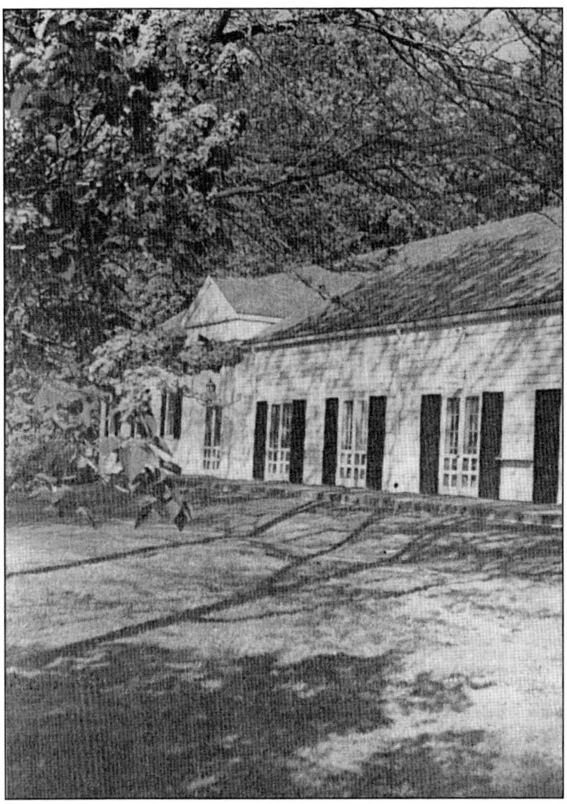

Music Mountain, located in Falls Village, has been in operation since 1930. Its founder was Jacques Gordon; he and his wife Ruth created what has become home to the oldest continuing chamber music festival in the United States. It is the permanent home of the Gordon String Quartet, and is the only cultural institution ever built by Sears Roebuck, which at the time was in the business of building houses. Gordon Hall is shown here.

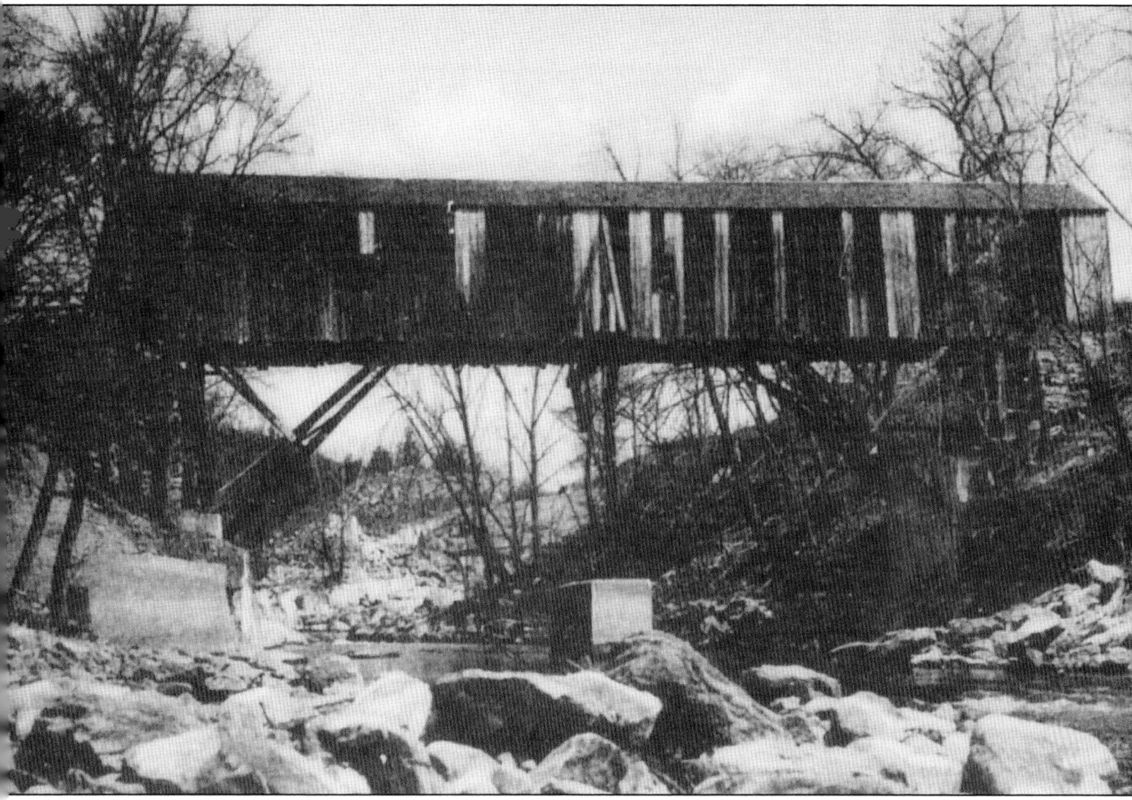

Known as Bull's Bridge in Kent, this is one of the bridges that George Washington crossed on his way to the battle at Fort Ticonderoga. Kent was settled in 1738 and was one of the area's major producers of iron.

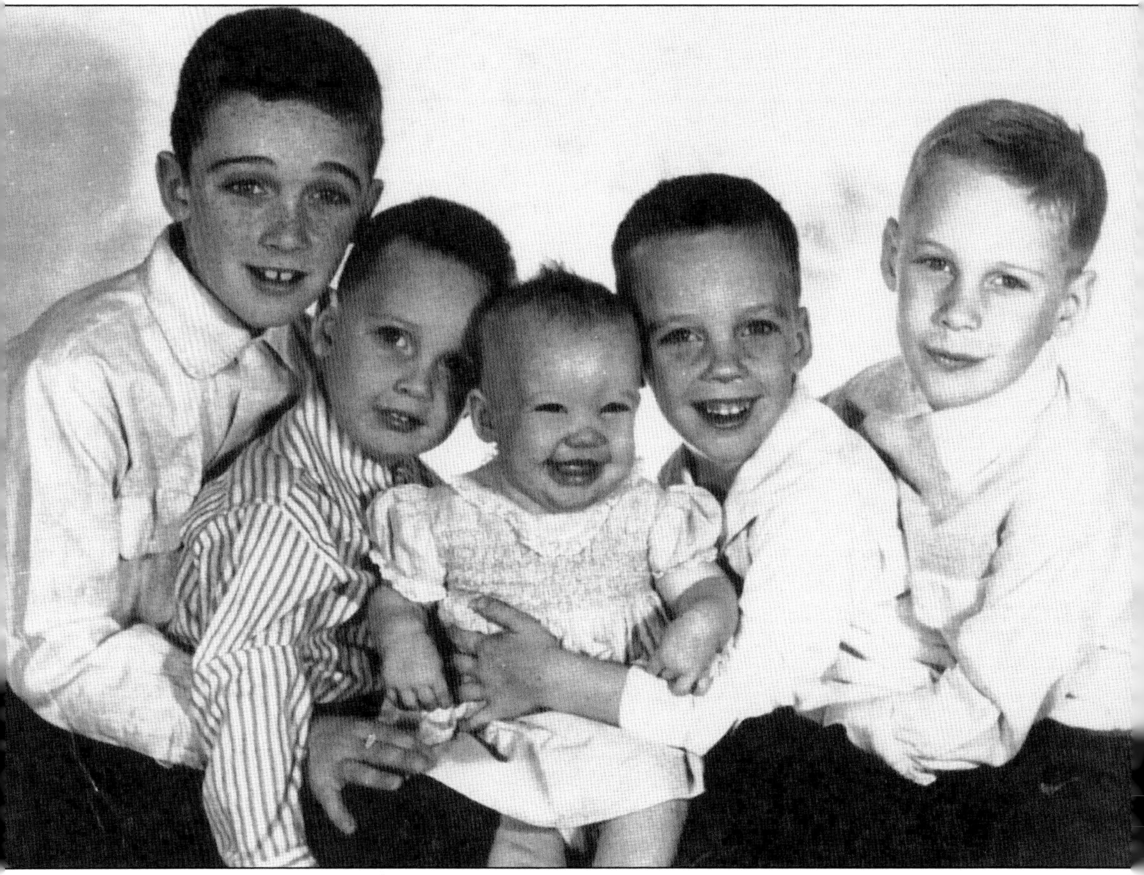

These are the children of Attorney Thomas F. McDermott Sr. and his wife Vina, at the time he assumed the role of clerk of the Superior Court in Litchfield in 1958. The family moved to East Street into a home that was once known as Aunt Kate's Boarding Home. From left to right are: Thomas Jr. (who is currently an attorney in Waterbury and Litchfield); Greg McDermott; Betsy (the author of this book); John; and Peter. Vina McDermott was born in 1962 and is not pictured here. Aunt Kate's is well-remembered in Litchfield as a place where "marriages were born." Operated by Katherine Fitzpatrick, many young men would come to spend time there over the weekends and to court Litchfield's young ladies. The marriages of Hank and Gertrude O'Donnell, George and Isabel Murphy, and John and Lillian Cooney were among those that were supposedly encouraged by this beautiful setting. (Courtesy of Alice Kelly Lenox.)

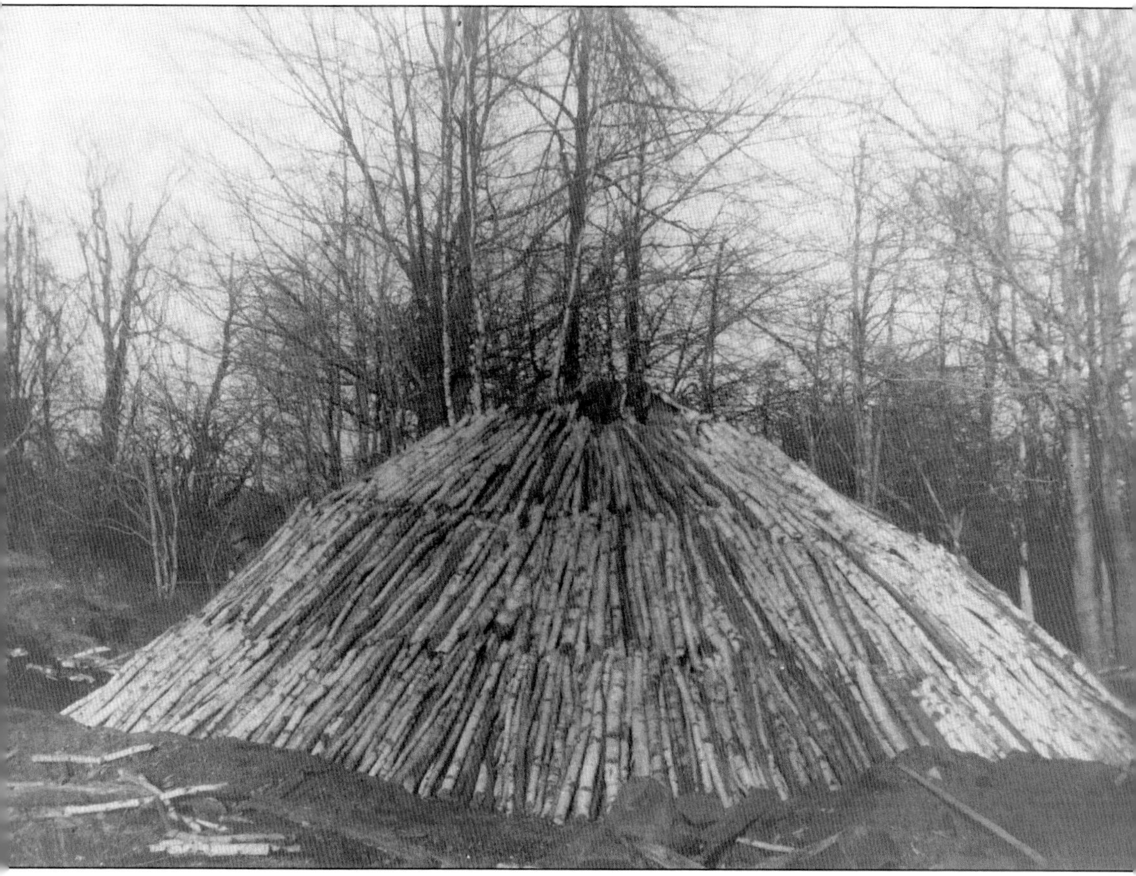

Part of the process of making charcoal is shown here at the Hogan Farm in Burlington in about 1920. (Courtesy of Alice Szczesniak.)

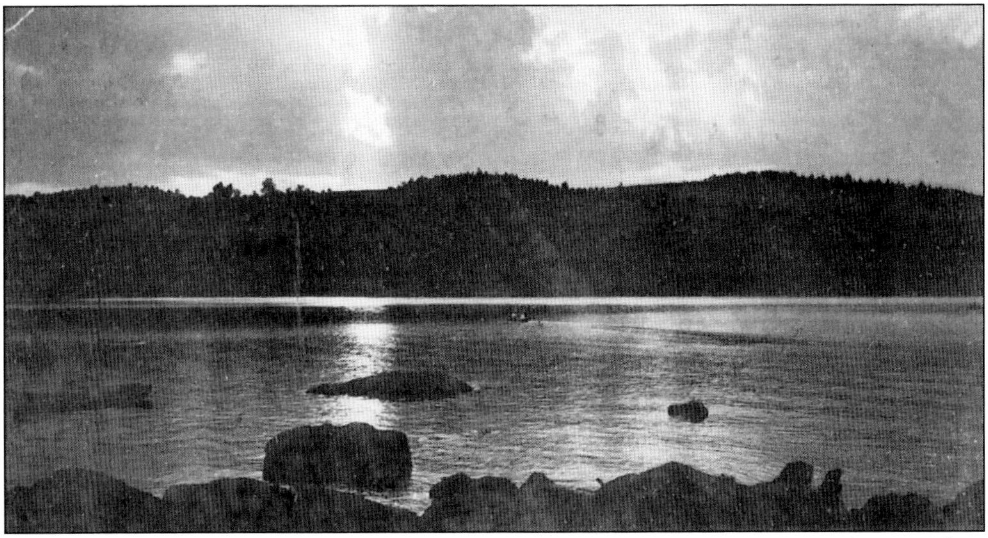

A moonlit night over Highland Lake in Winsted was captured by an enterprising photographer. Highland Lake drew a lot of summer visitors then, and it continues to do so today.

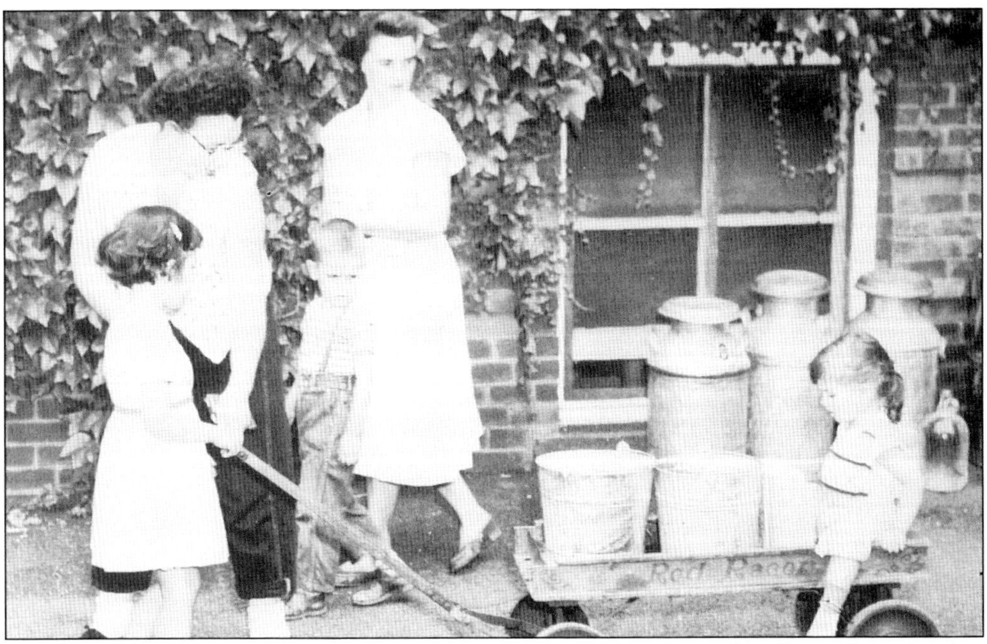

Mothers and their children bring home uncontaminated water and milk to their families following the Flood of 1955.

Four

A Time to Dance, A Time to Mourn

It was not an uncommon practice
for young boys to skinny-dip in the many old swimming holes
throughout the Wolcottville area.
Since towels and bathing suits were not "allowed,"
the boys would fold their clothing in neat piles left along the banks
and run around to dry off.
On some days, according to Charles Johnson,
one or more of the boys would find their clothes
tied up into numerous hard knots
which they needed to use both hands and teeth to untie.
The others boys would stand about
chanting "chaw beef, chaw beef."

(As paraphrased from Memories of Wolcottville by Charles Johnson,
used with the permission of the Torrington Historical Society.)

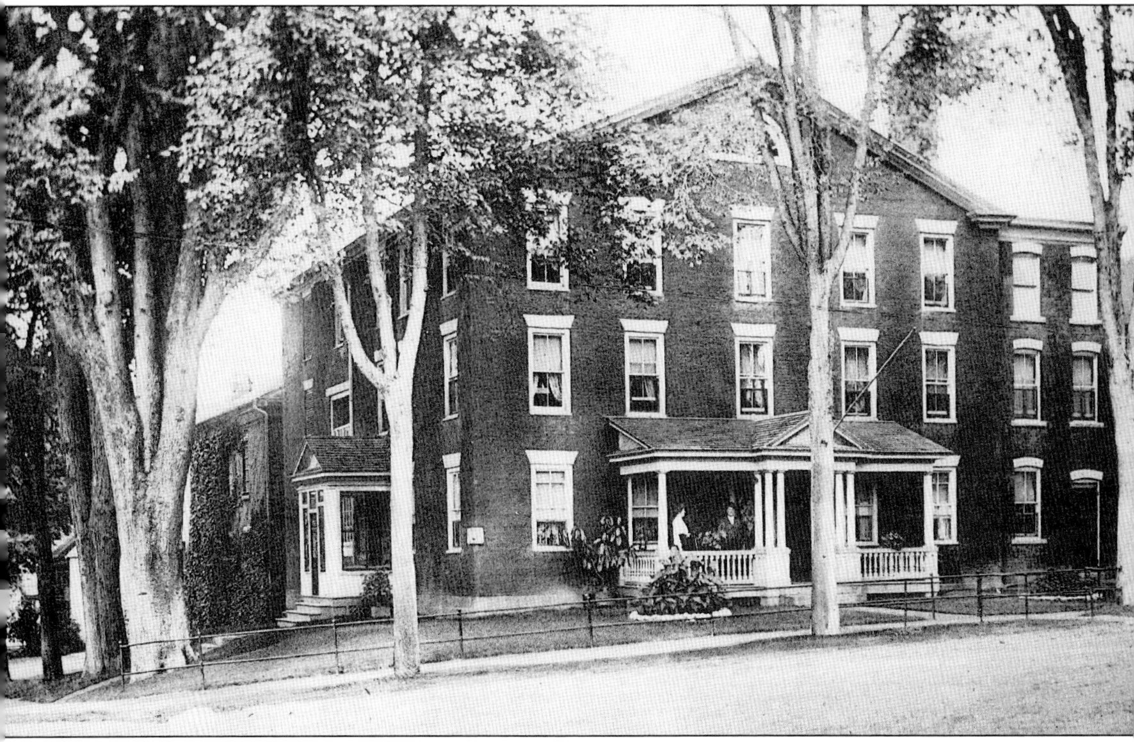

The Litchfield County Jail, erected in 1811, is the oldest public building in Litchfield. It has the distinction of sharing an adjacent wall with the First National Bank. It now serves as a residential program for women experiencing problems with substance abuse.

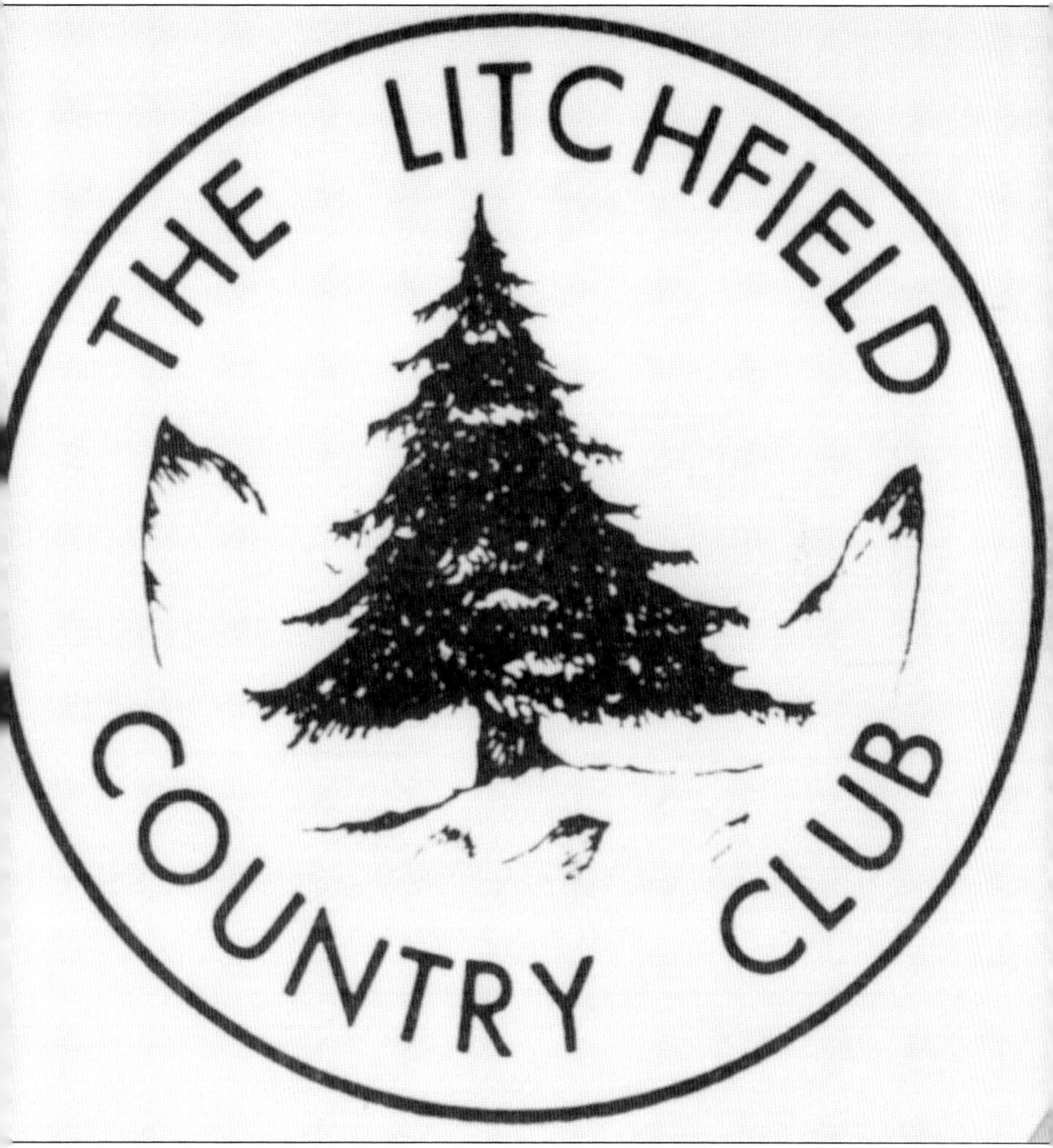

The Litchfield Country Club has been active now for over one hundred years. It began operating in 1892 at the urging of Alexander McNeil. From 1893 until 1914 the Connecticut State Tennis Tournaments were held here. Between 1898 and 1904, Litchfield became divided socially between its east and west sides, to the point that summer visitors became offended by the competitive efforts between the two. In 1916, Alaine White, through his role with the White Memorial Foundation, offered the Catlin Farm and house for a golf course and clubhouse. White later donated pine trees. In 1943, President Alexander Dostin agreed to an 18-hole golf course and in 1952 a liquor license was obtained. The Litchfield Country Club celebrated its 100th anniversary on September 9, 1992. Committee member Betty Merz provided this information in the form of a brochure written by the Anniversary Committee.

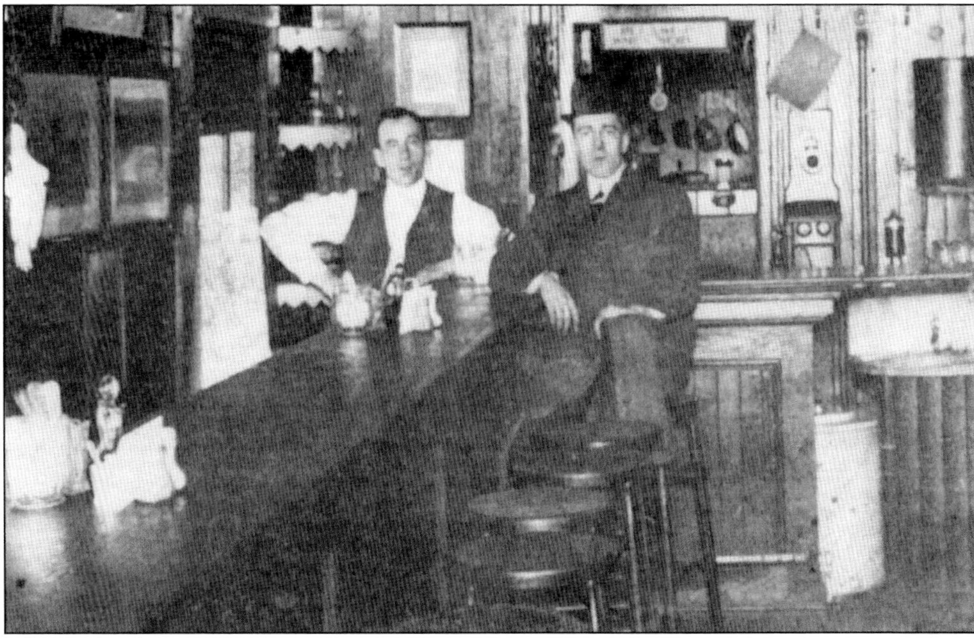

A bartender and customer share a quiet moment in a Torrington tavern. Although the author is not certain, the tavern may be the Yankee Pedlar, which was located within the Conley Inn.

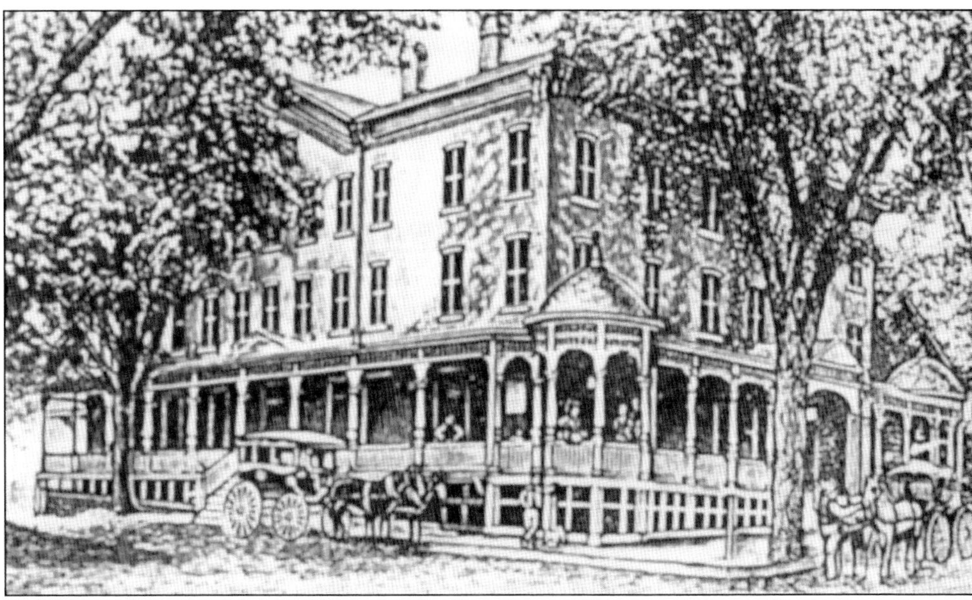

The Conley Inn was owned and operated for many years by the two Ruben brothers (Arthur and Gerald) who also operated a photographic studio in Torrington. Regretfully, ownership of the Conley Inn recently changed hands.

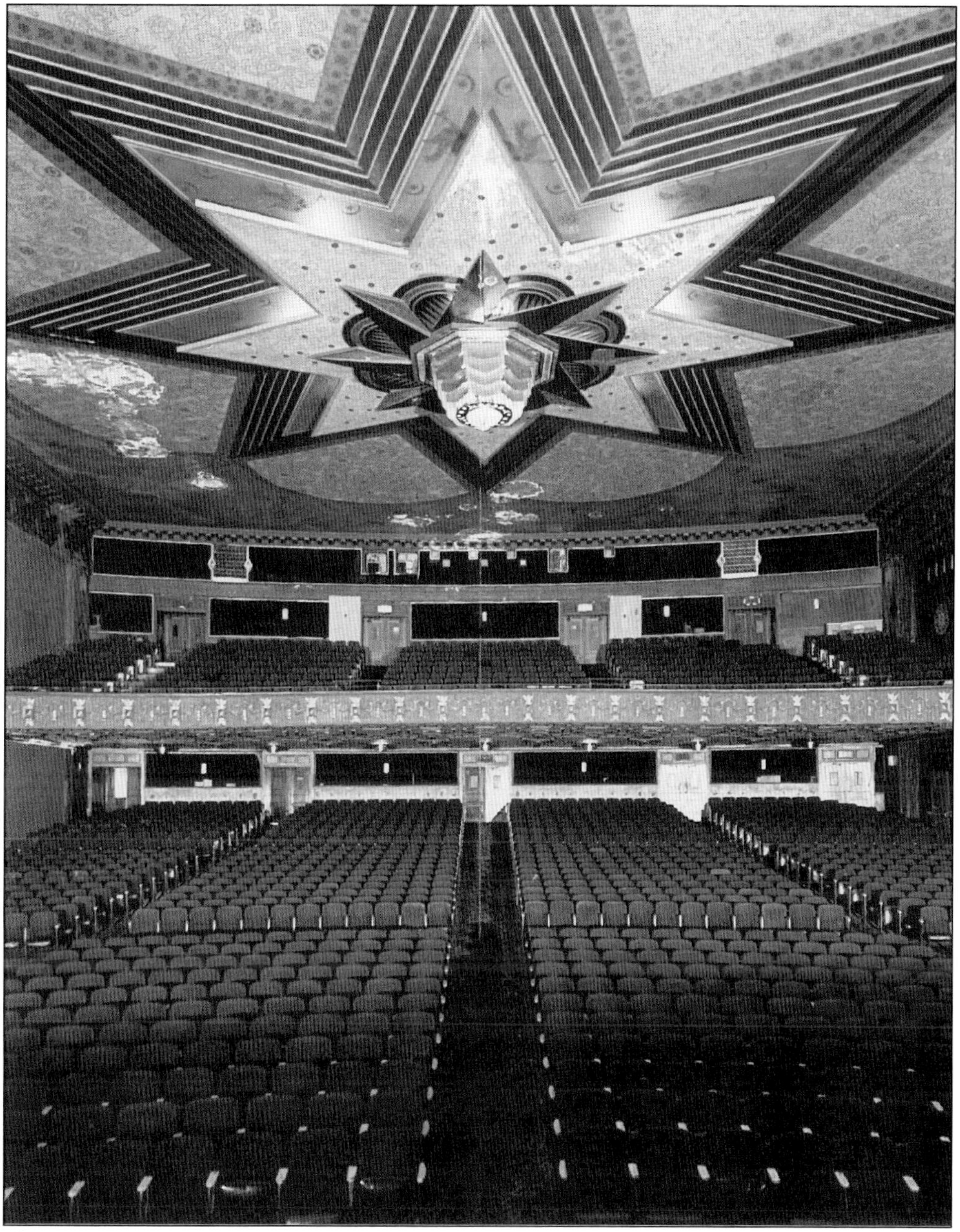

The Warner Theatre, located on Main Street in Torrington, began operating in the 1930s, when the entertainment business was booming. During the heart of the Depression, Warner Brother's Studio paid $750,000 to build this elaborate structure. The Warner's design is known as Art Deco and it was at one time one of the largest theaters in Connecticut, having the capacity to seat over 1,700 individuals. Beginning as a movie theater where Saturday matinees could be seen for just 50¢, it quickly advanced into offering operas, ballets, on/off broadway hits, etc.

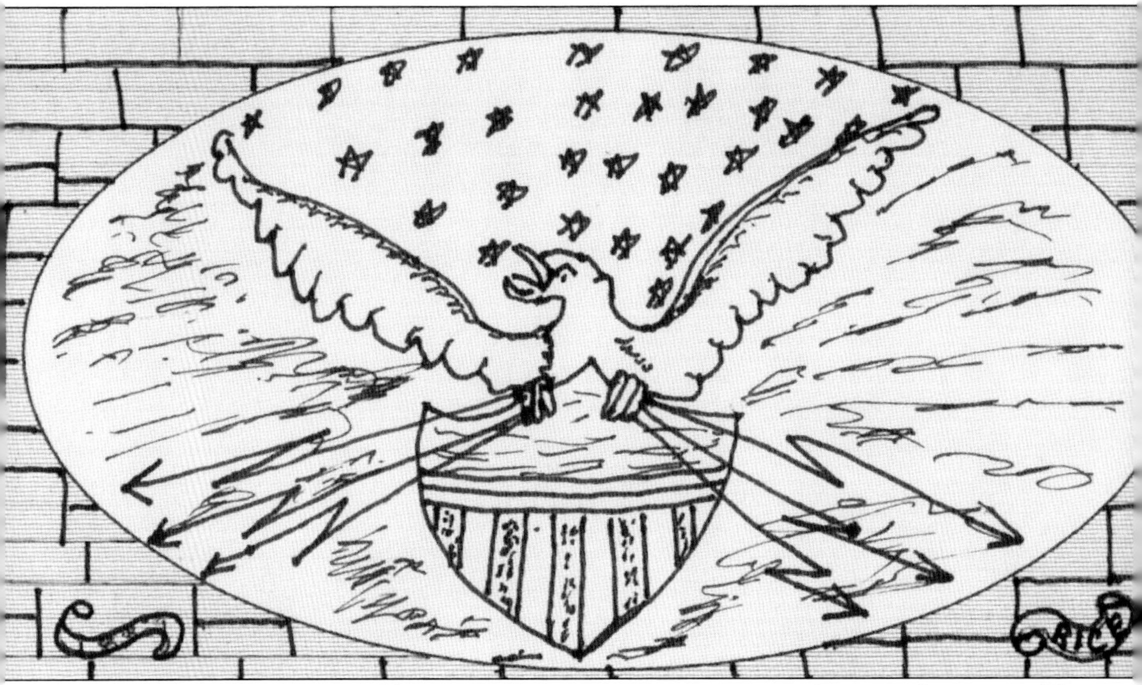

The original sign of the Old Pinney Inn in Riverton was just recently put up for auction. This nineteenth-century sign was painted by William Rice and is 3-by-5 feet. It is considered a classic piece of "Americana." Four bullet holes, the result of a clash between the owner and local militiamen back in the 1800s, make the sign even more attractive. According to historian Douglas Roberts, Reuben Pinney (the owner) was tending bar when some militiamen came in for a drink. The house rule stated that no loaded weapons were allowed within the tavern. The militiamen thereby "unloaded" on the sign.

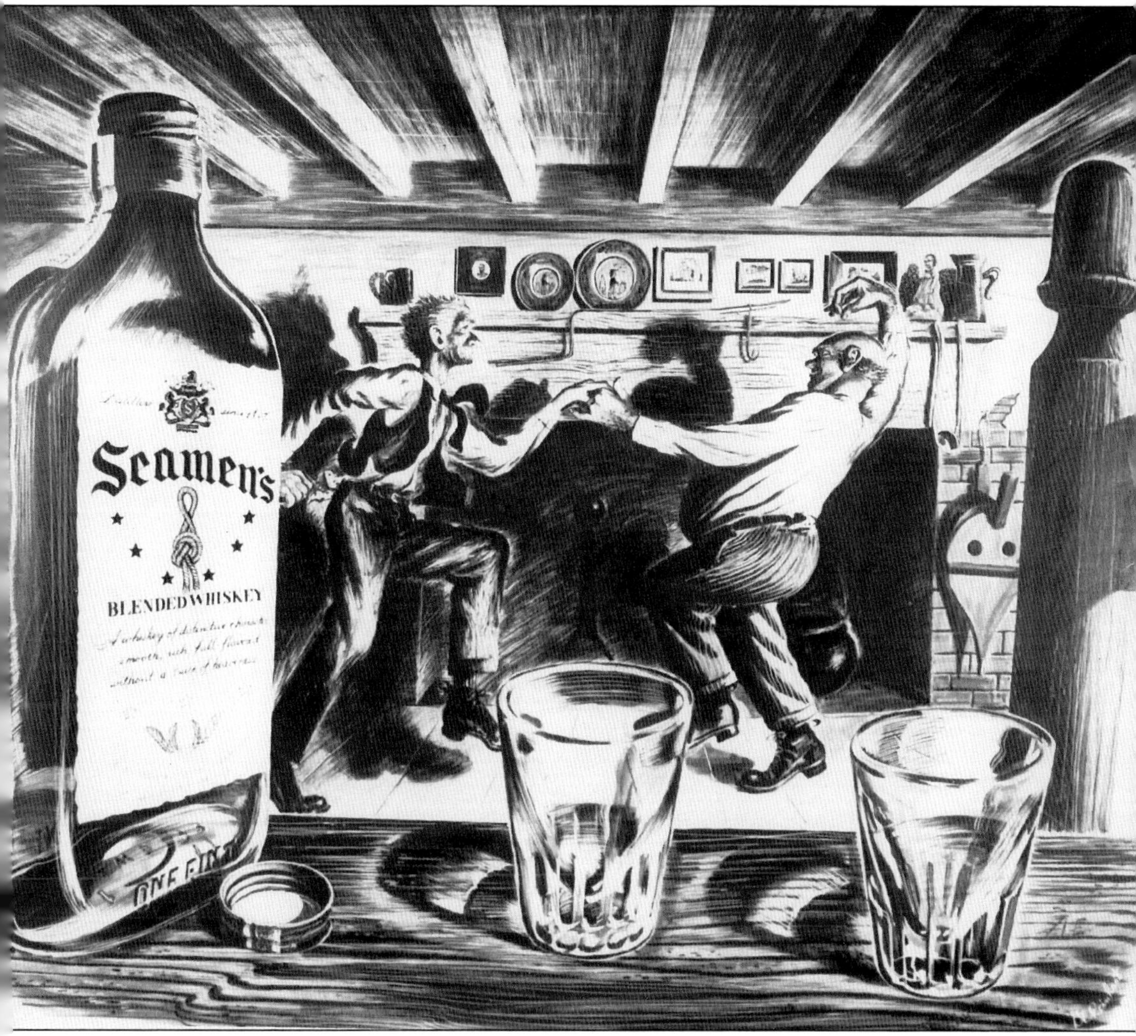

This lithograph was created by artist Carl Reinhart as a "spoof" on Seagrams Whiskey. The late Reinhart, who retired and spent his final years as a landscape artist in Cornwall Bridge, had spent many years in New York involved in advertising art as well as other artistic endeavors. (Courtesy of Andrew Charleton.)

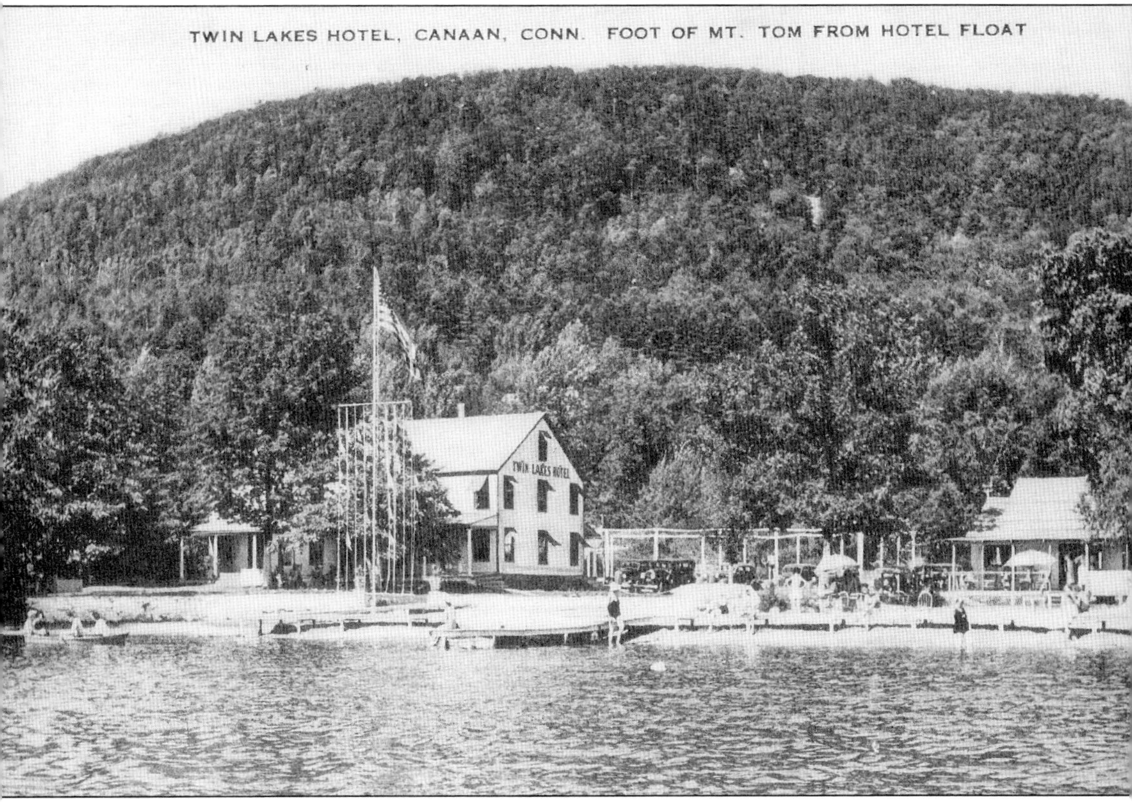

This view of the Twin Lakes Hotel in Canaan was taken from one of the hotel's floats. A major attraction for summer visitors, the hotel was located at the foot of Mt. Tom. Within the town of Canaan there exists a cemetery which contains the gravestone of Captain Gerston Hewitt. Hewitt pretended to be the "village idiot" and wandered about Fort Ticonderoga under the direction of Ethan Allen. His "act" was a cover to allow him to secure plans and report defenses to Allen.

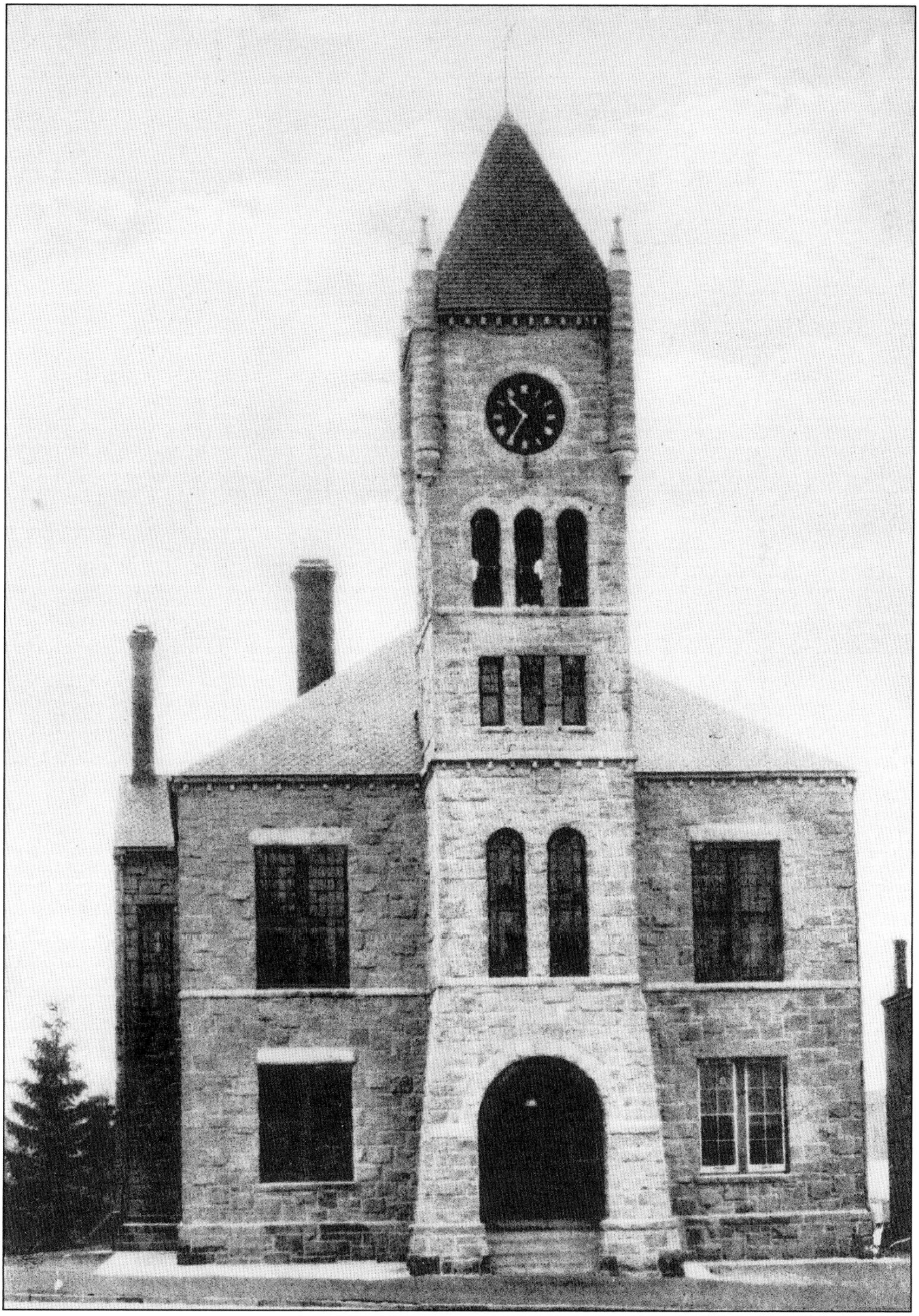

The Collinsville Green was photographed during the centennial celebration held on July 6, 1906. At that time, Collinsville was part of Canton, Burlington, and Harwinton. It was named after Samuel Collins who, with his brother David Collins and cousin William Walks, established an axe factory, which was the beginning of the well-known Collins Company.

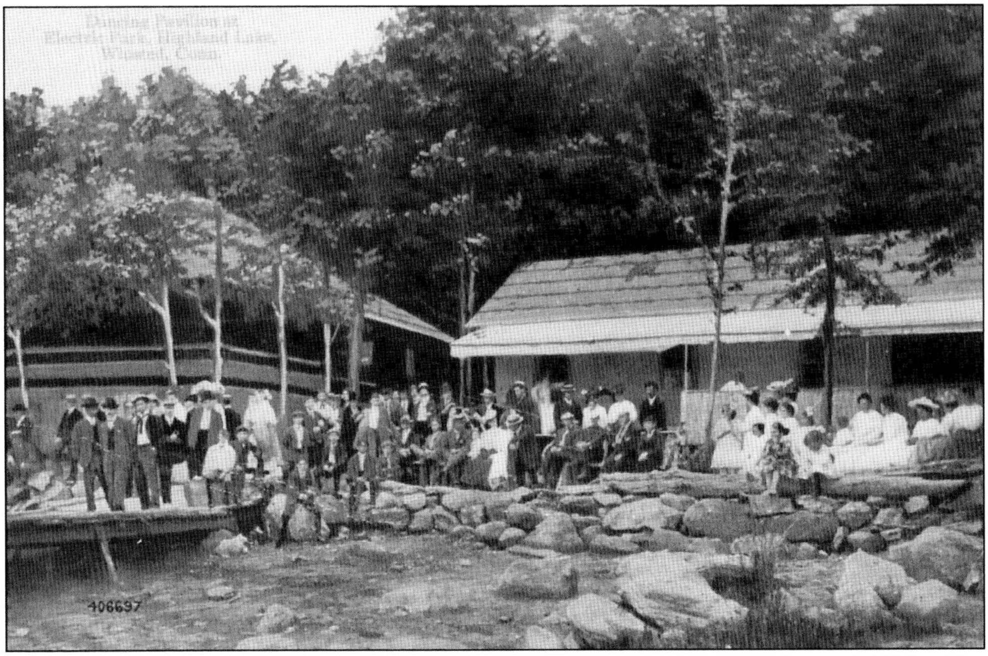

This dancing pavilion was located at Electric Park in Winsted during the mid-1900s. The nation was between wars, and the entertainment business throughout the Litchfield Hills was beginning to blossom.

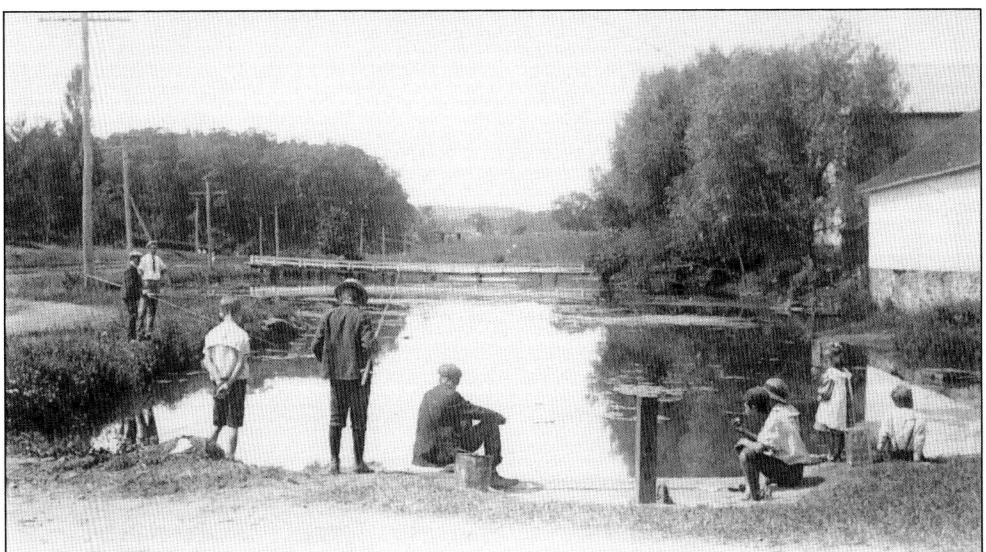

In the early 1900s town fishermen gathered in Lakeville to share fish stories and conversation—and to occasionally catch fish.

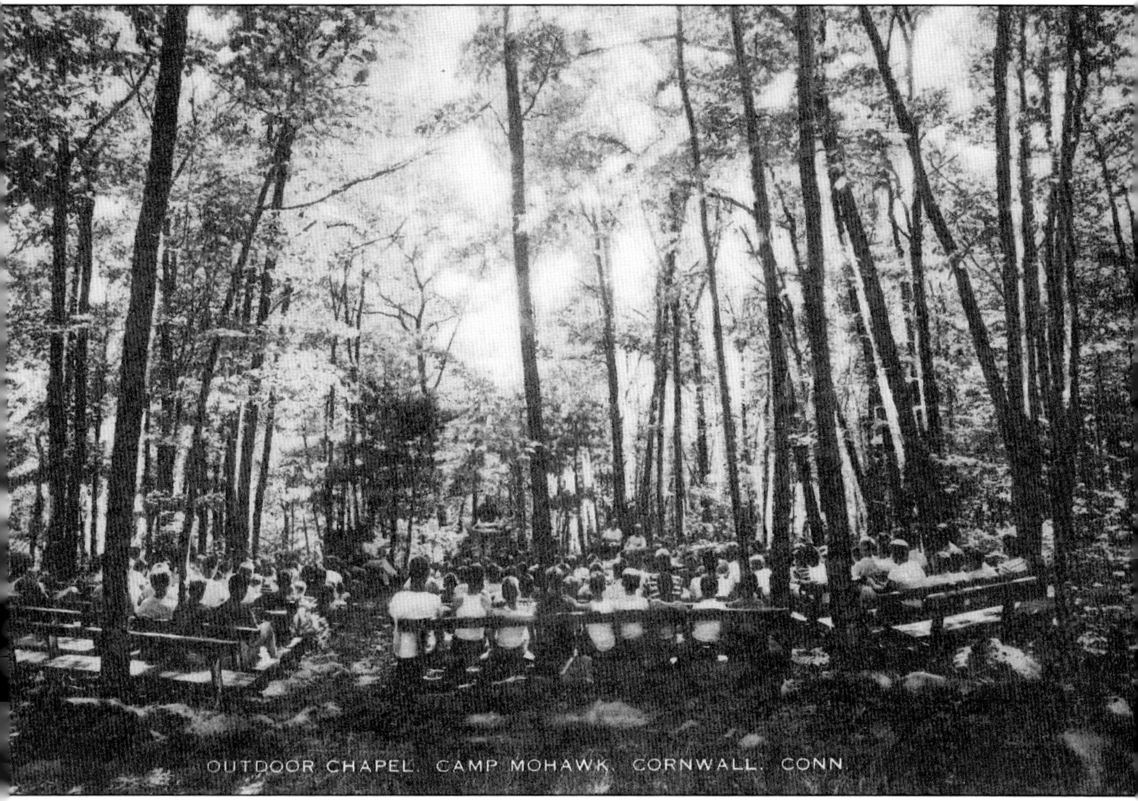

This photograph was taken at the outdoor Mohawk Chapel. The Nathana Merwin Case Chapel and stone pulpit were dedicated in 1937. Nearby was the Mohawk Summer Camp for the Litchfield and Fairfield County YMCAs. Located in Cornwall, the camp has been in operation since the early 1900s. The meetings at the chapel did much to strengthen Methodism in that area.

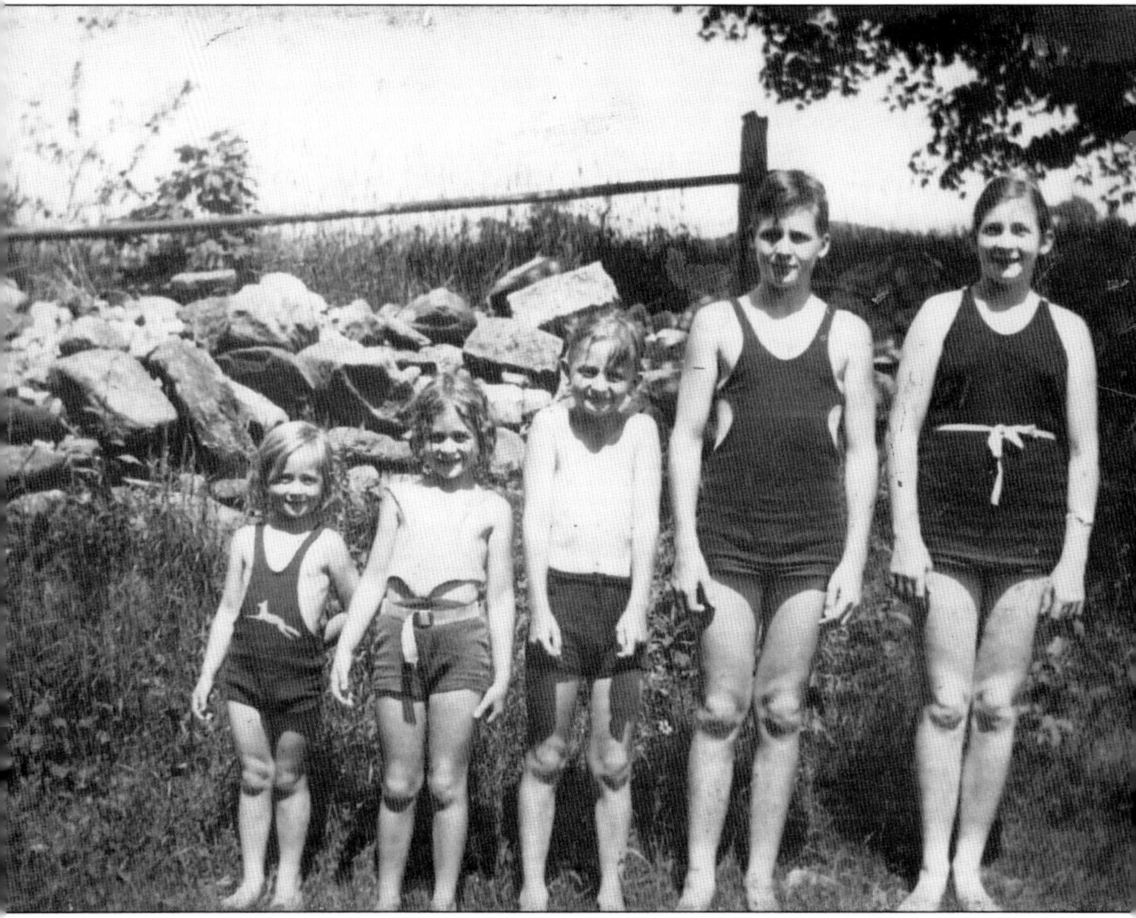

The last swim of the year in the Housatonic River is celebrated by the children of Flora Brown in 1935. From left to right are: Alice, Matthew, John, and Betty. This photograph was taken in Puffingham of Cornwall Bridge. (Courtesy of Alice Szczesniak.)

Five

A Time to Love, A Time to Hate

It became quite common for the young men
who attended the Tapping Reeve Law School
to pursue and even wed the young women
in attendance at the Sarah Pierce Female Academy.
The academy, being situated next to the law school,
allotted plenty of time for frivolity among the students.
This was a time when the poetry of Lord Byron
made young girls swoon
and the air was light with romance.
Sarah Pierce was born in Litchfield
to John Pierce and his first wife, Mary Patterson.
When Sarah was only fourteen years old, her father died.
Sarah began her teaching career in Litchfield out of her own home.
The school grew rapidly, necessitating the establishment
of the Litchfield Female Academy in 1827.
At one time, there were 131 students at the academy.
Religious instruction was given by Lyman Beecher
in return for his own daughter's tuition.

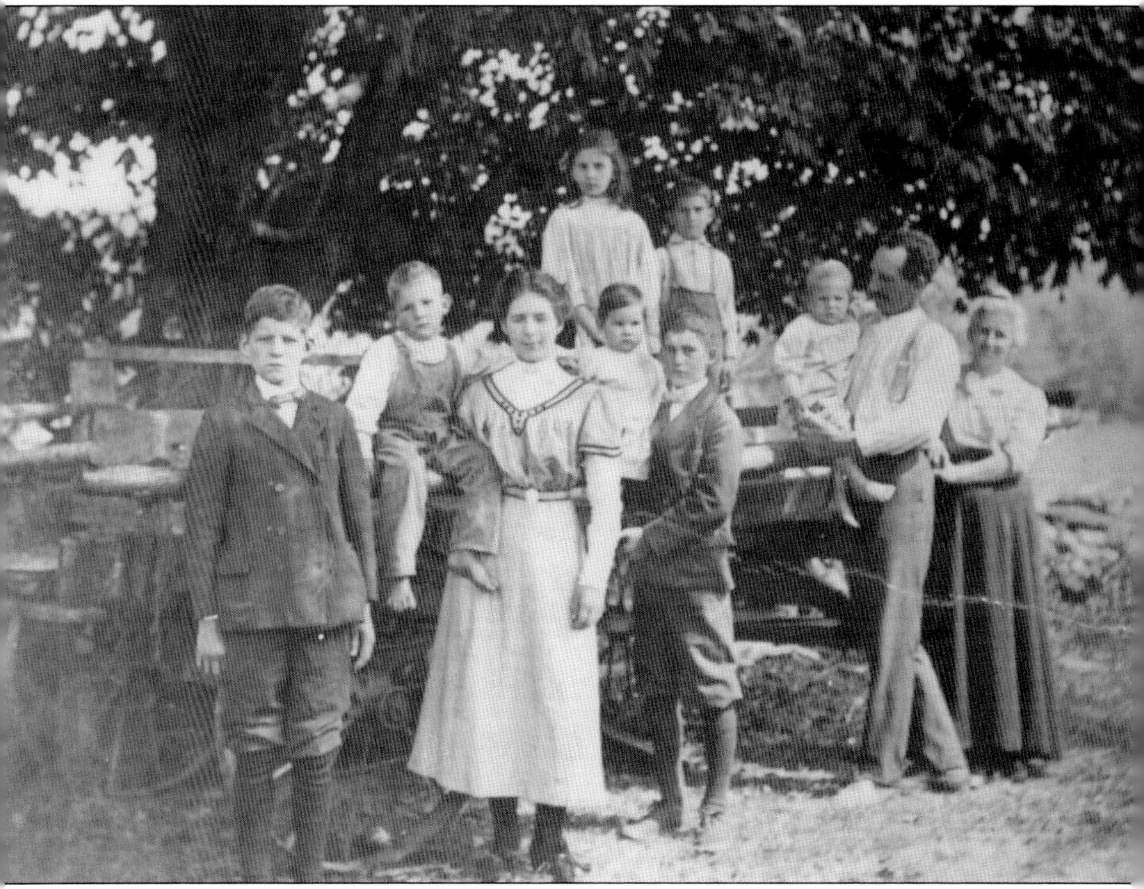

This photograph of the family of David and Alice Strong features eight of their eleven children. The children include Eunice (1896), Donald (1897), Noble (1899), Ruth (1901), Philip (1903), Andrew (1907), Harley (1909, held by his father), Rebecca (1910), Rachel (1911), Connie (1915), and Nathan (1916). (Courtesy of Paula Strong Zehring.)

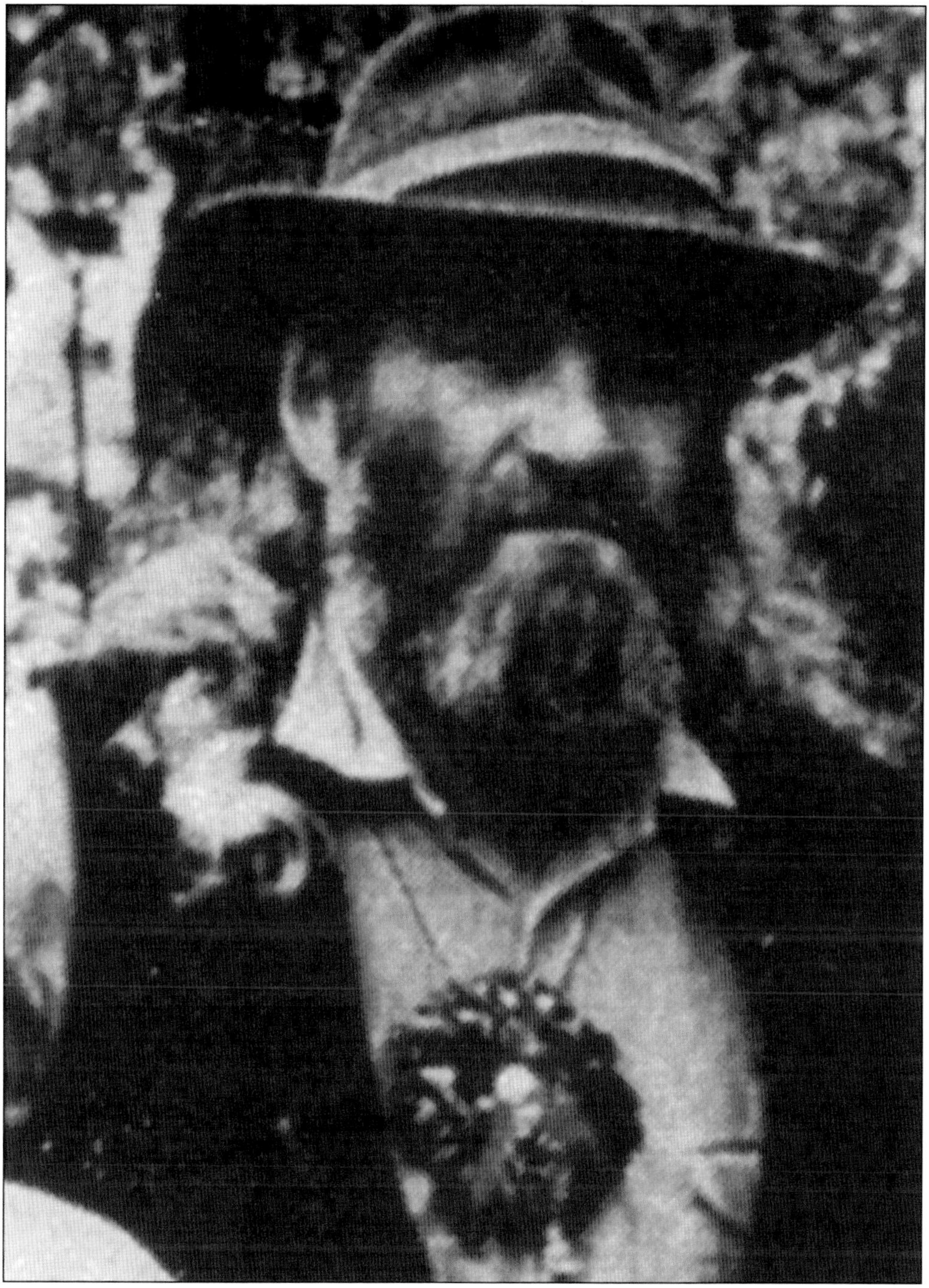

Nate Strong is thought to be the last male descendent within the line of the Elder John Strong family. Nate strongly resembles Elder John Strong, who is recognized as an ancestor of all the known families with the surname in New England and virtually all over this country. Born in Taunton, England, in 1605, Elder John (the son of Richard Strong) came to New England with his sister on March 20, 1630, in the ship *John and Mary*. The early Strong settlers and their descendants are scattered throughout the history of the Litchfield Hills area.

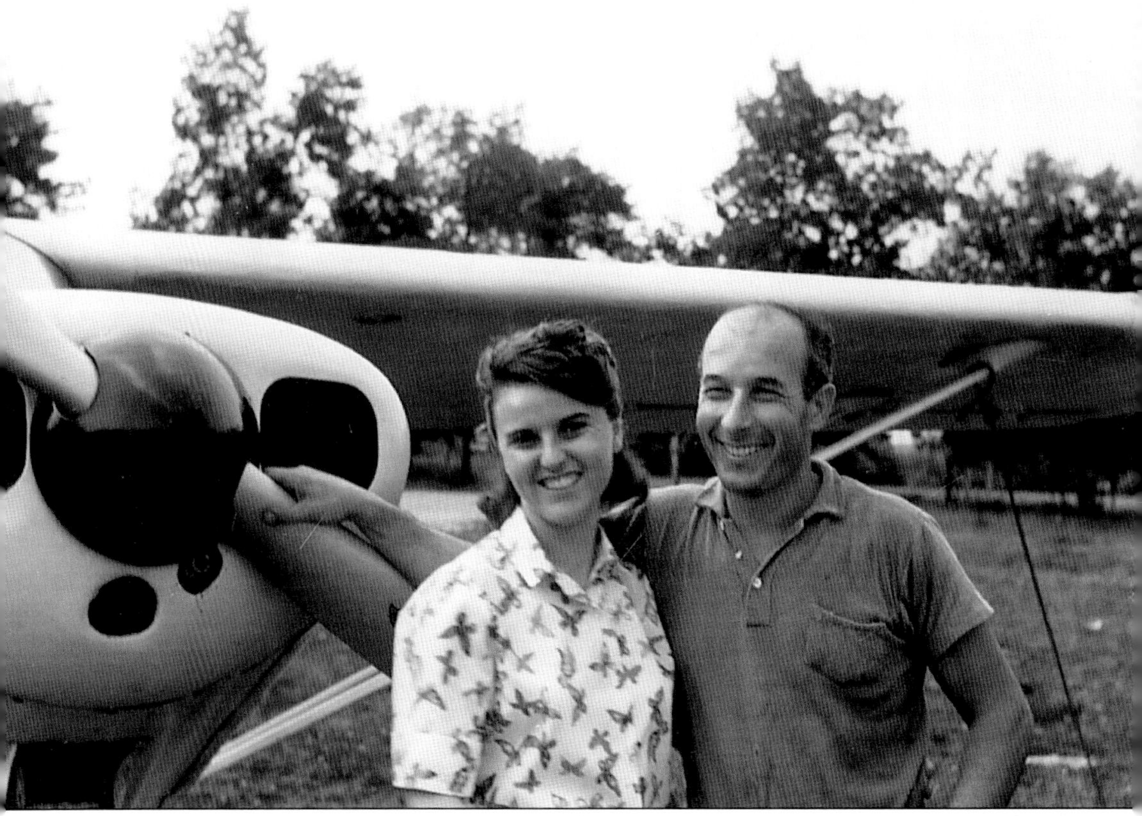

Fred Pesce (shown here with his now deceased wife) was at one time a young, aspiring pilot who later instituted the beginnings of what became known as Johnnycake Airport in Harwinton. With a twinkle in his eye, Pesce recalled the time that he and his wife flew over the stretch of land that was at the base of Johnnycake Mountain and he stated "that is where I want to keep my first plane." He approached the owner of the land, who was also the owner of Hogan's Cider Mill (located just across the street), and together they made what Pesce calls "a gentlemen's agreement" about a 1,000-square-foot plot of land. Others soon followed and the small area of land grew into a small commercial airport. Pesce, with a grin, recalled some of the celebrities who landed at or flew out of Johnnycake Airport and how much effort it took to clear the land for the runway. Today, the continued existence of Johnnycake Airport is up to the litigators, the courts, and those who trust and depend on its survival.

Charles Barber and his brother Henry also flew out of Johnnycake Airport. The Barber brothers owned a Stinson voyager. When Charlie got his own plane, he and his wife Margaret flew together in his Cessna 172. According to Margaret, she and Charlie often flew to Martha's Vineyard or Block Island for supper on Sunday afternoons. They flew as far south as Florida and as far west as Kansas.

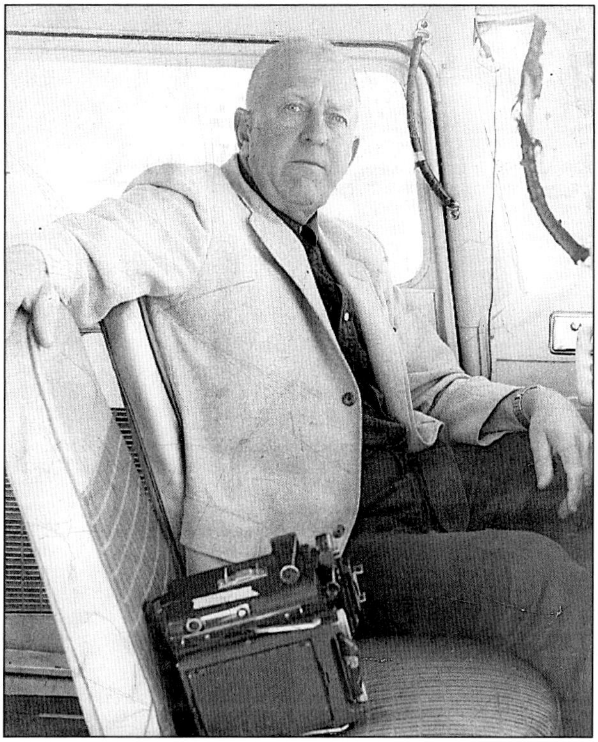

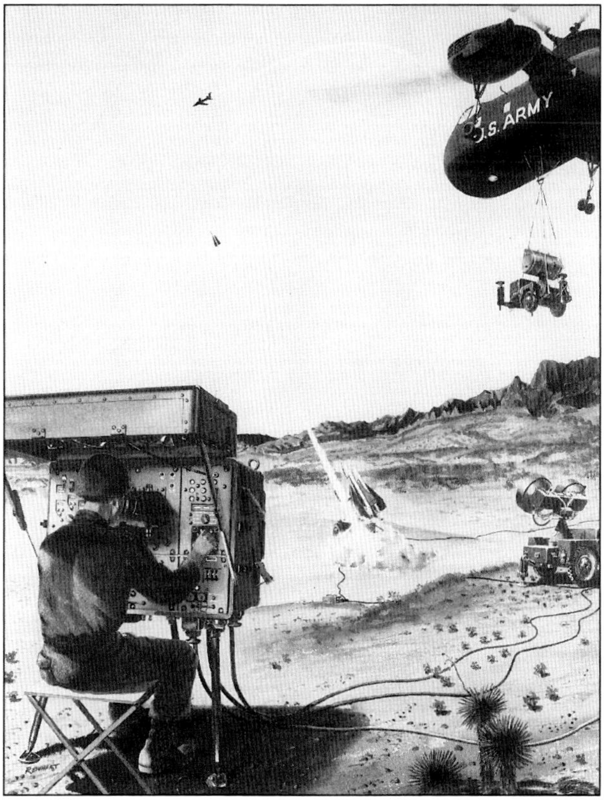

Reinhart worked during the post-war years of the 1950s on assignment from the Chrysler Corporation's missile division. His field drawings brought him commendations from Warner Von Braun.

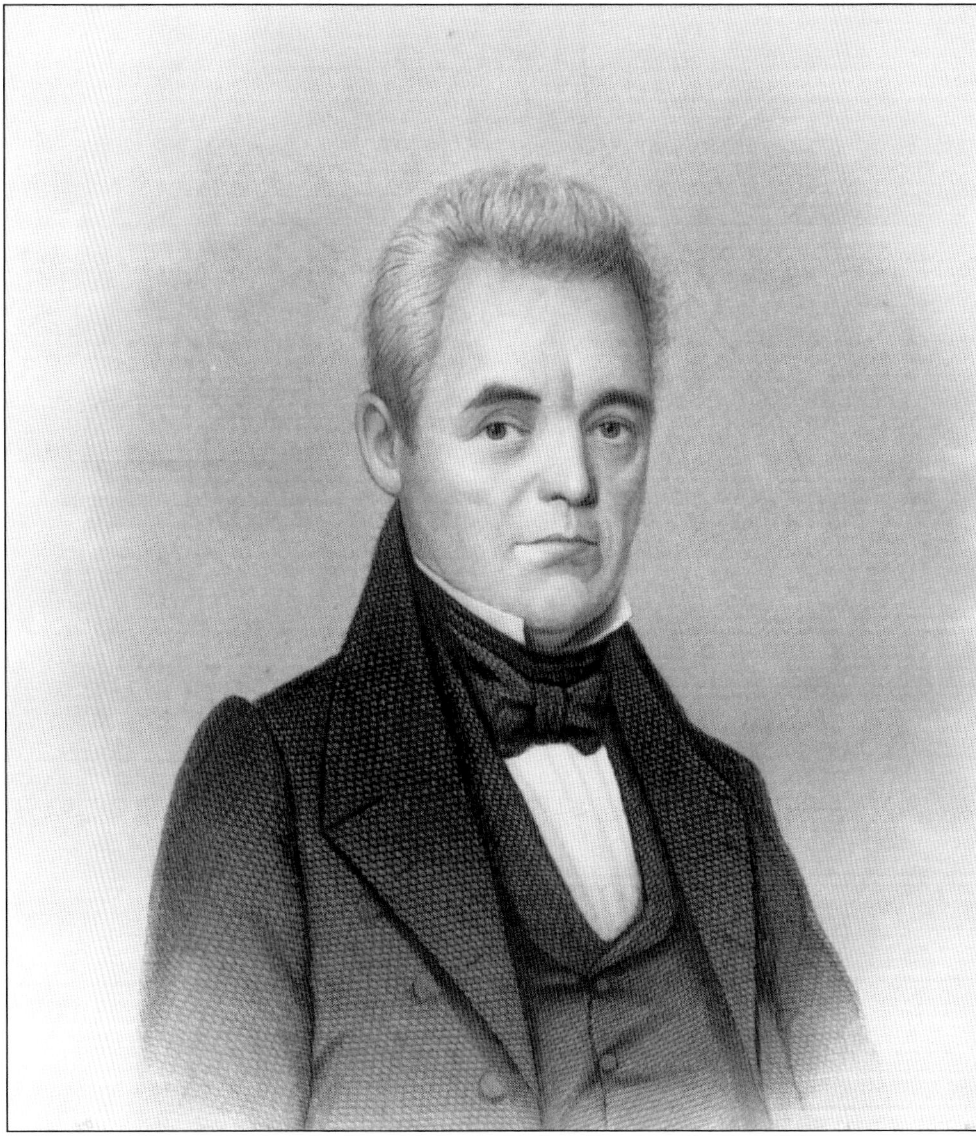

Morris Woodruff (the son of James Woodruff) was born in Litchfield on September 3, 1777. He was educated at the Morris Academy and brought up to be a merchant. General Morris Woodruff served as the judge of the county court for the eleven years prior to his death.

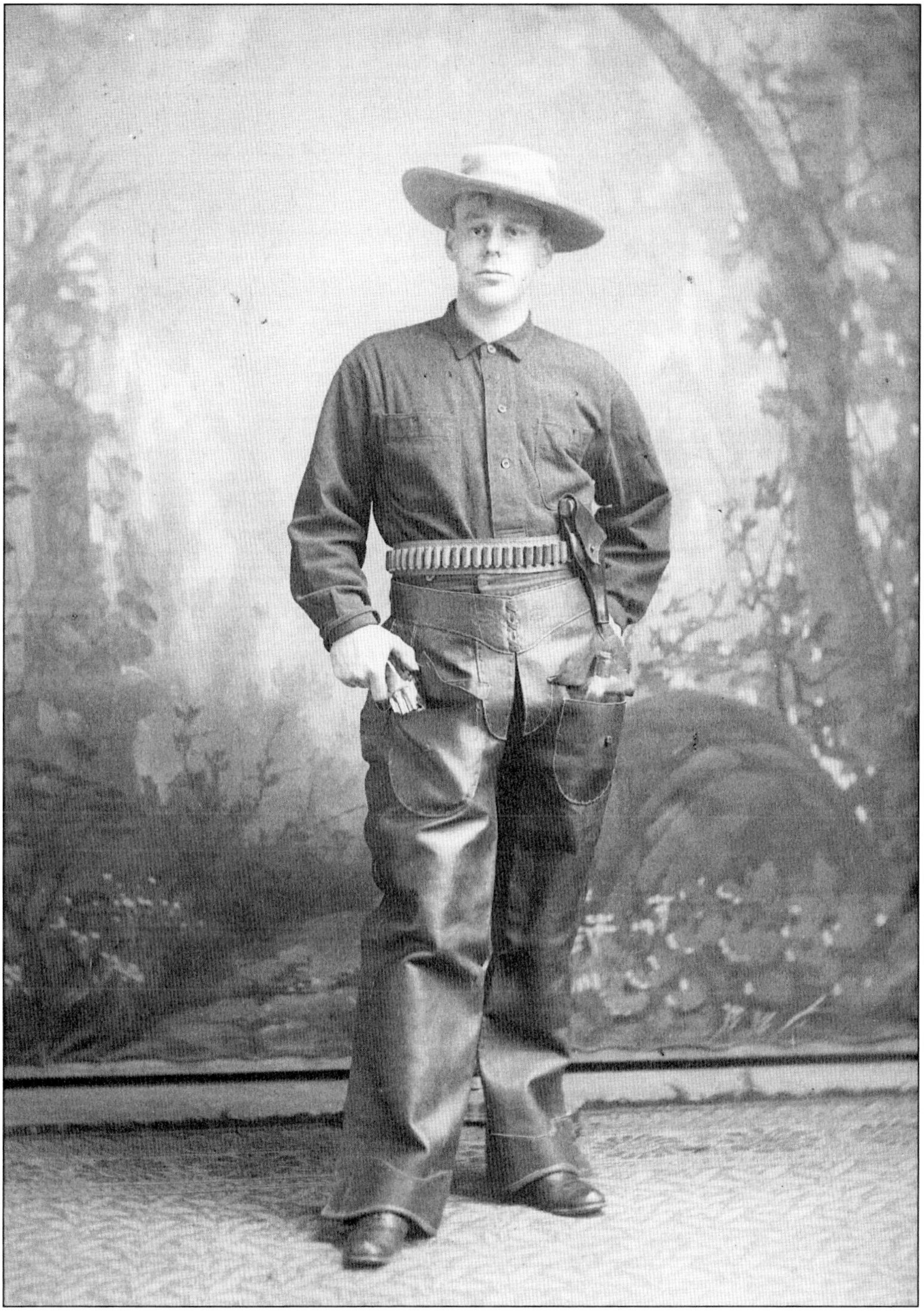

James Woodruff, a graduate of Amherst College, is shown here sporting a "western" look.

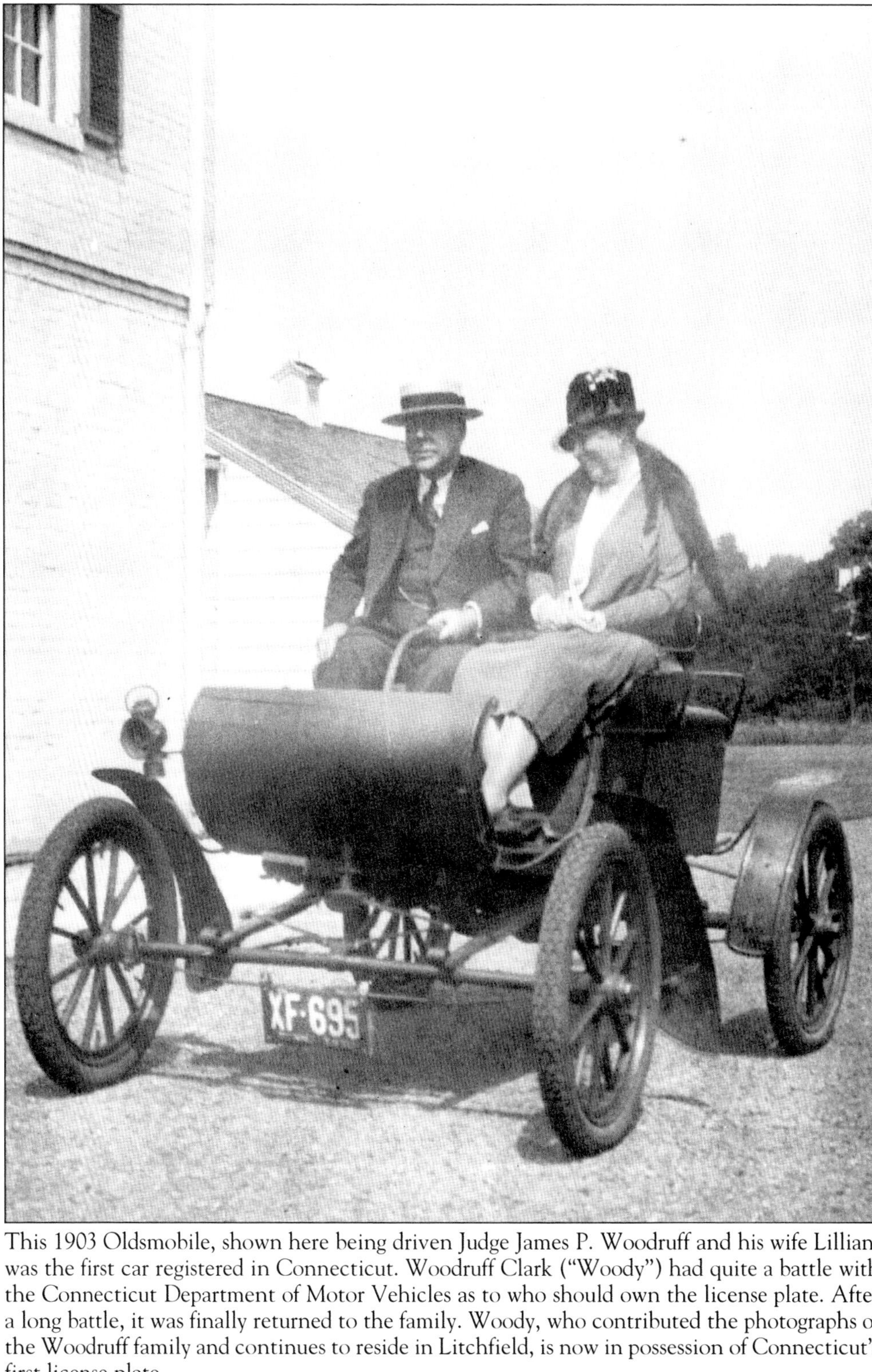

This 1903 Oldsmobile, shown here being driven Judge James P. Woodruff and his wife Lillian, was the first car registered in Connecticut. Woodruff Clark ("Woody") had quite a battle with the Connecticut Department of Motor Vehicles as to who should own the license plate. After a long battle, it was finally returned to the family. Woody, who contributed the photographs of the Woodruff family and continues to reside in Litchfield, is now in possession of Connecticut's first license plate.

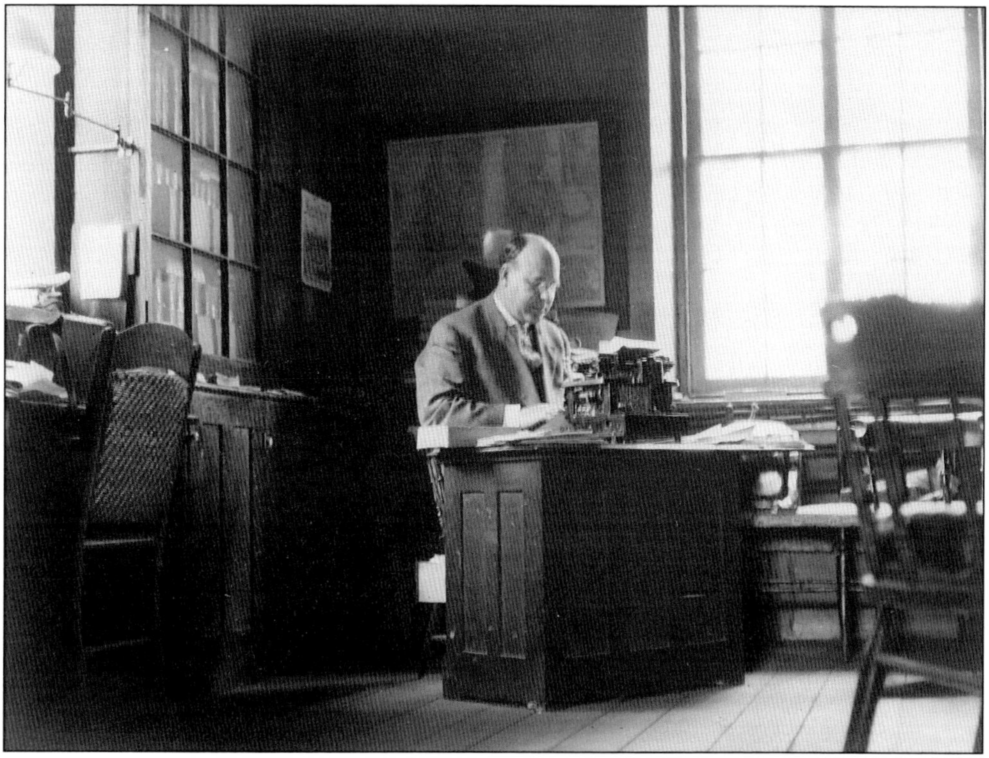

Judge James P. Woodruff is shown here working out of his office in Litchfield.

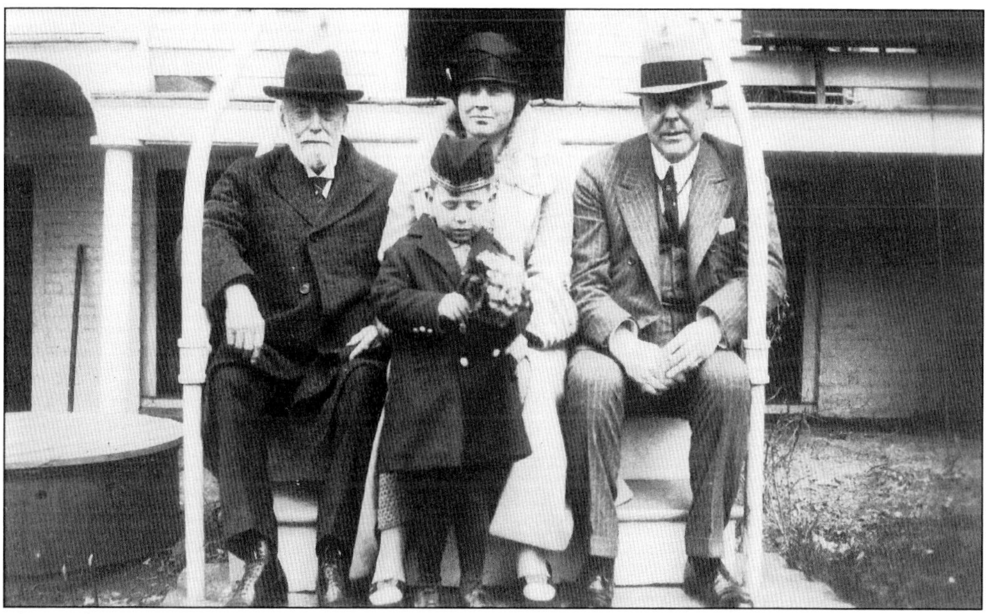

Shown here on the steps of the Woodruff residence are, from left to right: George Morris Woodruff, Lillian W. Clark, James P. Woodruff, and Woody Clark (seated on his mother's lap). Woody was a long-time postmaster in Litchfield.

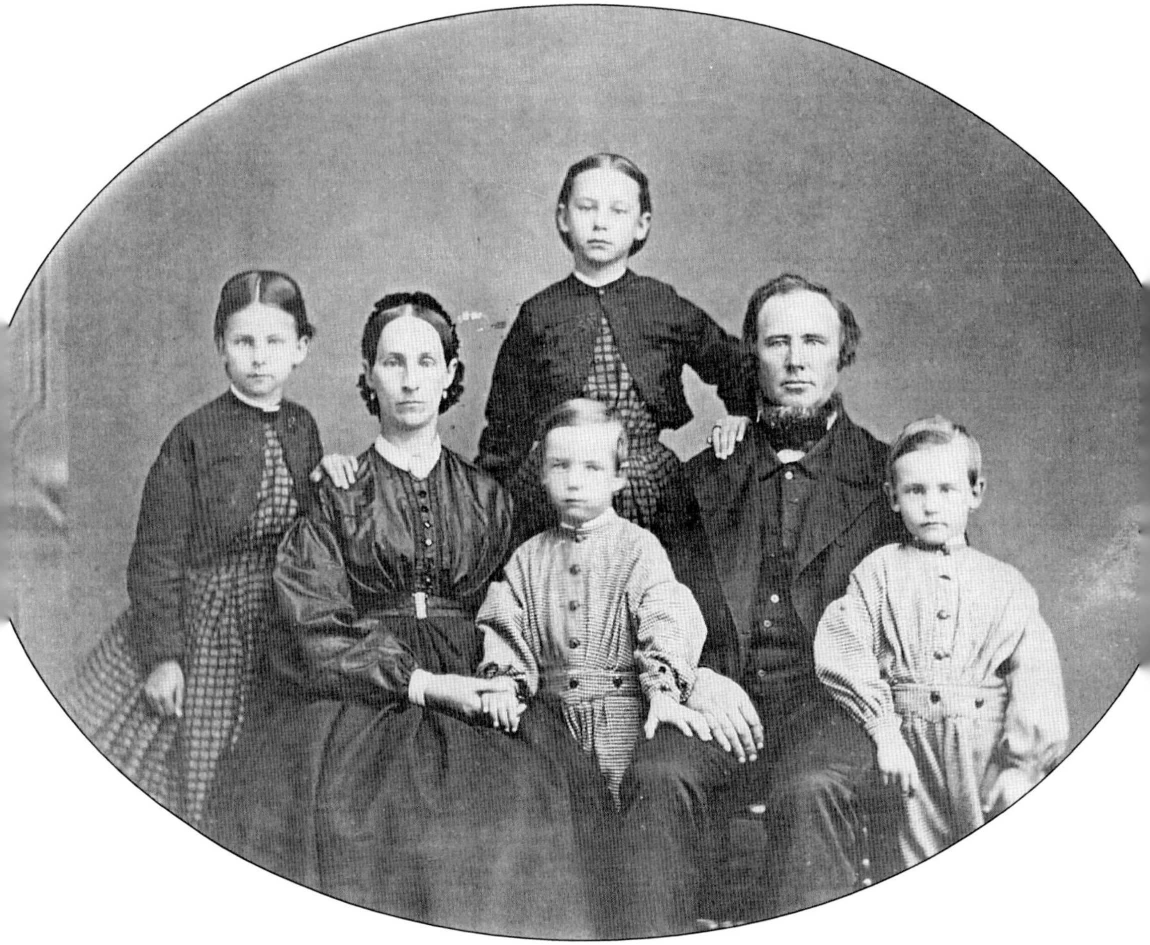

This portrait of the family of Alvin Beach Dickinson was offered by Arthur W. Sweeton and Eunice Sweeton from Canton Center. In the top center is Louise (who married Edmund Newcomb), Mary (who married George Andrews), Sarah Thankful Law (with the twins Frederick and Franklin), and Alvin. Mary Andrews stated that Sarah spent her married life in the "old homestead" in West Goshen.

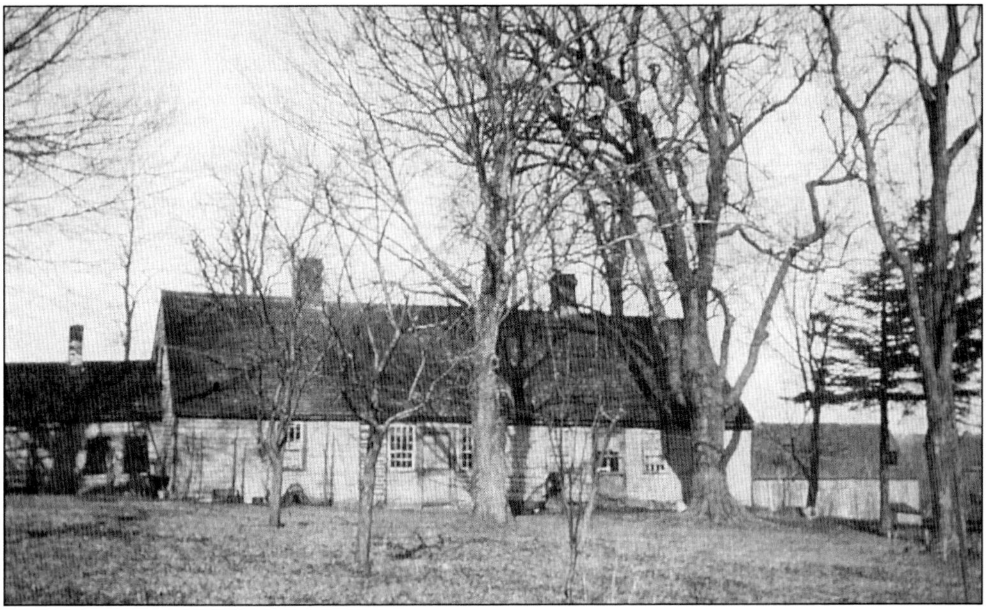

The home of the Alvin Beach Dickenson family was located in Goshen. Dickenson was born on September 15, 1828, and died on January 13, 1909. He was the great-grandfather of Arthur Sweeton, who has contributed much to this book. As the "keeper" of her family's history, Eunice has been able to trace her family's roots back to Nathaniel Dickenson. Born in England in 1600, Nathaniel emigrated to this country and died in Hadley, Massachusetts.

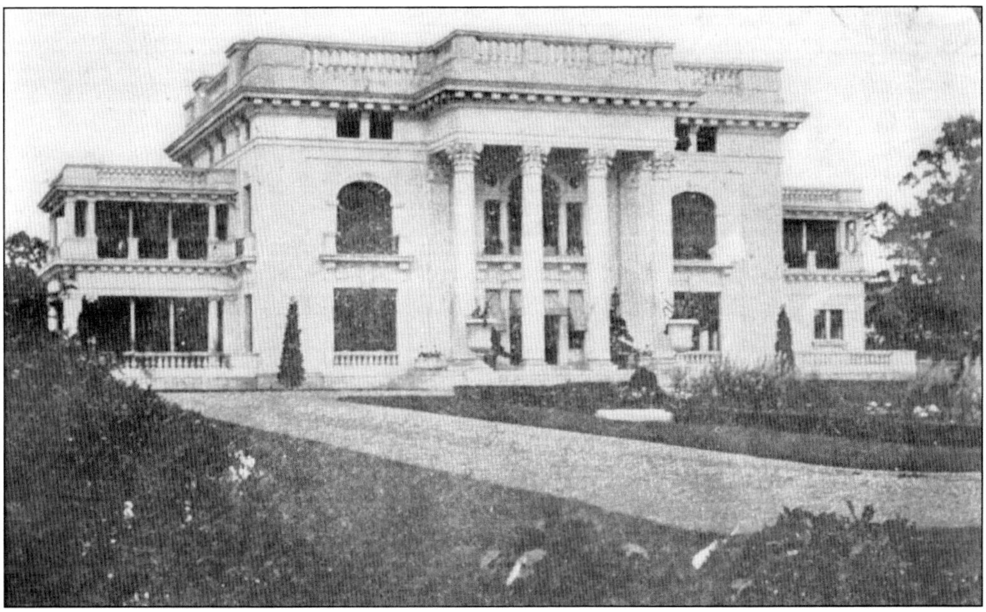

The "Filston" was the residence of the Colgate family in Sharon. Sharon flourished during the eighteenth century as a manufacturing community. Stoves, tools, cigars, and wooden mousetraps were among the many items made here. Benjamin Hotchkiss invented the exploding shell in Sharon, and his brother Andrew developed the repeating rifle and an air-cooled machine gun. Andrew was born almost completely paralyzed and devised his own "adaptive equipment" to enable him to function.

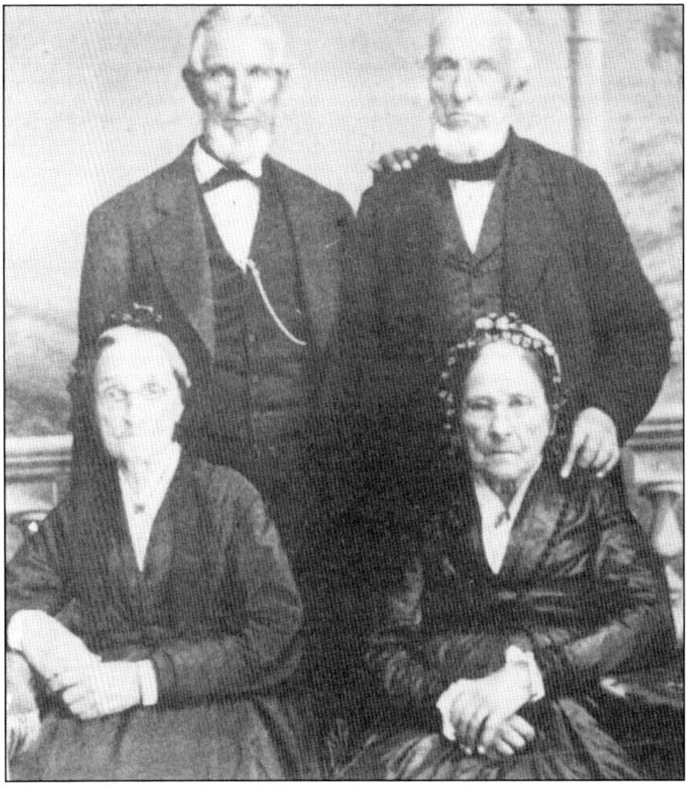

This is the Coe family. From left to right are: Asabel Coe (1799–1884); Israel Coe (1794–1891); Flora Coe Stocking (1797–1894); and Chloe Coe Mott (1792–1871). Israel Coe was the founder of the Coe Brass Company, which produced, among other products, brass kettles.

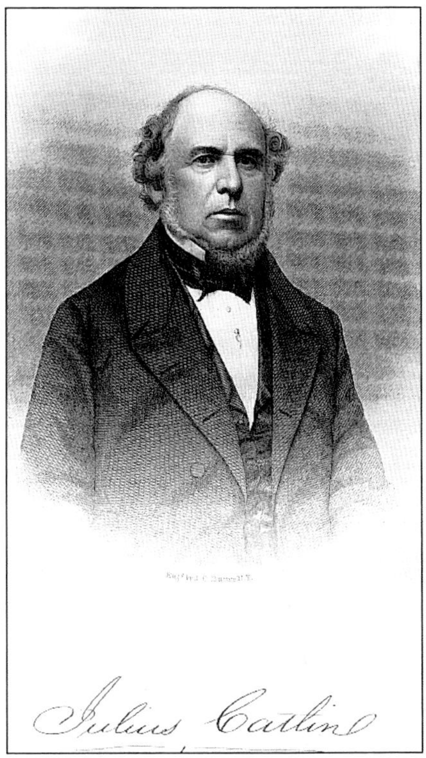

Julius Catlin (the son of Grove Catlin) was born in Harwinton in 1799. He remained in the Litchfield Hills area until mid-adolescence, when he ventured off to Hartford and became a successful merchant. Though he did not return to the area, he always held fine memories of his childhood. He wrote to a friend many years later: "My recollections of Litchfield are indeed pleasant. I love its very name and shall ever take a deep interest in the place."

Six

A Time to Build Up, A Time to Break Down

"NEWS FLASH:
August 10, 1955 Commemorated as The Great Flood of 1955
** Claimed at least 75 lives and left thousands homeless in Norfolk.*
** Norfolk suffered $500,000 worth of damage including*
the house that Betty Curtiss lived in that was swept down the river.
** What had been small, sleepy brooks*
turned into raging torrents of water traveling as fast as 50 miles per hour.
** Rte. 44 was completely wiped out.*
** In Winsted, 170–200 businesses were destroyed*
and at least 20 people died.
** Winsted suffered damages estimated to be between 25–50 million*
dollars as the waters of the Mad River spilled over
sweeping much of downtown Winsted away."

The real story of the flood, however,
was that of the volunteers who worked together,
providing food and shelter for the victims,
and the industries and businesses who banded together
to rebuild their storm-torn cities.

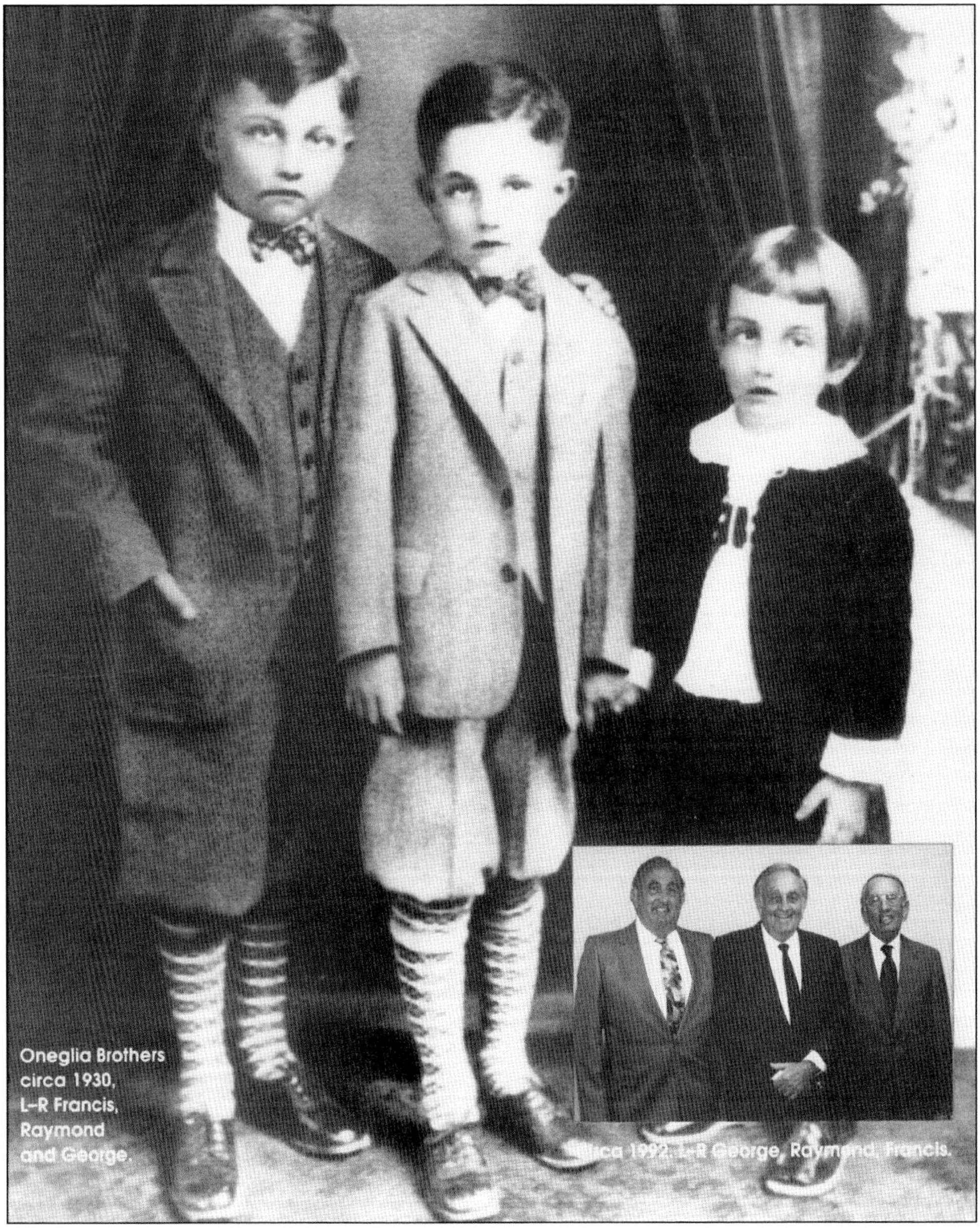

The O'neglias of the O'neglia and Gervasini Construction Company are shown here in 1930. A later photograph shows Francis, Raymond, and George long after they had formed one of the county's most prestigious and successful construction businesses, concentrating most heavily on commercial and industrial building, heavy highway and bridge construction, and the distribution of construction material. It is a family business that has been operating for over seventy years.

Andrew O'neglia Sr. befriended Flaviano Gervasini while working in a large contracting firm. Both had aspired to own their own business. Together they formed O&G in 1923. Andrew Sr.'s three sons are shown on p. 70. They began hauling sand and stone to construction sites and soon owned two trucks and a steamroller. Tragedy struck when Gervasini was killed when the truck he was operating was hit by a train. Andrew and his family became more determined than ever to go forward.

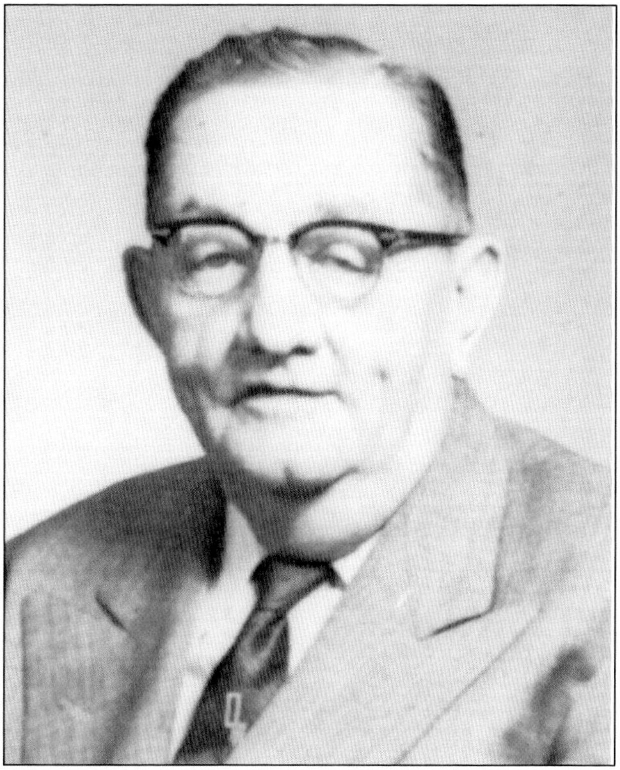

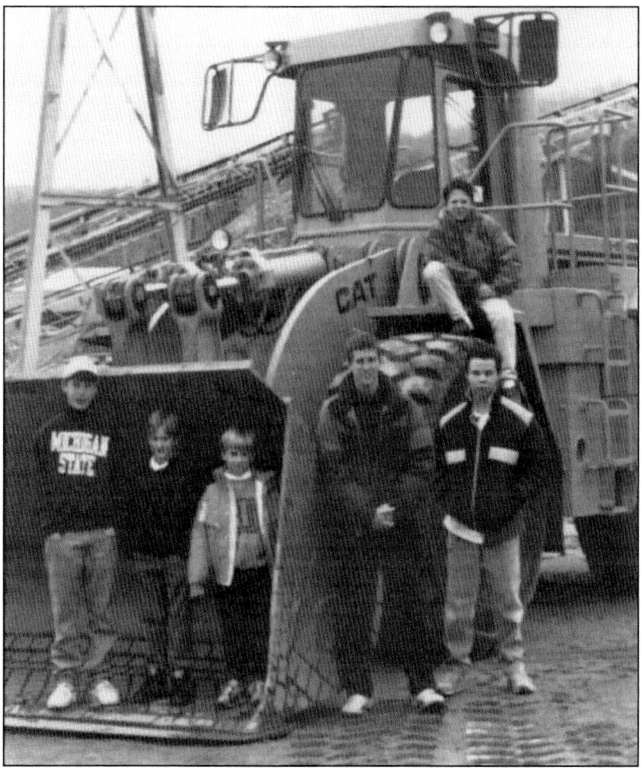

The fourth generation of the O'neglia family is just as compassionate about keeping the family business alive and thriving as the previous three generations were.

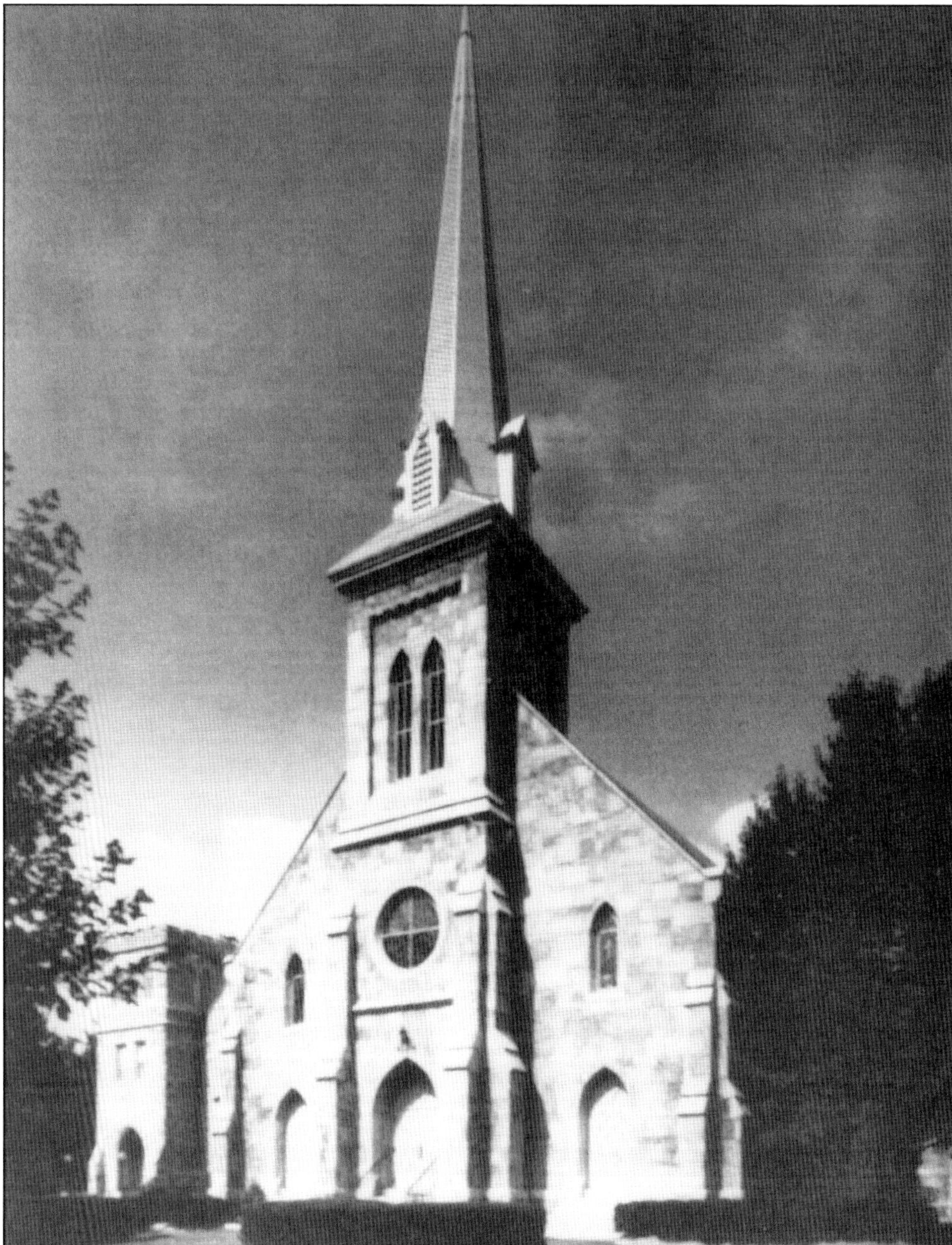

The Center Congregational Church of Torrington was rebuilt after the original structure was destroyed by fire in the late 1950s. This was one among hundreds of projects that O&G became involved in: others included the Union Train Station in New Haven, the Bushnell Plaza office and residential complex in Hartford, and the Hartford Civic Center (after its roof collapsed).

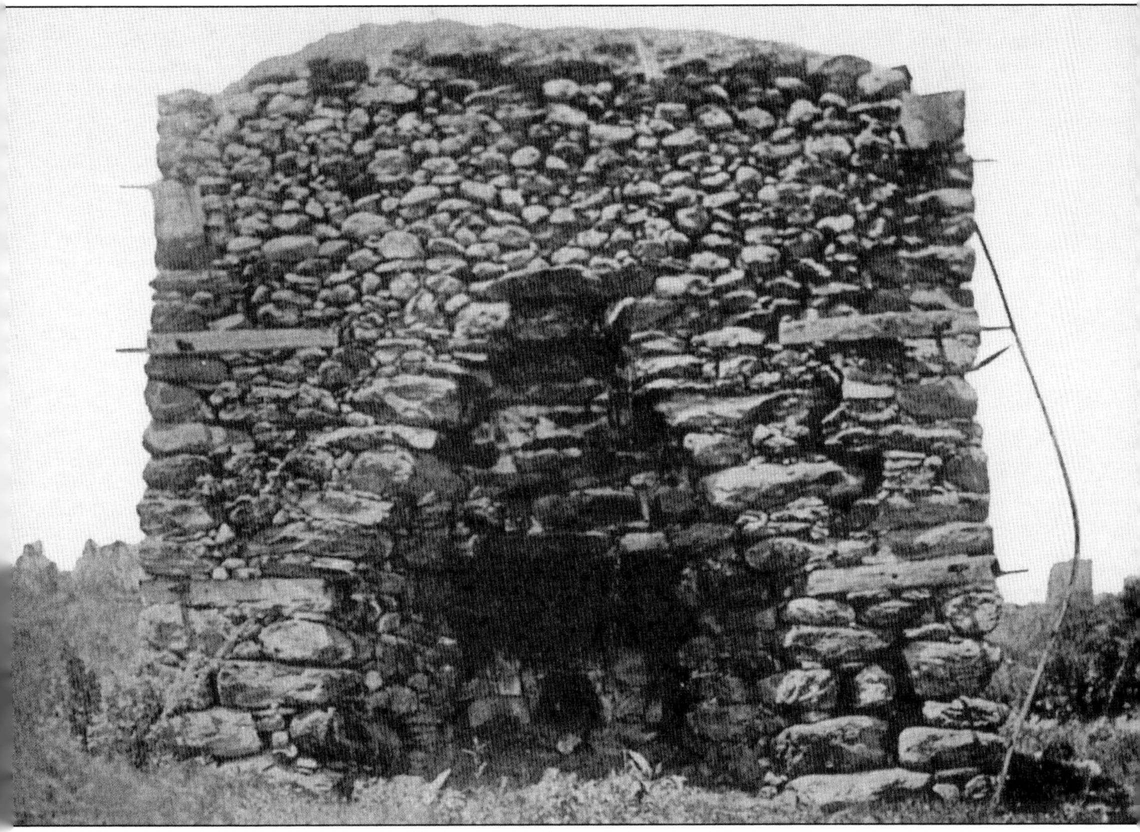

The Lakeville/Salisbury area was well known and the perfect setting for iron mines and forges; the Lakeville Iron Forge (shown here) was one of them. William Storrs Lee, in *The Yankees of Connecticut*, describes what was seen across the hills of northwestern Connecticut during the American Revolution, even in Litchfield: "At night, the sky around Salisbury glowed as if it were reflecting an eternal inferno, by day the sky was yellowed by the smudge from the furnace and the grunts of the furnace bellows and the unearthly screech of the revolving waterwheels." The iron furnaces poured out cannonballs and cannon barrels, which were then used by Washington's army and American fighting ships.

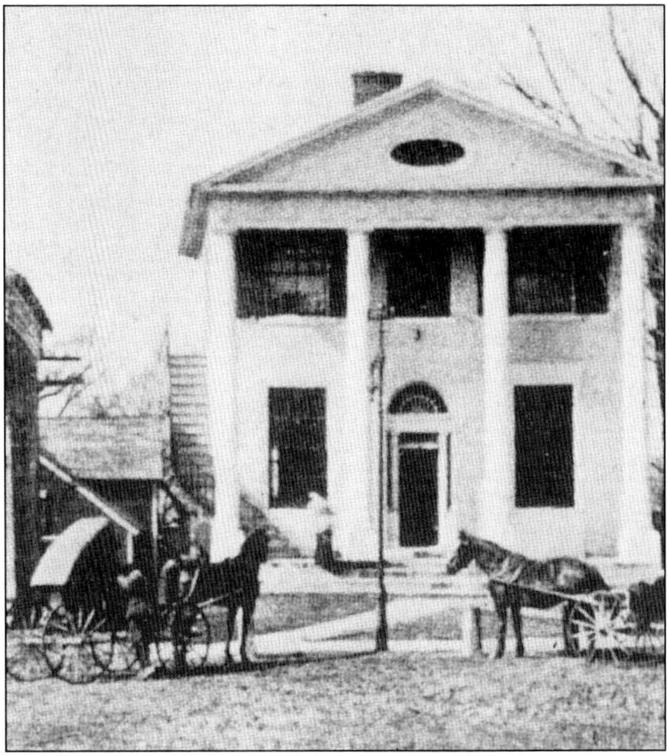

The First National Bank of Litchfield has been in continuous operation since 1814. It shares an adjacent wall with what was once the county jail (an interesting concept to be sure).

The Center Congregational Church is located on the green in Riverton.

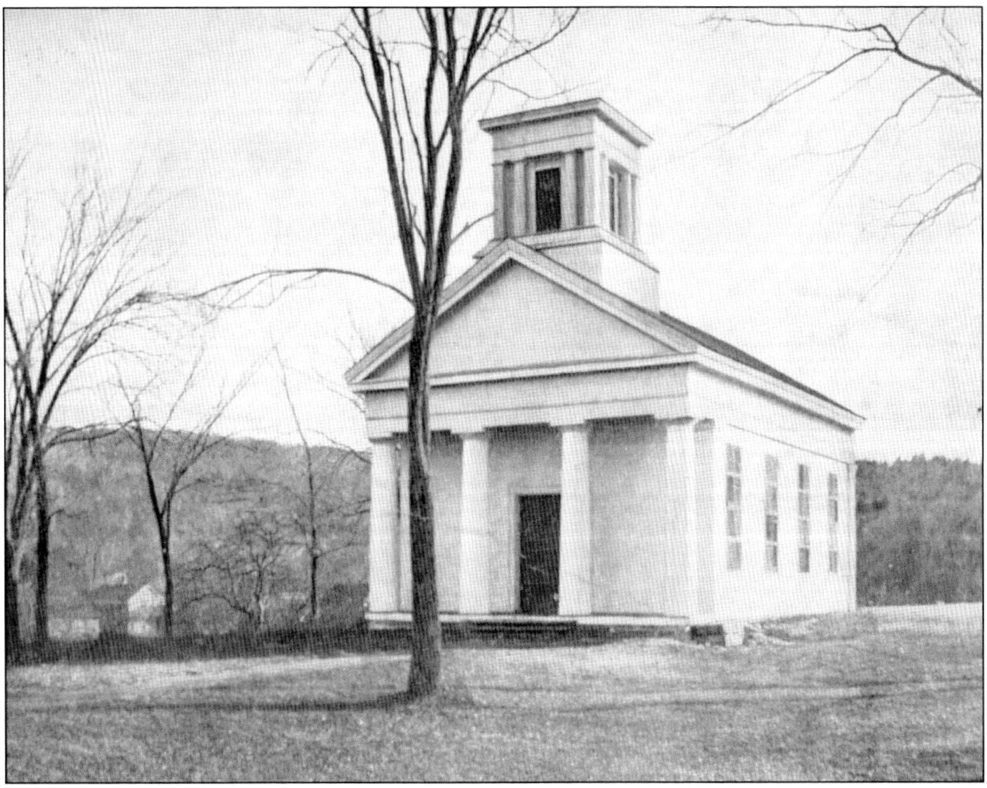

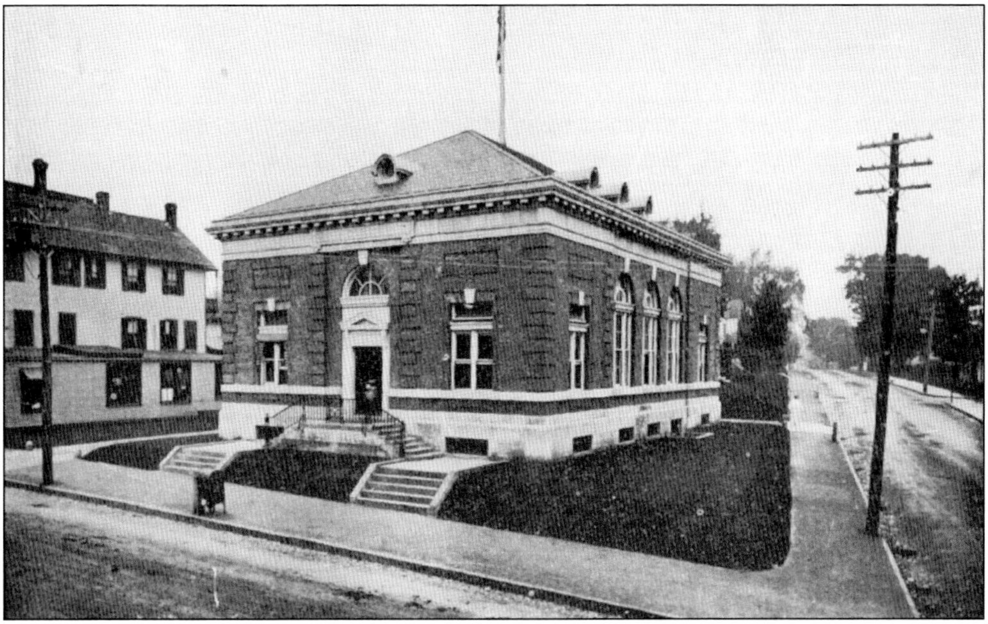

The Torrington Post Office is shown here at the time of its erection in 1909.

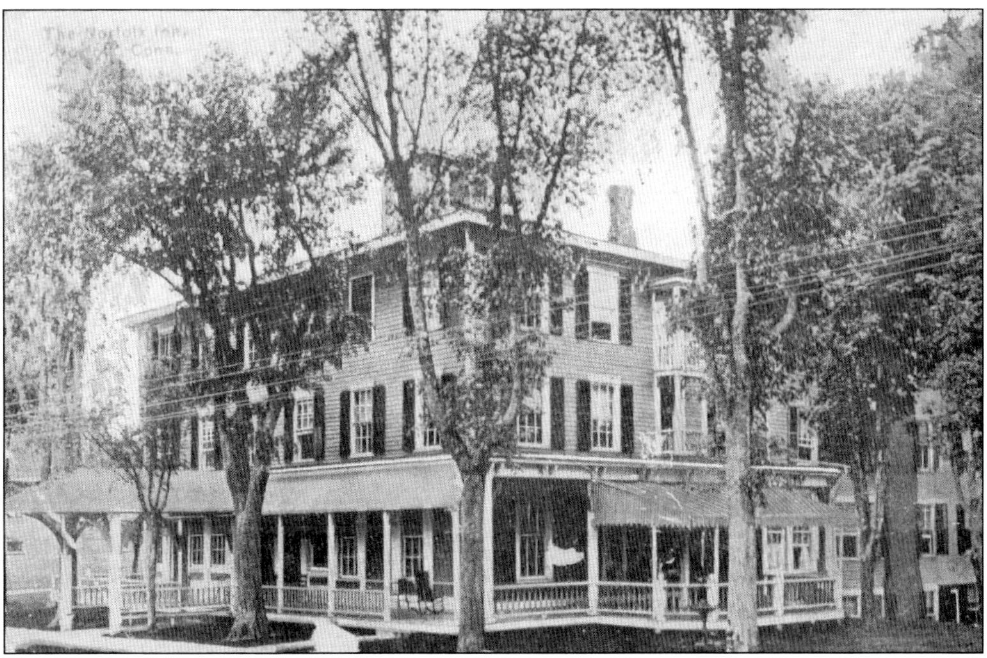

In the 1700s the Norfolk Inn was located in an area where making maple sugar was common. Clothing was made of home-grown wool and flax which were then spun and woven. Norfolk was devastated during the Flood of 1955.

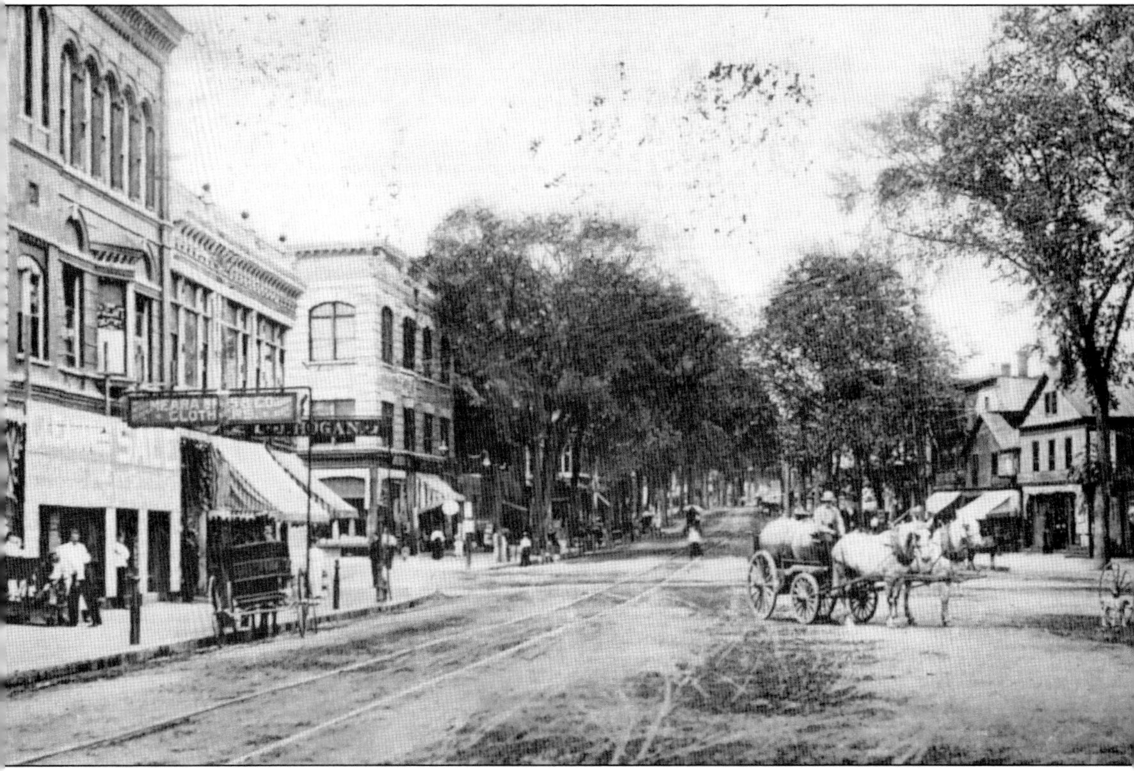

This view shows Main Street in Torrington at the turn of the century. The name "Torrington" was taken from three Saxon and Briton words: "Torr" (meaning "hill"), "ring" (meaning "circle"), and "ton" (meaning "town"). Thus, "Torrington" means a "hill-encircled town." In the late 1800s, Torrington's population doubled. New immigrants during this period included the Poles, Czechs, Slovaks, Italians, and Lebanese. With their cultures they brought their skills as stonecutters, masons, and carvers. By 1923 the population had grown to 23,000 and Torrington was chartered as a city. The city experienced a "new look," which reflected the Art Deco theme of that period. It was in 1931 that the Warner Theatre was built.

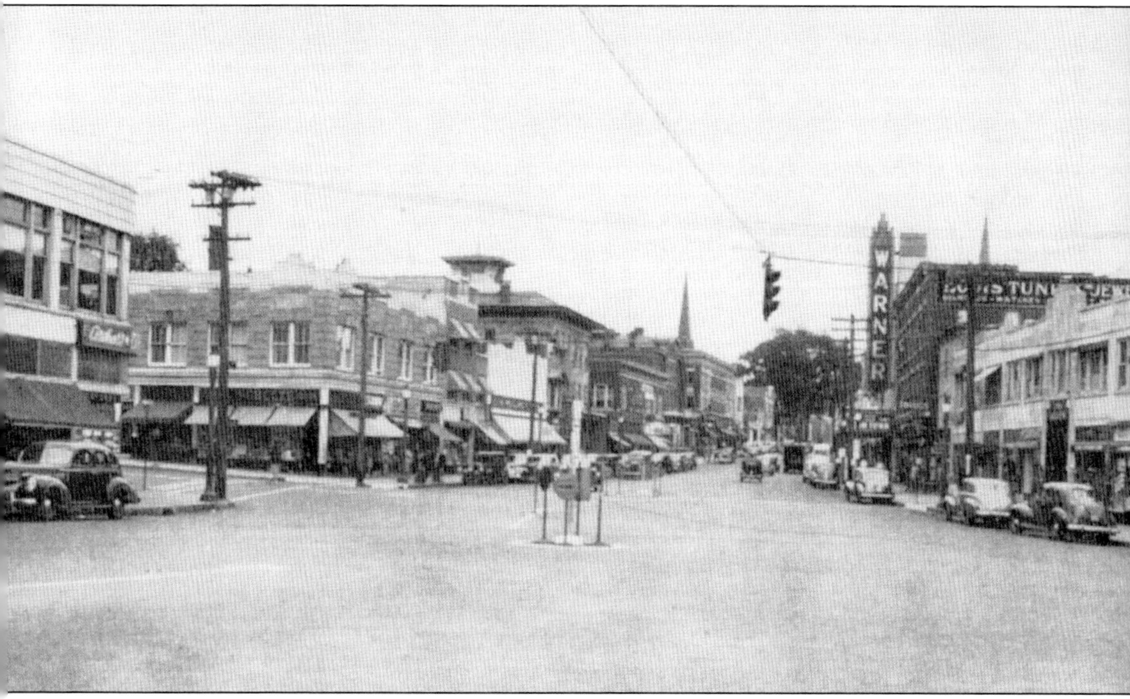

Main Street in Torrington is shown here during 1940. Most of the businesses that lined Main Street were family businesses, many of which were in the process of closing at this time (just another "sign of the times" and days gone by). During the 1940s, the industrial population of companies in Torrington increased. In general, growth began to "slow down." With the Flood of 1955, the city experienced a severe setback in the areas of industry and commerce. The backbone of Torrington has always been manufacturing, however; some of these companies were started in the early 1900s and are still in operation today.

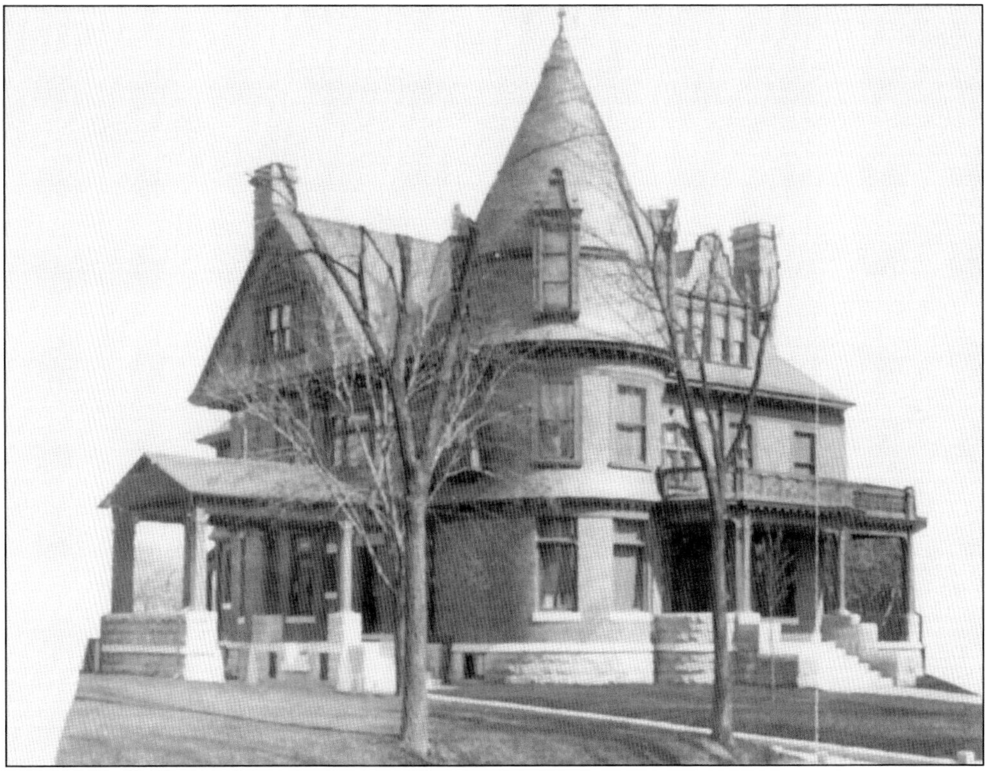

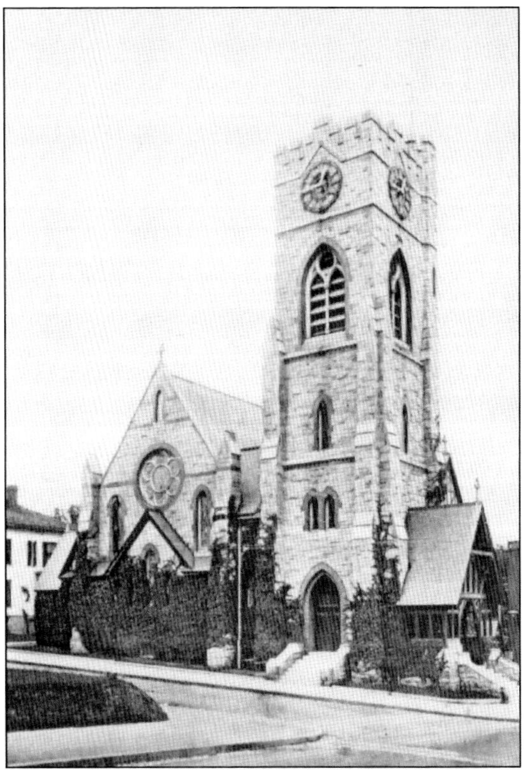

The Hotchkiss-Fyler Museum continues to grace Main Street in Torrington with its original Victorian style. Mr. Orsamus Fyler, a successful businessman and politician, decided to build this family home in the 1890s and contracted one of Connecticut's finest architects to do so. The house was also the home of his daughter Gertrude and her husband. When Gertrude passed on in the 1950s, she left the home to the Torrington Historical Society to be kept as a museum.

The Trinity Episcopal Church of Torrington was erected in 1898 on the corner of Water and Prospect Streets. When a typhoid epidemic broke out in the fall of 1911, over 323 people were stricken—36 of them died. The governor refused to allow the armory to be used as a temporary hospital so the Trinity Parish House, which had been constructed only a short time before the epidemic occurred, was used as one.

This view shows Torrington's YMCA in the early 1900s. The building was erected in 1890.

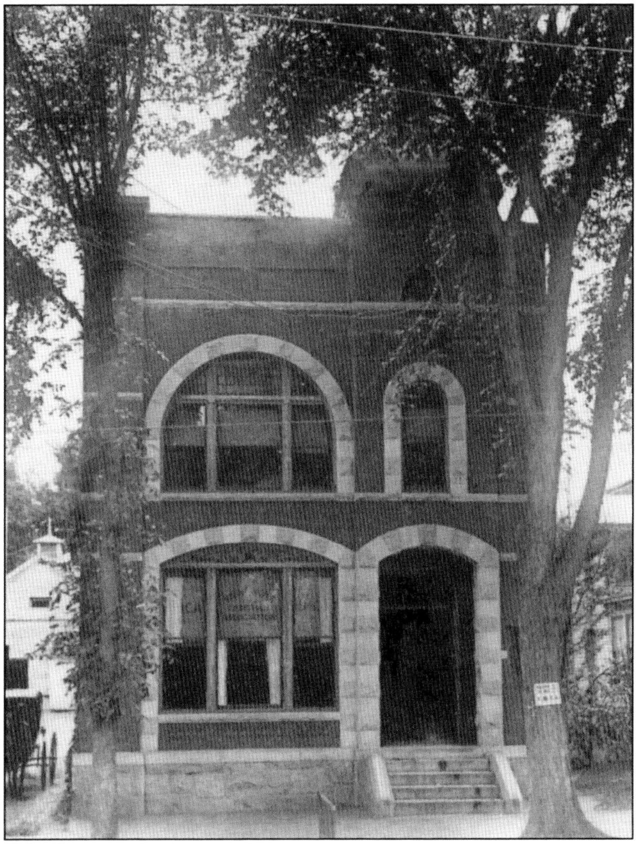

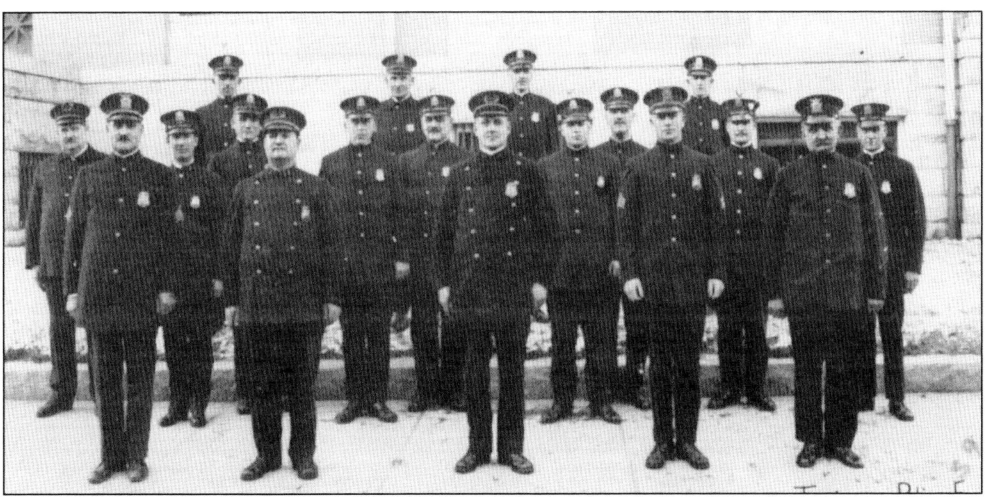

The Torrington Police Department posed in front of City Hall during the early 1900s.

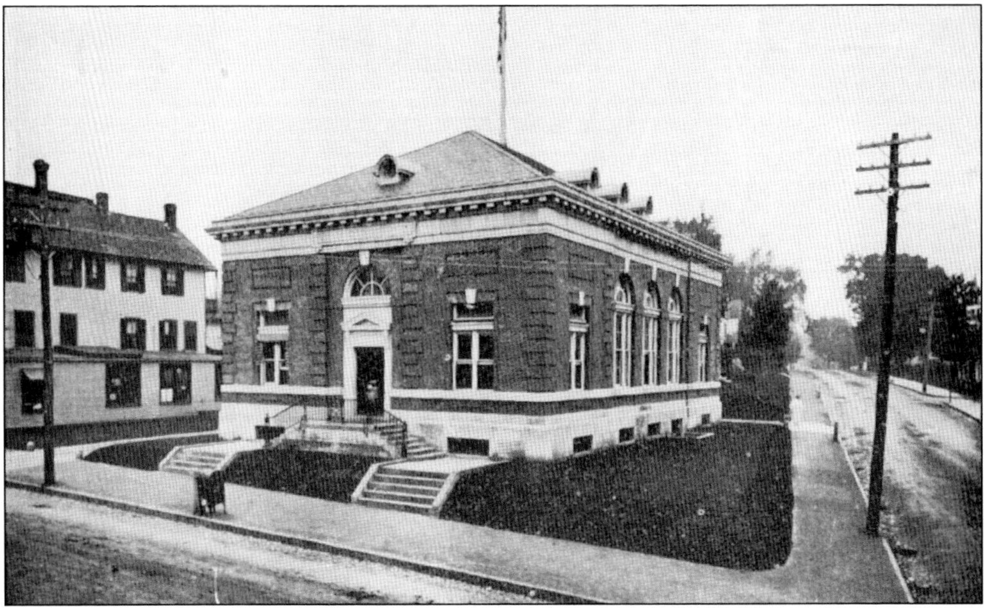

Torrington had post offices in Wolcottville, Torringford, West Torrington, and Burrville. The postmaster of Torringford at this time was Nathaniel Smith, who held that office for forty-six years.

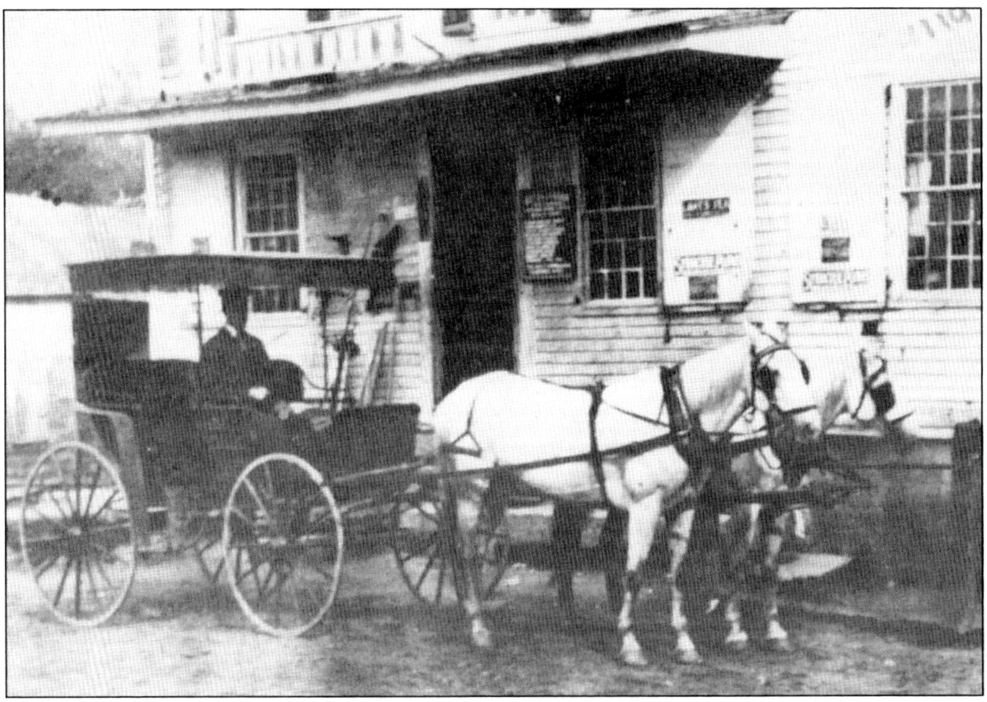

The Goshen Post Office was used as a stagecoach stop in the years before rails and trolleys.

Seven

A Time to Create, A Time to Destroy

Tales abound around a small community that once existed within Cornwall known as "Dudleytown." Dudleytown was settled in the mid-1750s by members of the Dudley family. Many believe that this once thriving community fell victim to evil: some say it was because "ghosts"; some say it was due to witchery and evil curses; and others believe a strange, unknown illness spread through, claiming the lives of area inhabitants.

A statement released by the Cornwall Historical Society says that these stories are nothing more than "garbage" written by gullible authors. Early settlers farmed on high ground, which which was thin and rocky. Thus, when farming failed, the residents moved elsewhere. The buildings collapsed and the fields reverted to forests, creating the feel of a "ghost town."

The tales of curses and plagues no longer hold any credence—except, perhaps, to the thrillseekers and tourists who visit this location in search of their own answers.

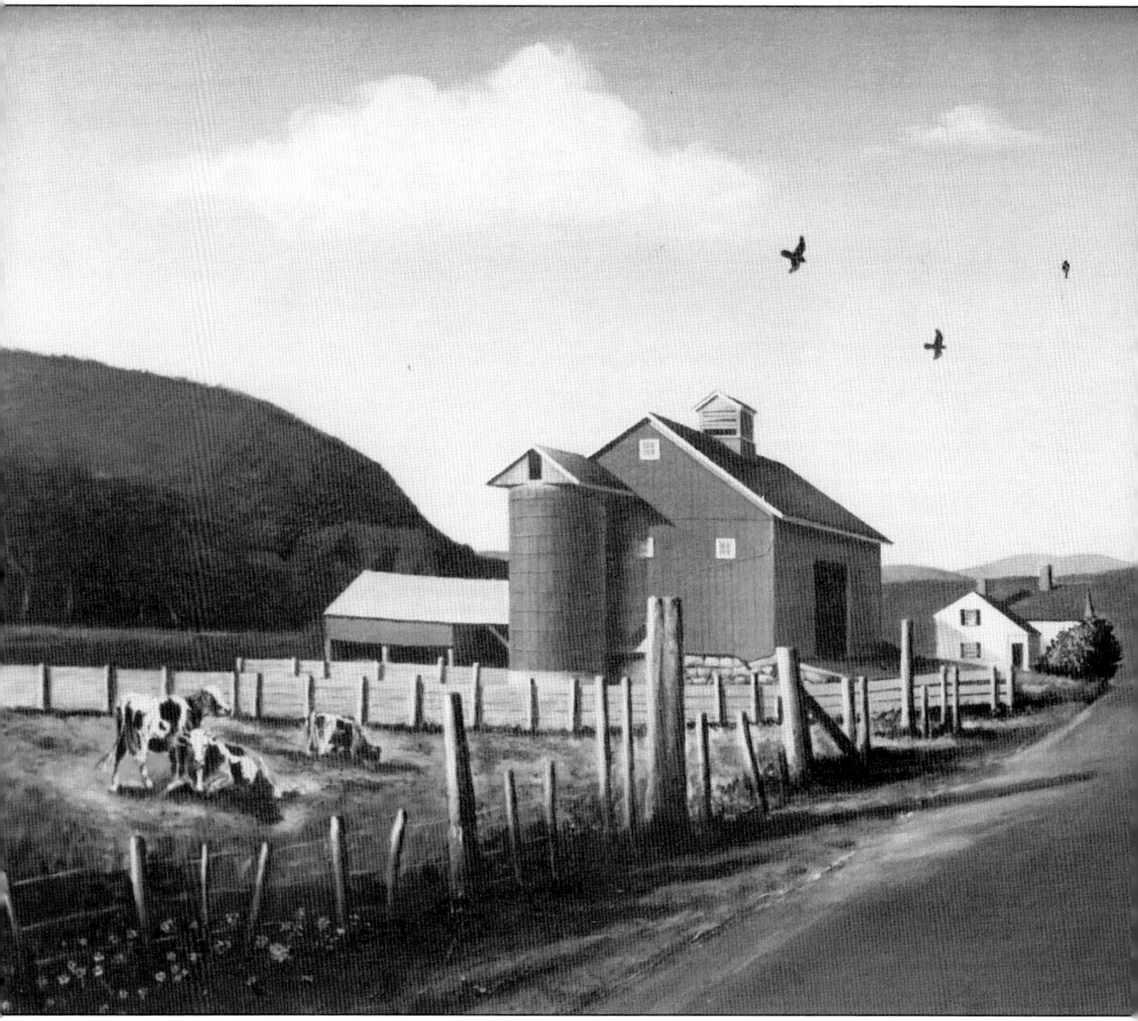

This sample painting by the late Carl Reinhart of Cornwall Bridge depicts the quiet serenity and agricultural nature of his surroundings. During his retirement years, Reinhart began a second career as a landscape artist.

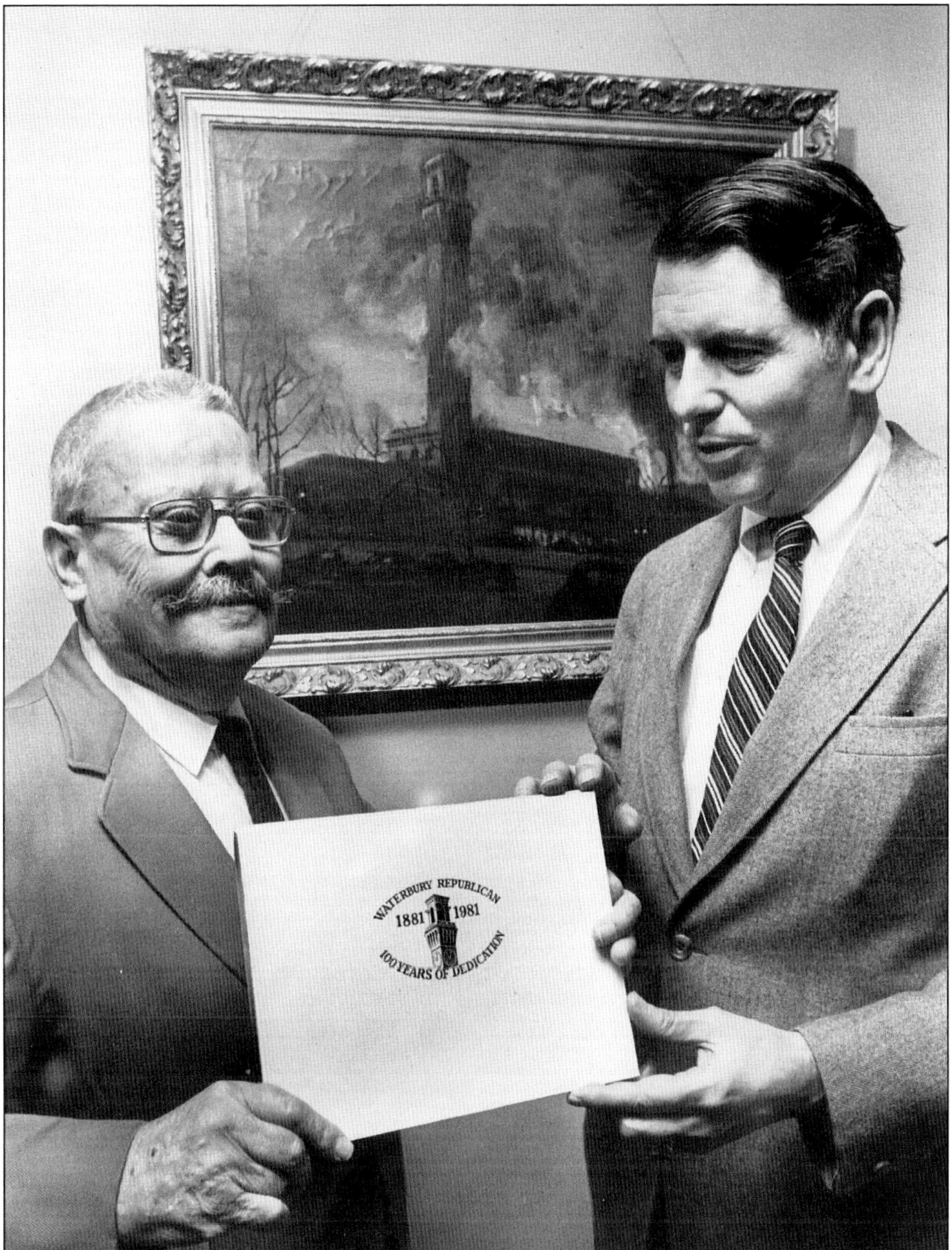

Reinhart is shown here receiving his reward for being the winner of the Waterbury Republican's 100th Anniversary Logo Competition.

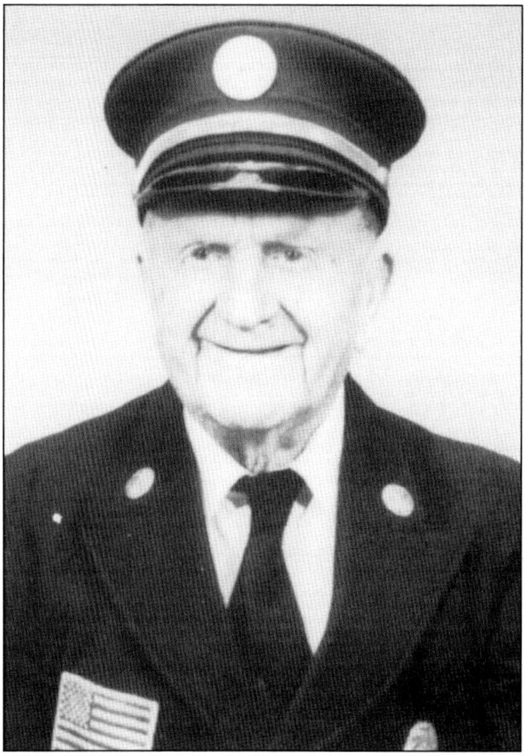

Norman "Brother" Barbar was the chief of the Harwinton Fire Department for thirty-eight consecutive years. "Brother," as he became known to the locals, lived across from the Harwinton Fire Department with his wife Frances and their two children, Norman Jr. and Carolyn (who have since moved on into adulthood). Brother was chief when the Harwinton church burned to the ground in 1949. He also became known as the town "dowser." The new chief of the Harwinton Fire Department is Fred Gottschell. Captain Bill Rinko spoke of how there was no ambulance service in Harwinton until 1967. Prior to that, ambulance services were provided by a well-known Torrington funeral home.

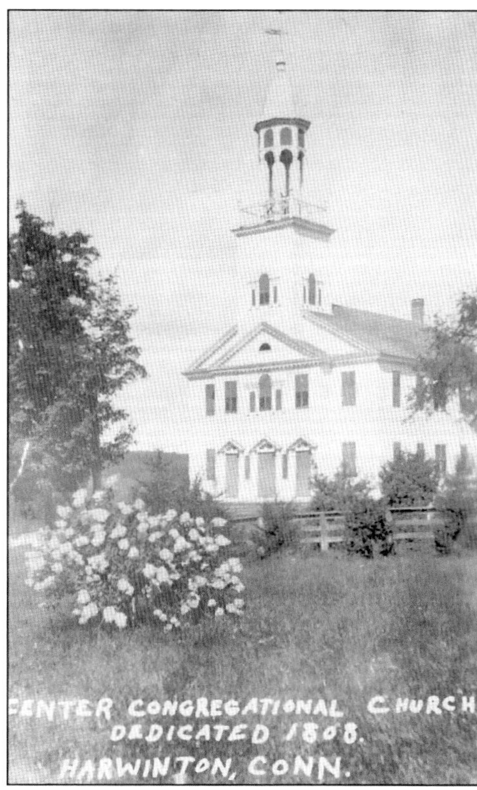

The Center Congregational Church in Harwinton was first dedicated in 1806.

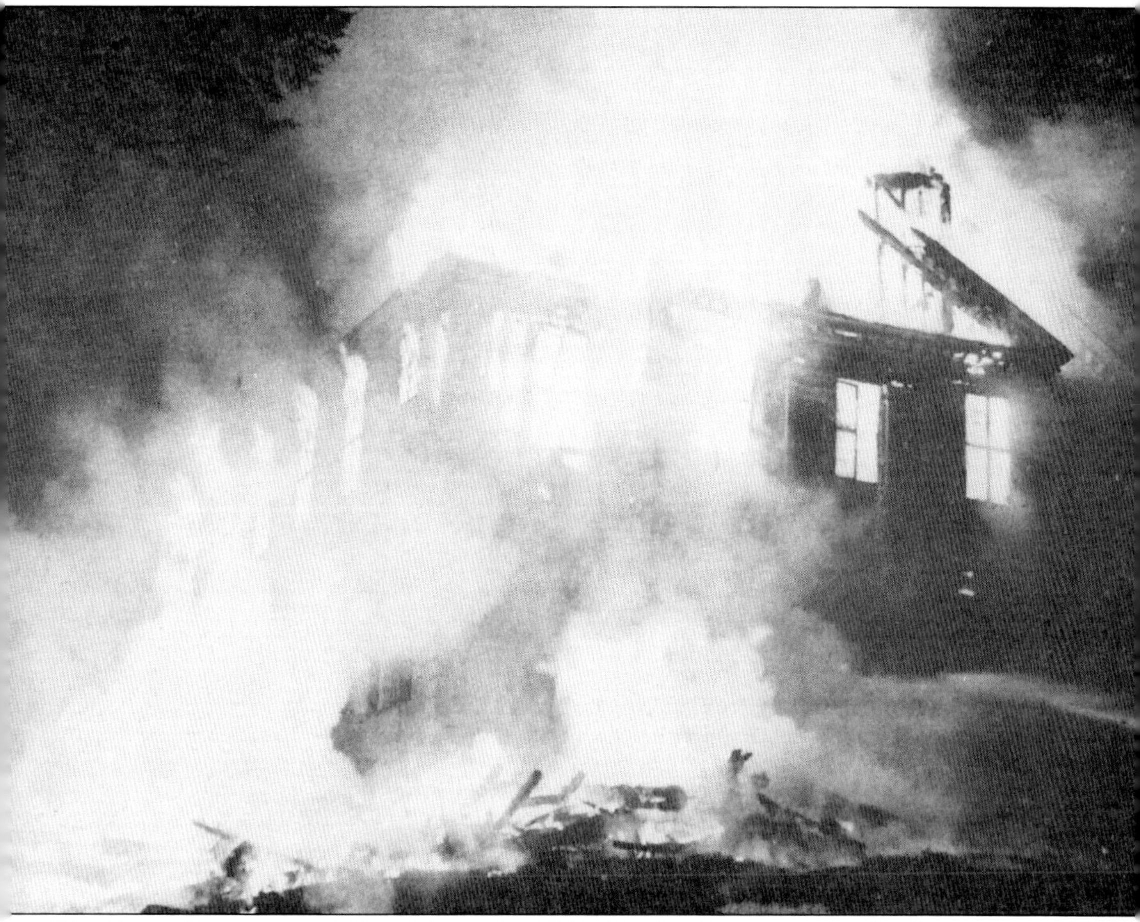

The Center Congregational Church burned in 1949. The church was a much valued institution in the community, not only as a place of worship but as a place to gather socially, hold town meetings, etc. Its destruction was felt deeply by the townspeople of the Harwinton area.

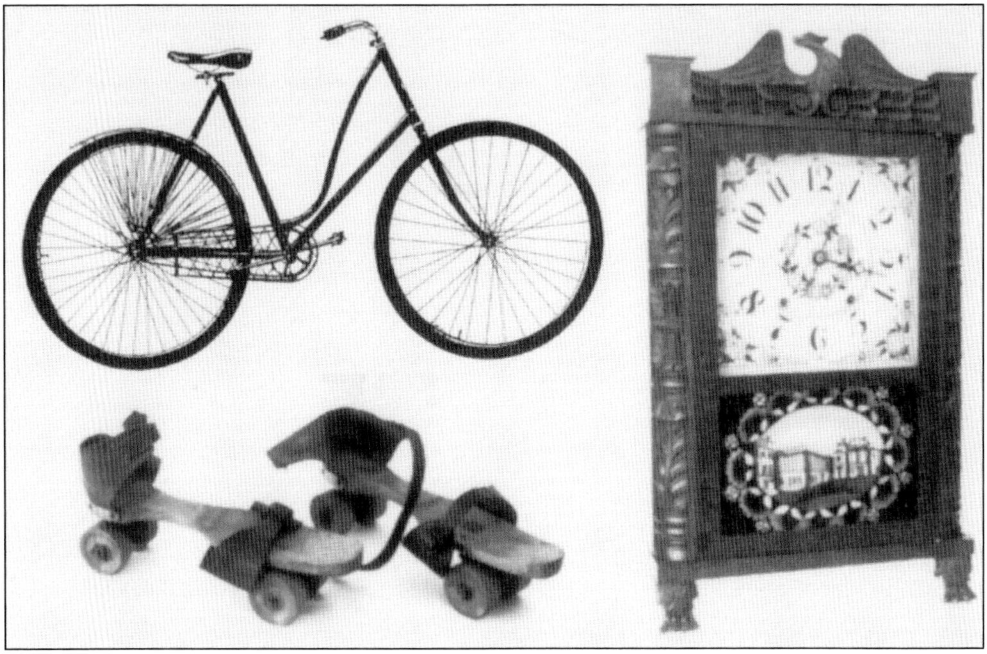

These products were produced by industries within the boundaries of Torrington. Torrington has been an industrial town for centuries; many of the original industries still exist and prosper, despite the considerable damage caused by the Flood of 1955.

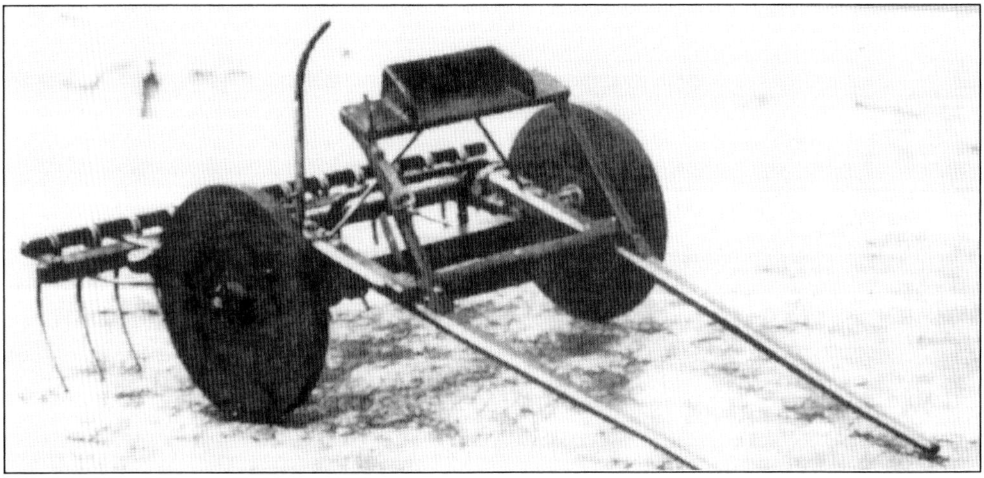

The hayrake was first manufactured in the town of Morris in 1918. Morris was primarily an agricultural community at that time.

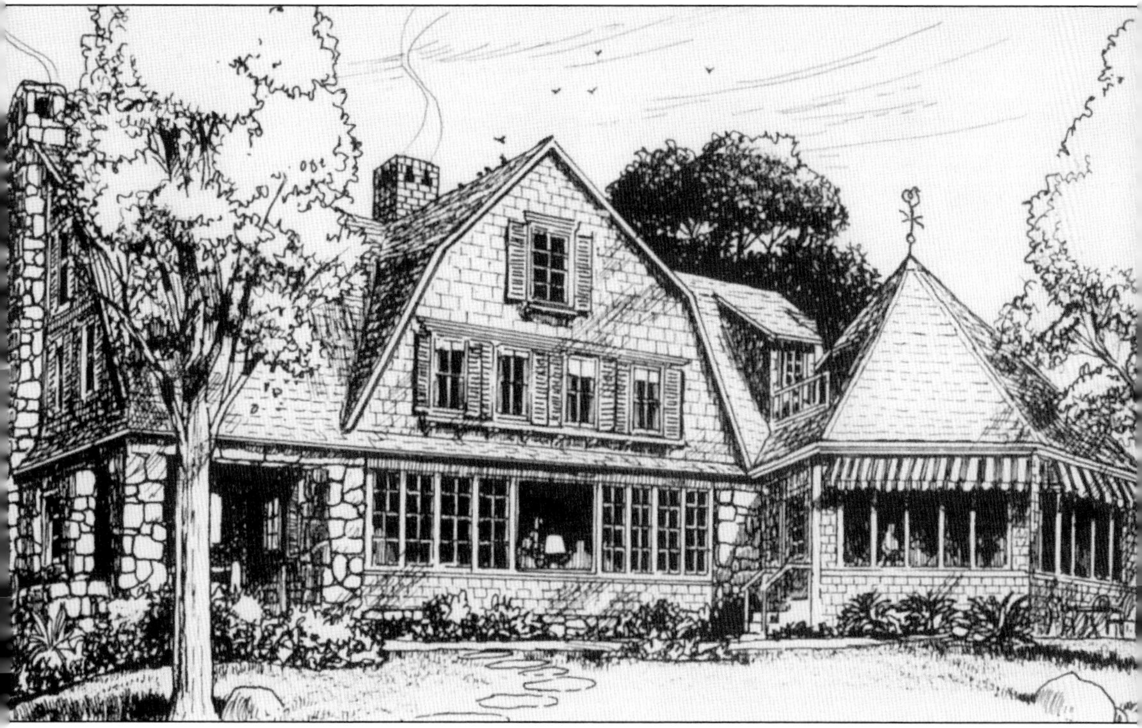

The Boulder's Inn is located in New Preston. It has been one century since it was first built as a private residence by Nelson Mead. Originally called Bush-Mead, it was named after two branches of the family. Nelson attended a private school known as the Gunnery. Eventually, six cottages were added to the original structure; the home opened to guests during the 1930s and it continues to operate to this day. Dick and Jane Lowe opened the main house to guests in 1951. At the time of its erection, Grover Cleveland was President and Victoria was the Queen of the British Empire.

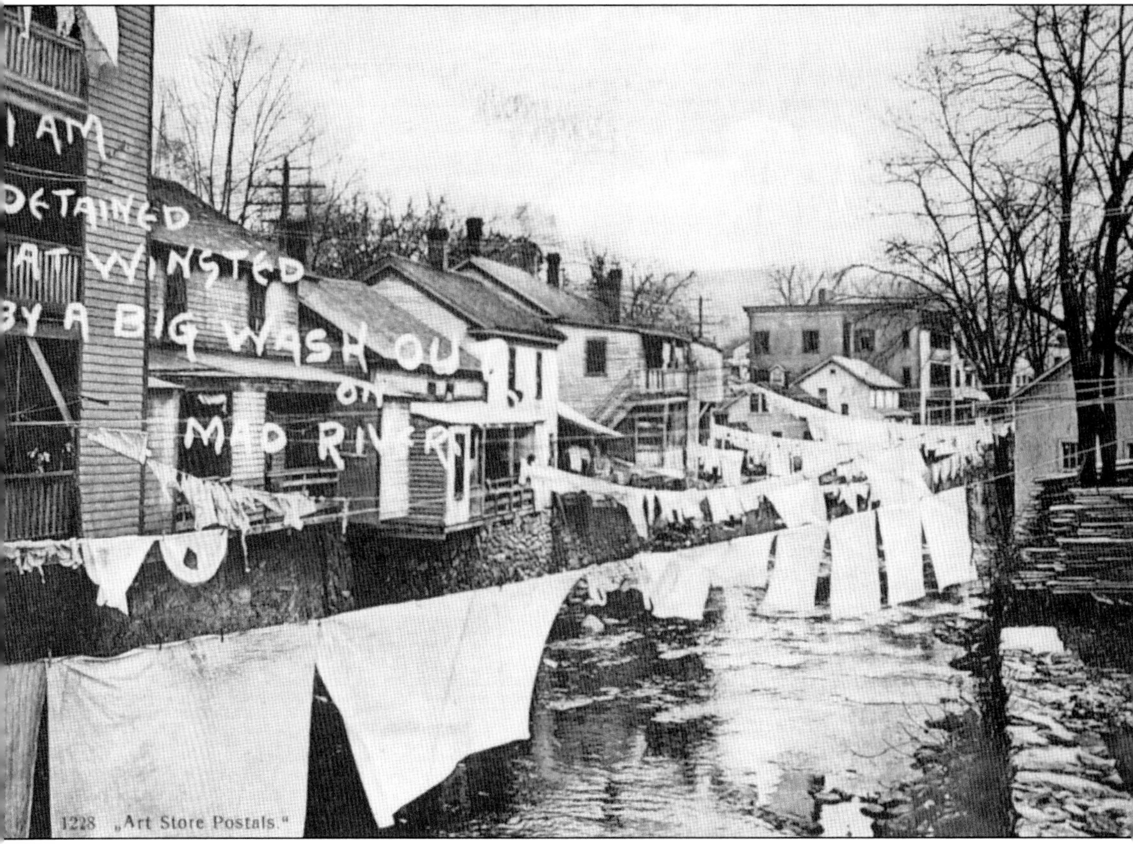

This is a humorous Art Deco postcard depicting the Flood of 1955. One wonders if the humor was appreciated at the time, as most residents of Winsted were badly impacted by Black Friday.

This toppled home was among many found in the area of Torrington, Winsted, and Norfolk during the Great Flood of 1955. In many areas of Torrington, houses were found on top of or leaning against each other when the waters began to subside. Several such scenes were in the area of Wolcott Avenue.

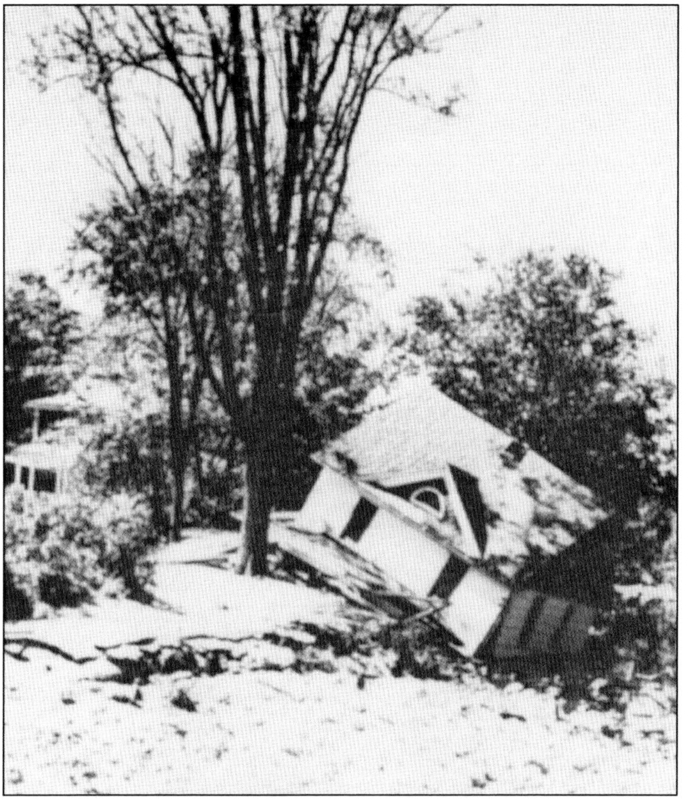

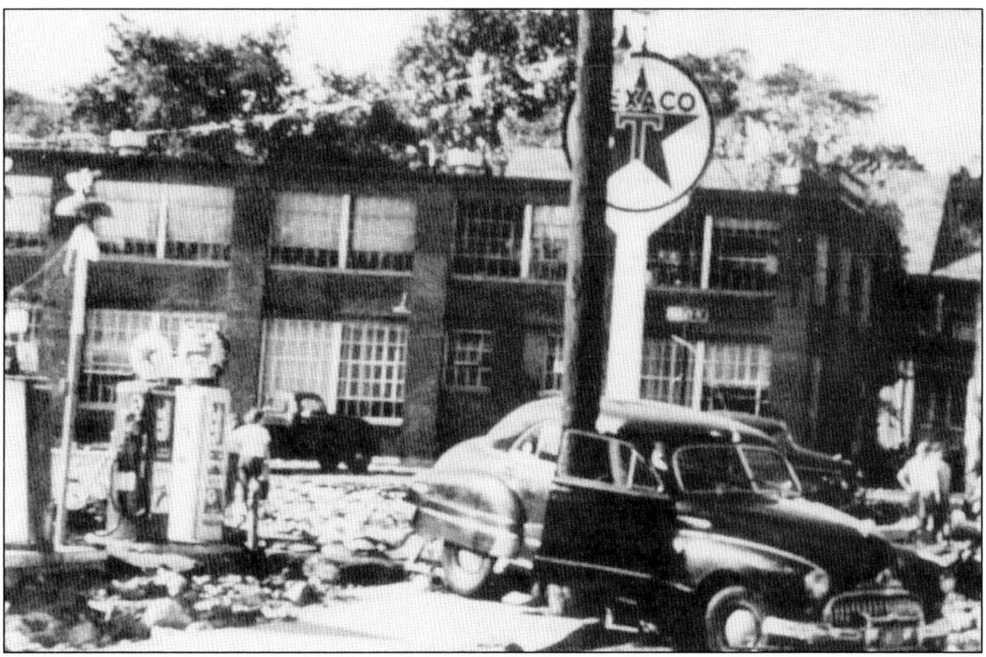

Another flood scene shows the devastation of Torrington. This car was found at a downtown Texaco station; streets had been washed away and along with them any parked or moving vehicles.

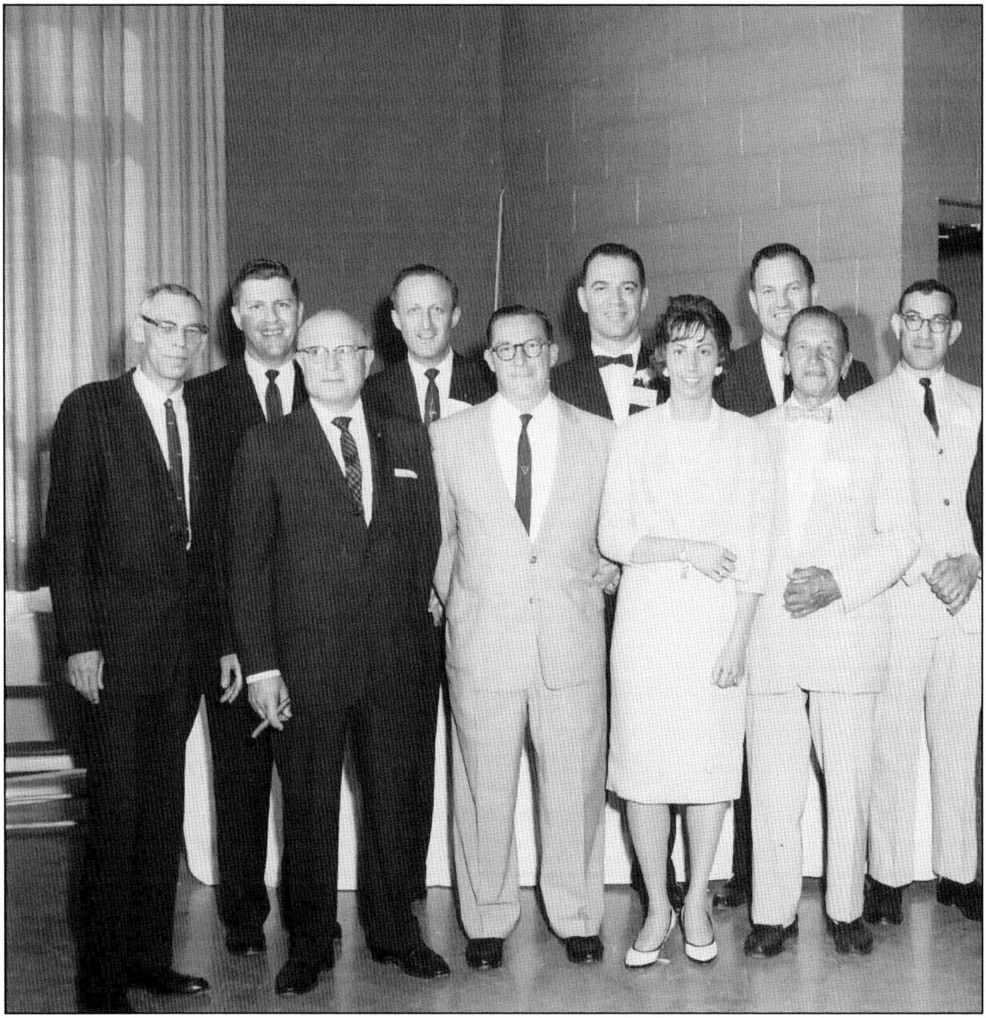

The rebuilding process, with preventative measures taken to insure that a disaster like the Flood of 1955 never occurred again, began soon after the flood waters receded. This included the formation of a Downtown Torrington Reconstruction Committee. Members of the committee are shown here during a groundbreaking ceremony in May 1962. From left to right are: (front row) Chairman James P. Houlihan, Vice-Chairman Sal Rubino, Treasurer Ernest W. Booth, Secretary Aurora Lanfranchi, property manager Paul A. Klampt, and Executive Secretary Director Frances Gillis; (back row) auditor Richard F. Wheeler, Commissioner Harold Reibman, land developer Leonard Farber, Assistant Treasurer Dr. James F. McKenna, and Recreation Director Marvin (Muff) Maskovsky. This photograph was offered by Mrs. Rubino from her personal collection and credited to Rubens Studio of Torrington.

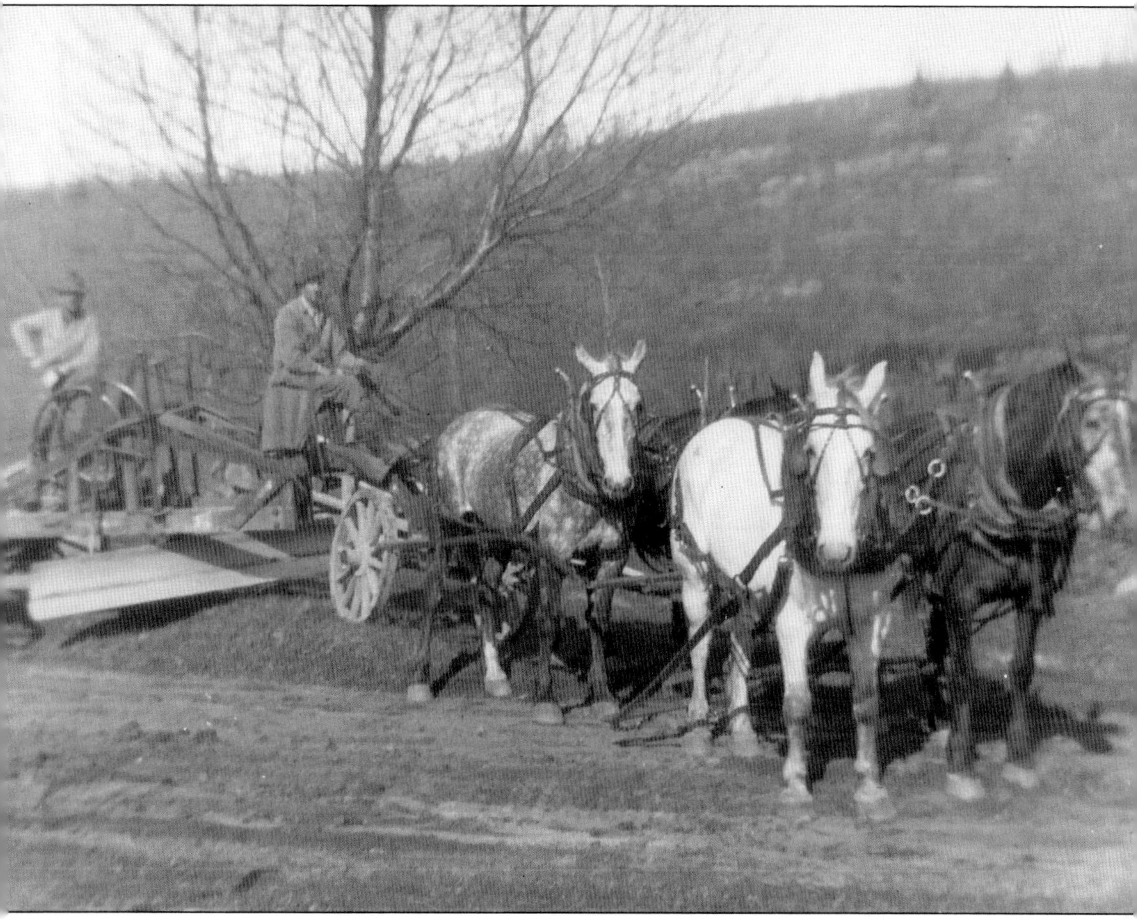

This is a 1920s "road grader," used for leveling old country roads while they were still made of dirt. It is very similar to modern road graders, except that it lacks gas power.

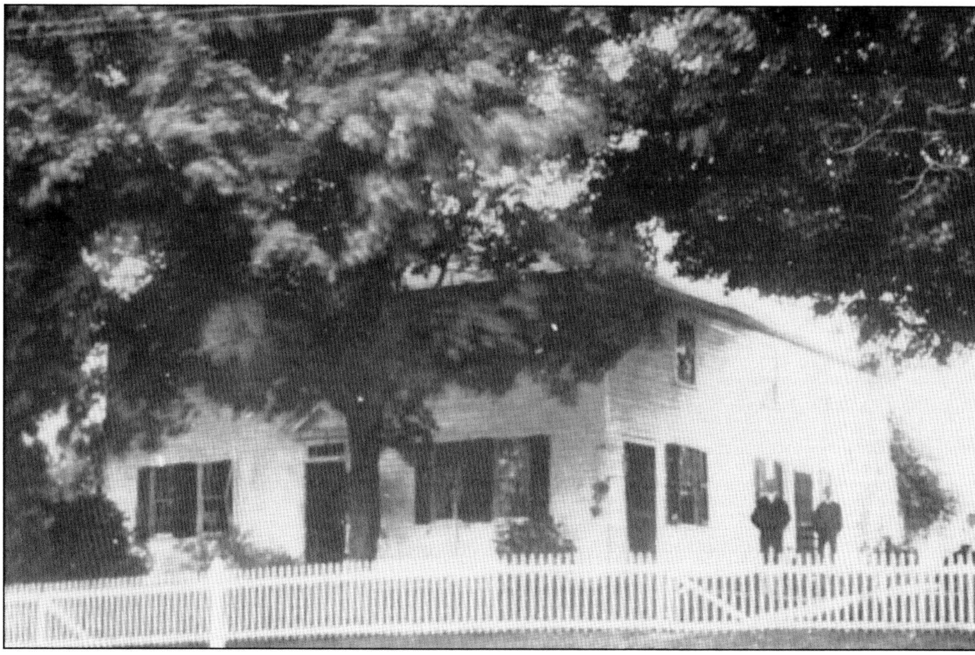

The Cogswell Tavern was built in New Preston in 1764.

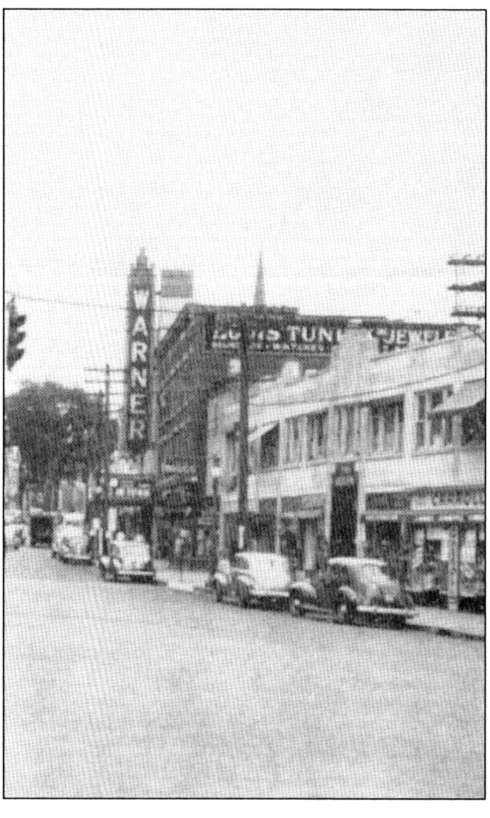

This view of Main Street shows the Warner Theatre. The Art Deco architecture of the theatre was characteristic of many Main Street buildings at that time.

Eight

A Time to Gain, A Time to Lose

Hazel Guilmart Osborn, granddaughter to Celestin Guilmart,
was the youngest of a large family that lived
in a legendary house known as Seven Gables
(not to be confused with the home in The House of Seven Gables).
This Victorian-style home was built in Hall Meadow,
the eastern area of the Goshen settlement.
Celestin Osborn, Hazel's grandfather, produced many items
including cheese boxes for Goshen's cheese-making tradition.
Hazel was carried into this eloquent home in 1900,
the year of her birth and the year that the house was completed.
She left in the early 1920s as a young bride.
Her widowed father went with her and the house was sold.
The Osborn family descended from some of the original setters
of the Litchfield Hills; Gleda Osborn, the family historian,
notes that her family goes back in history about 250 years.

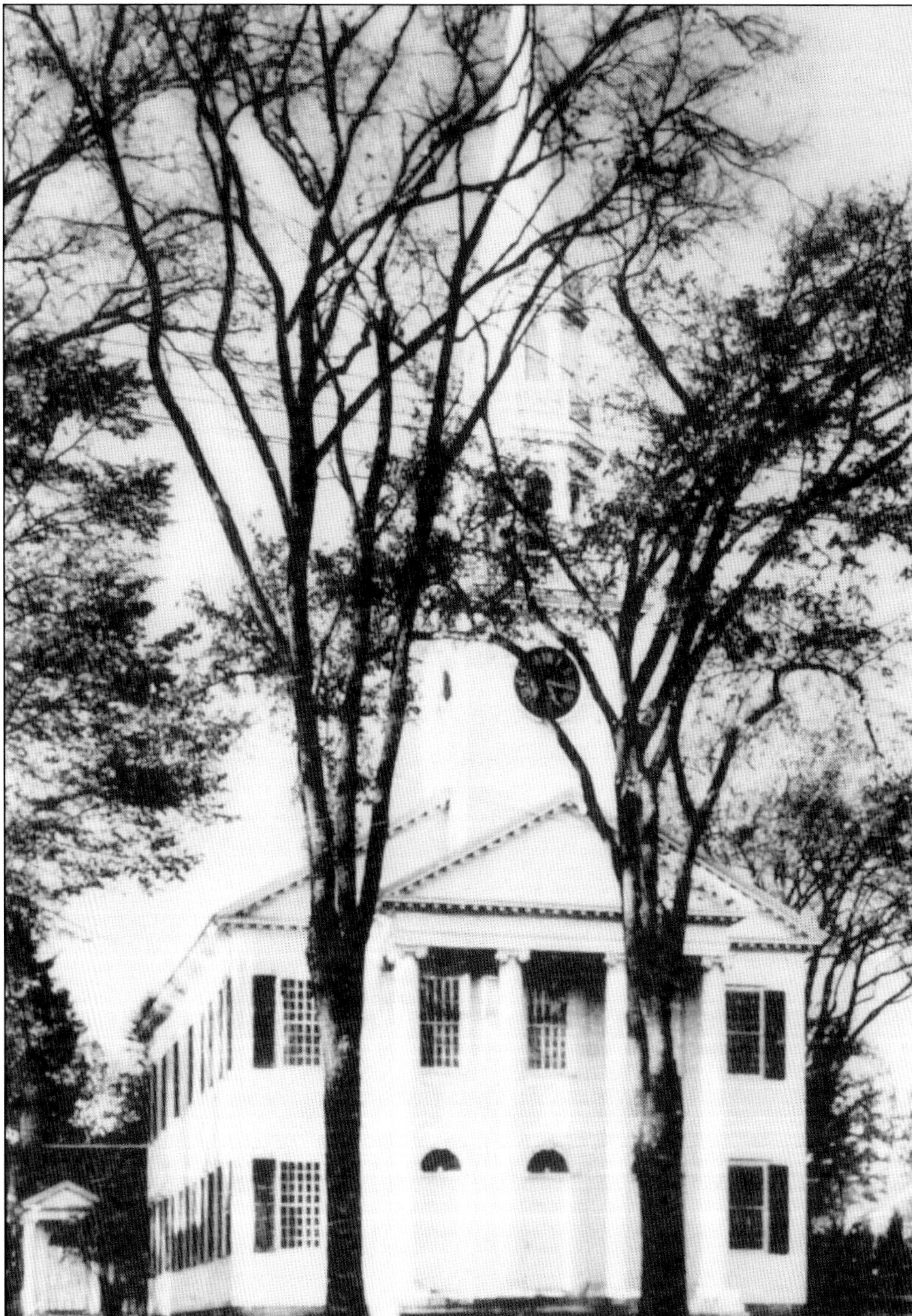

The First Congregational Church in Litchfield is probably one of the most photographed churches in New England. As evidence of the enlightened nature of the community, lightning rods were installed on some of the area churches just seventeen years after Benjamin Franklin's discovery in distant Philadelphia.

Ethan Allen was born in 1738 and moved to Cornwall as a boy. At the age of twenty-four, he helped in the construction of Connecticut's first blast furnace. On May 2, 1775, Allen joined the Green Mountain Boys and led eighty-five men to capture Fort Ticonderoga. The siege yielded 100 cannons, 10 tons of muskets and cannon balls, and a large quantity of gunpowder and small arms.

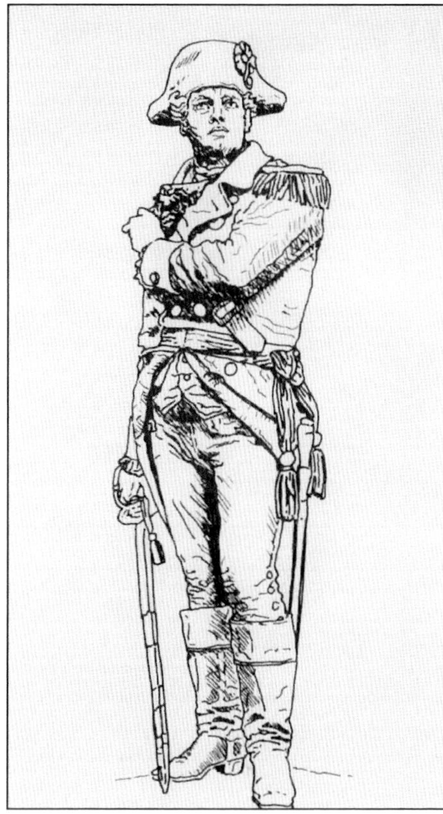

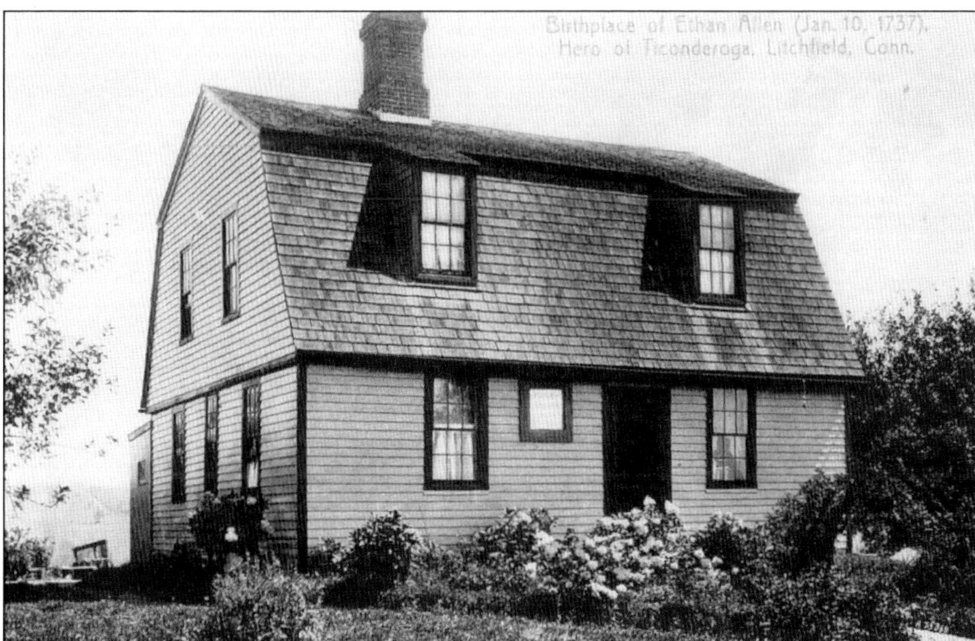

This is the birthplace of Ethan Allen in Litchfield.

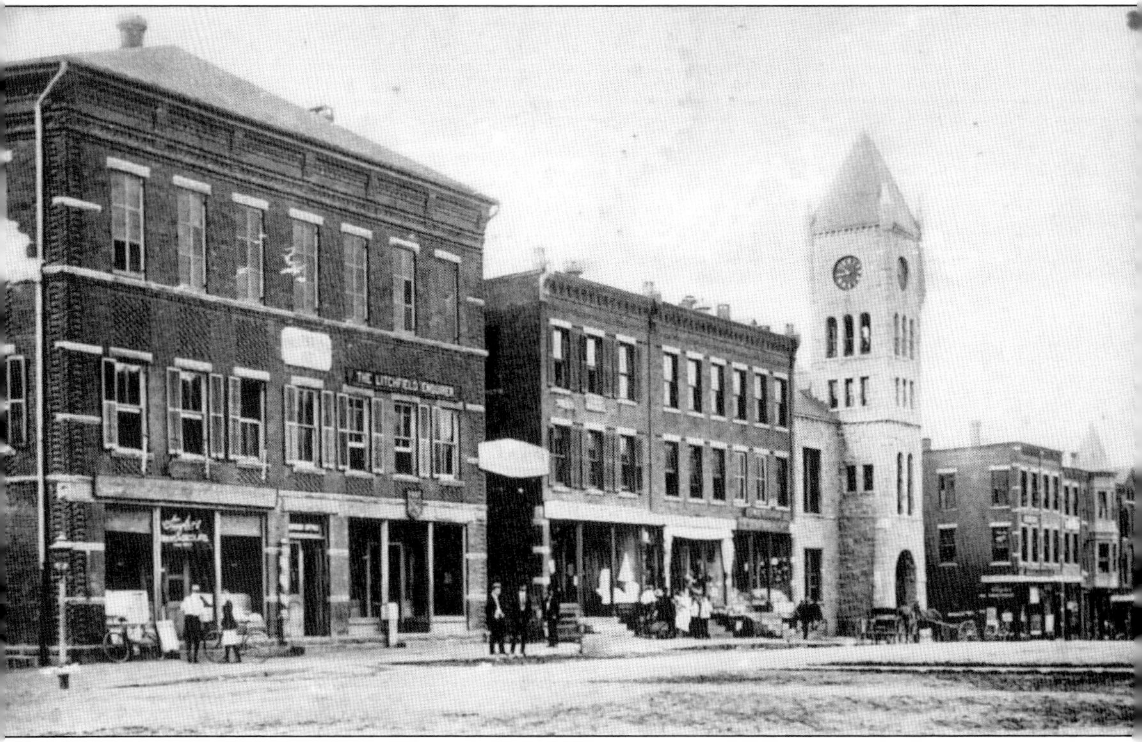

Note the granite and brick buildings in this photograph of Main Street in Litchfield; they were designed to protect the town from the fires that had burnt down the Main Street area on two previous occasions.

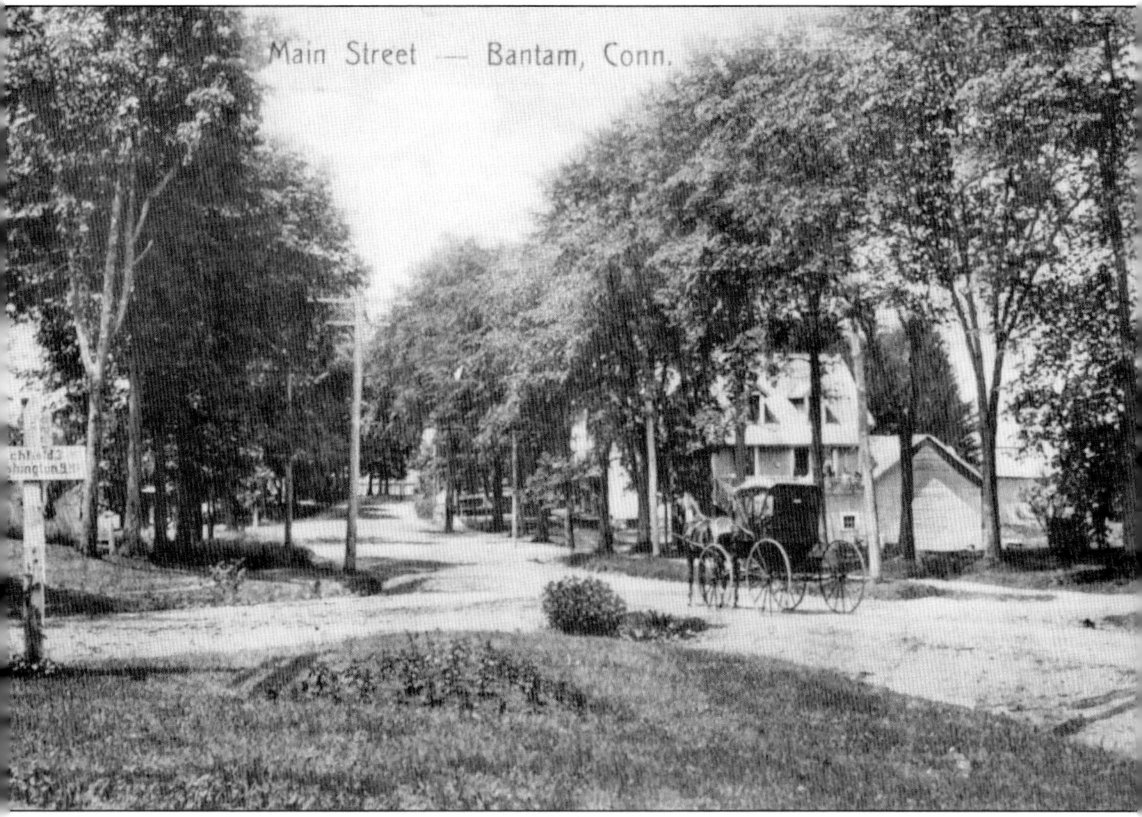

This is a view of Main Street in Bantam. Litchfield was once the name given to this area prior to its becoming an independent township. Many of the smaller communities changed names during the early settlement of the area. The Bantam Indians occupied Bantam in its early years. They reserved Mount Tom as hunting grounds, and used the peak, where the Mt. Tom Tower now stands, for sending out important messages by smoke signals. The Shepaug Railroad arrived here in 1872.

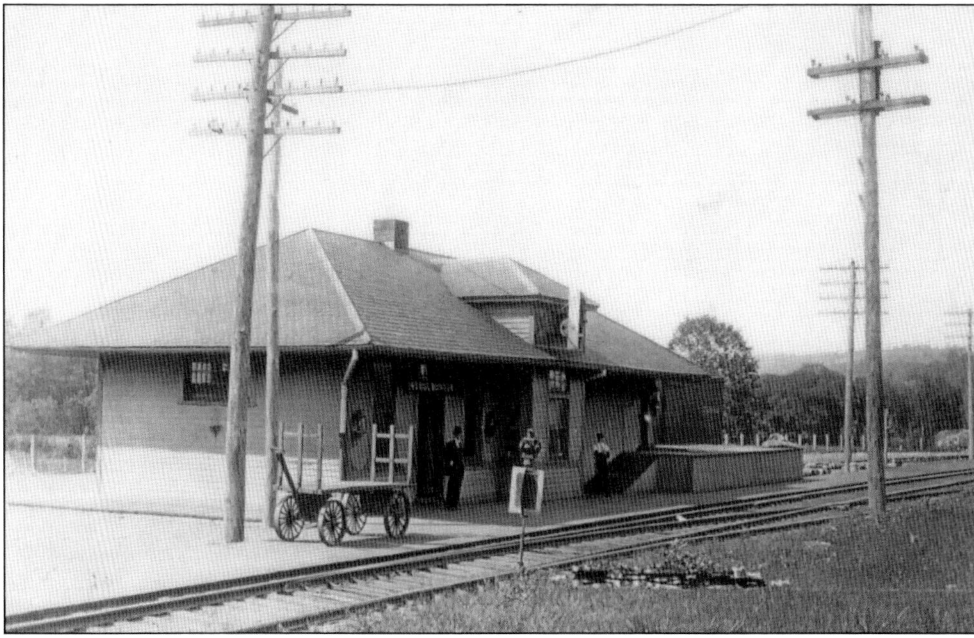

This trolley station in Litchfield was called the Still River Station. It was when trolley service first became available that Litchfield became a summer vacationland for many. There were many similar trolley stations throughout northwestern Connecticut connecting small towns to the larger cities.

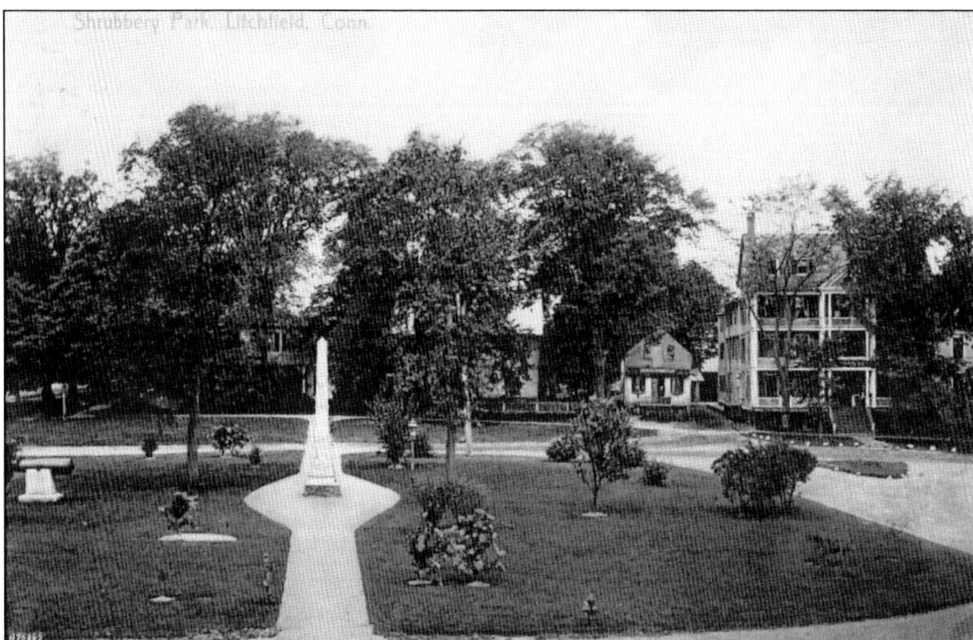

Once known as Shrubbery Park, the Litchfield Green is now decorated with monuments engraved with the names of those who have served in times of war, from the colonial days through the Gulf War. The old cannon on the green provides a place for youngsters to climb, parents to worry, and tourists to photograph.

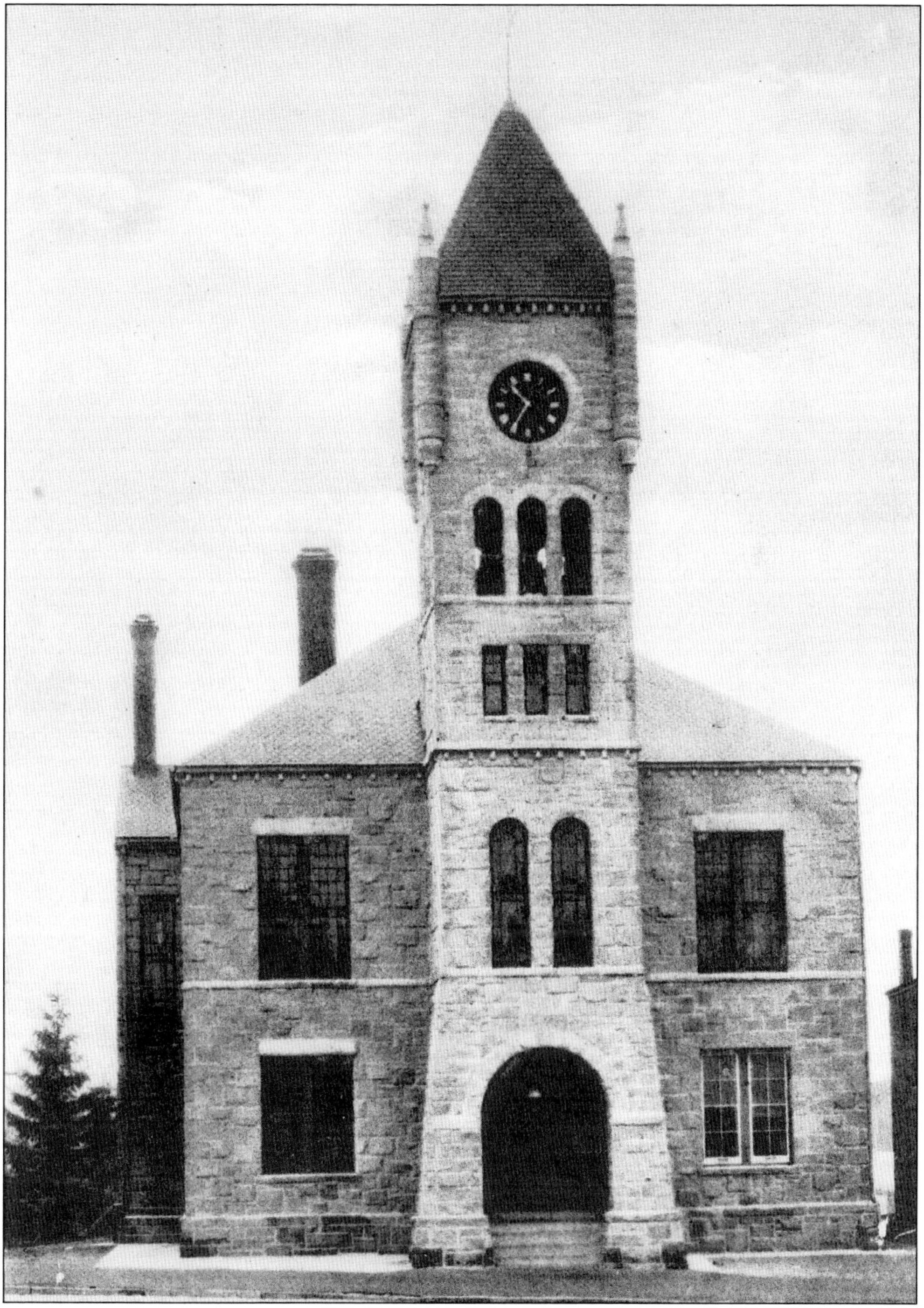

The Litchfield County Courthouse is shown here as it appeared in 1889. Two earlier buildings which had served as the courthouse had previously burned to the ground. One fire took place in 1879 and wiped out most of downtown Litchfield. Another fire occurred in 1886. The building shown here was built, as many of the other downtown buildings finally were, of granite (or bricks). It still serves as the primary courthouse for Litchfield County.

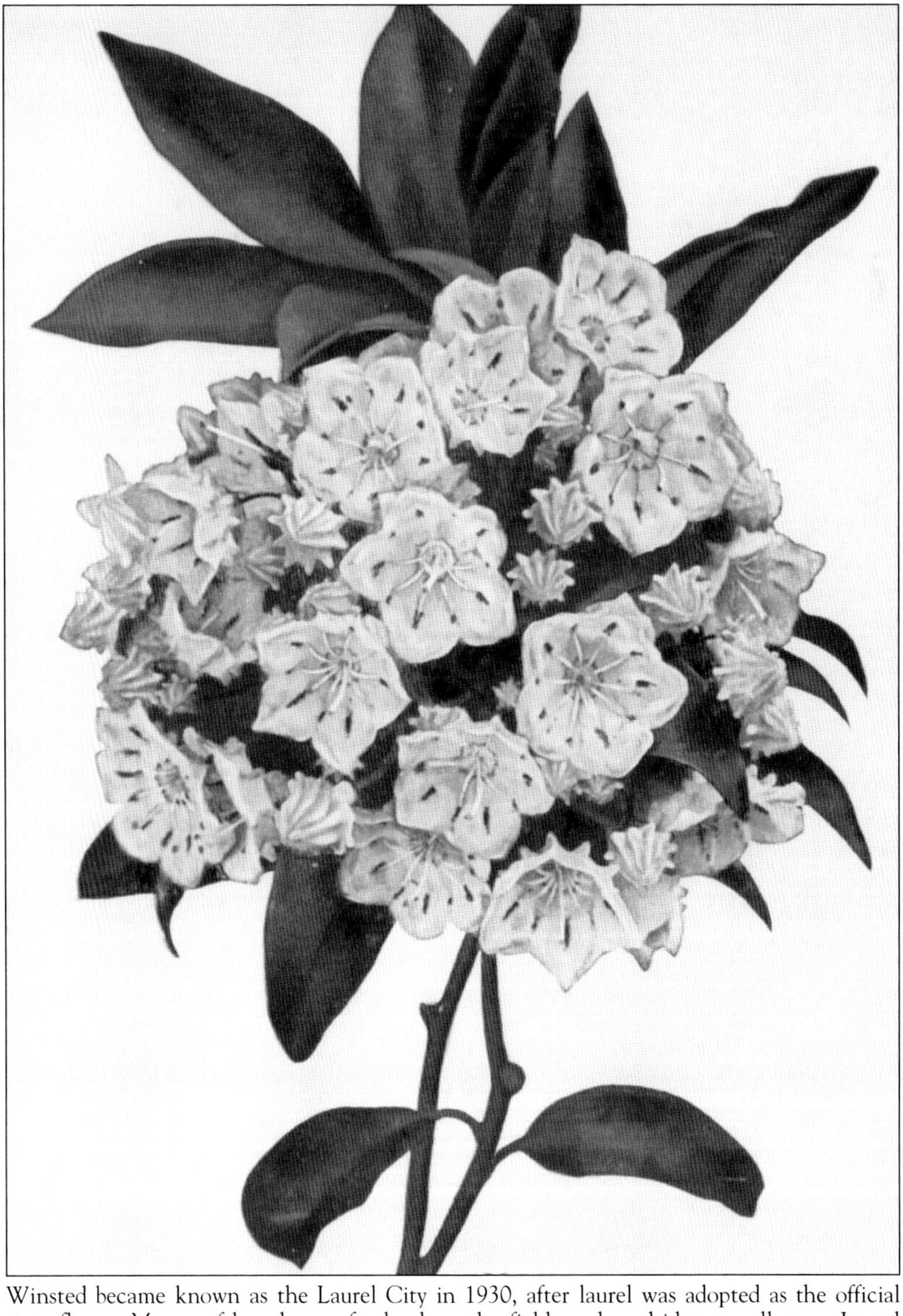

Winsted became known as the Laurel City in 1930, after laurel was adopted as the official state flower. Masses of laurel grow freely along the fields and roadsides as well as on Laurel Mountain. Annual celebrations include the "Laurel Festival," when an elected "Laurel Queen" rides through town on a throne atop a float. Other annual activities include a pet parade and many fairs.

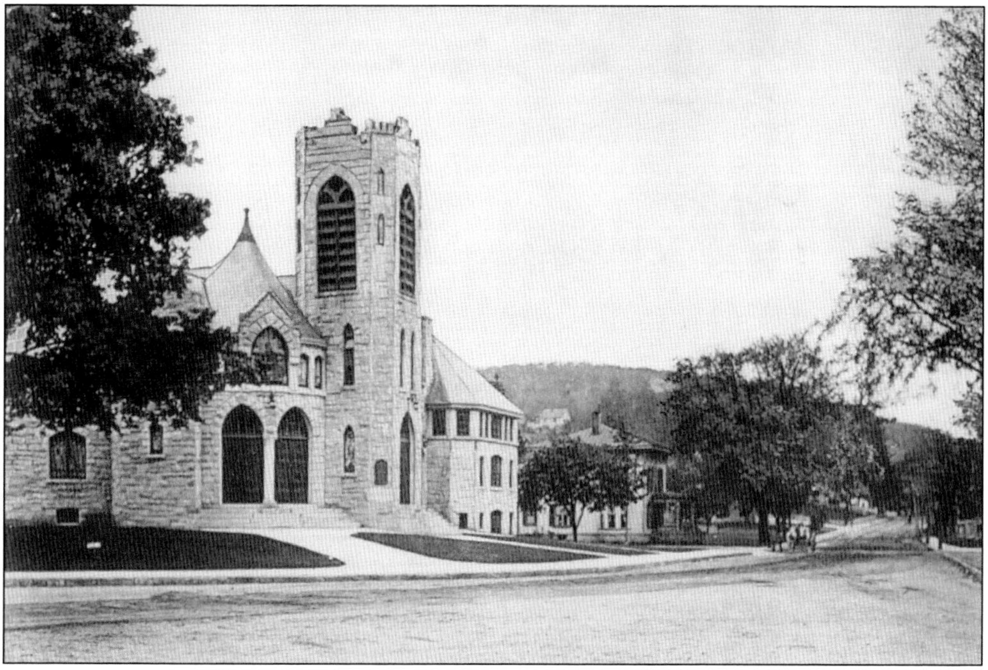

This is a view of the First Congregational Church in Winsted.

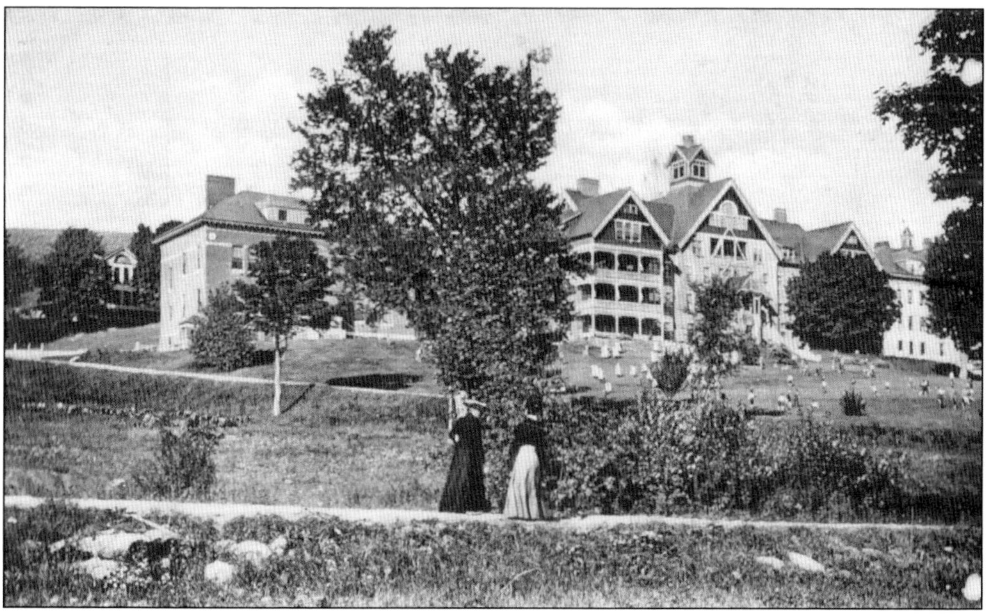

The Gilbert Home was founded by businessman William Gilbert as a home for orphaned children following World War I (*c.* 1915). It provided shelter, guidance, and nourishment for hundreds of children in need. The Gilbert School, which is tuition-free to Winsted residents and is supported by public funds, was also founded by Gilbert.

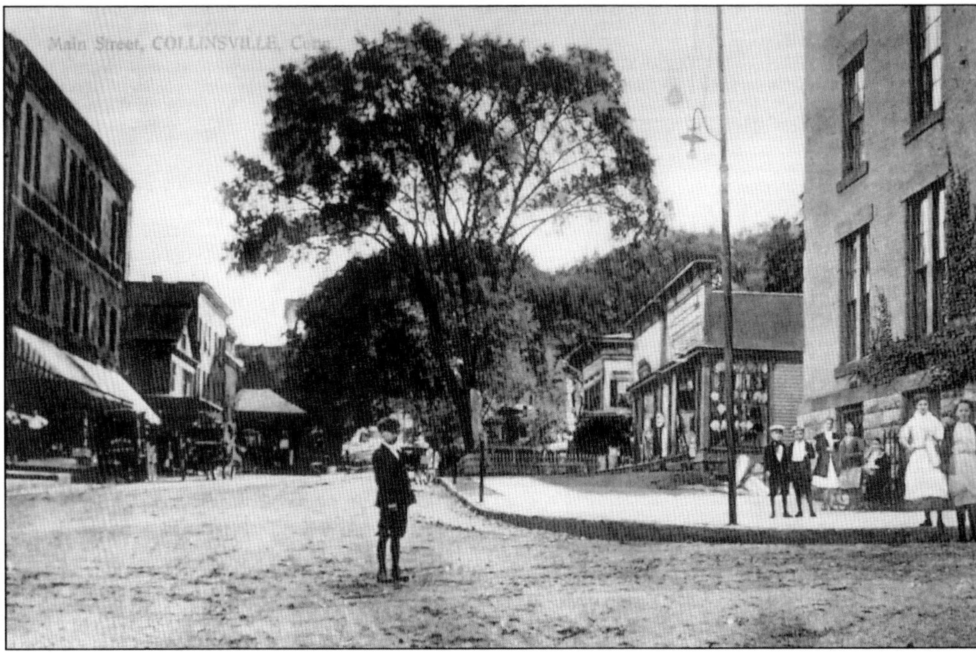

Main Street in Collinsville was captured in this turn-of-the-century photograph.

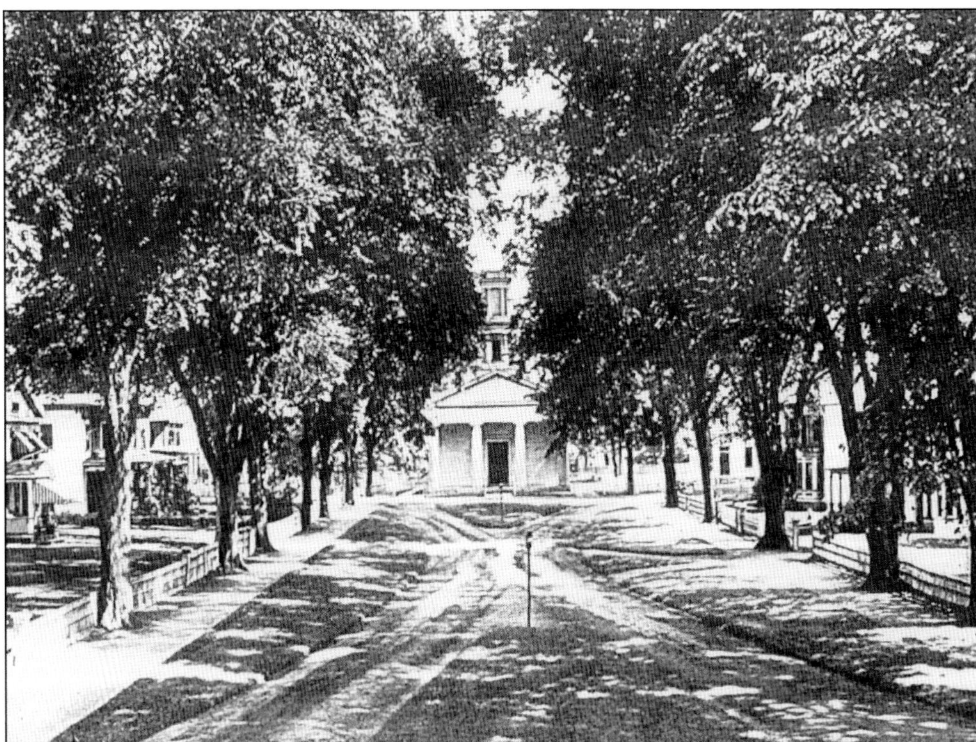

The street leading to the Collinsville church was lined with beautiful elm trees.

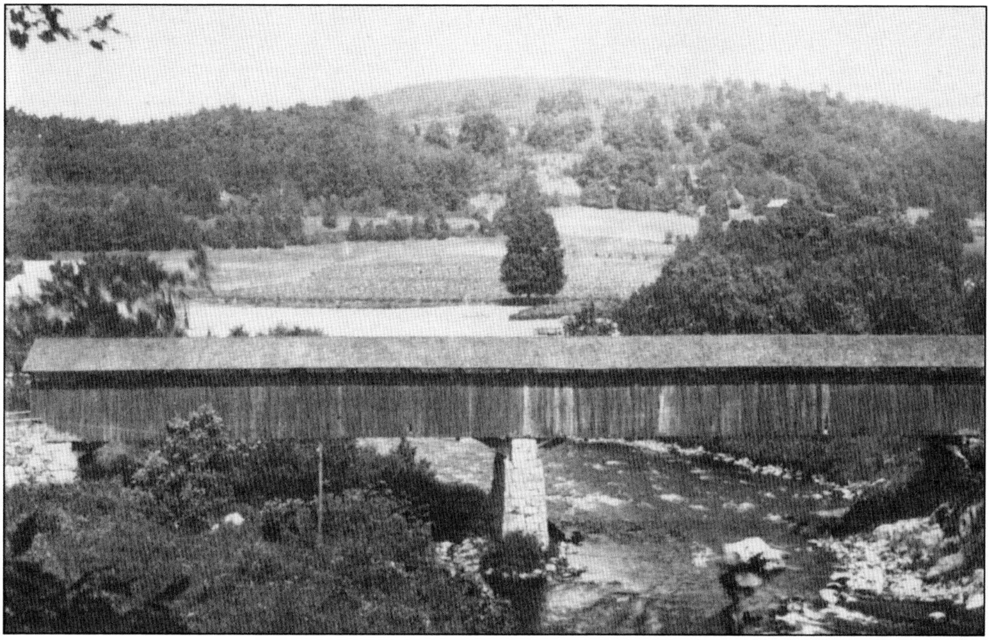

This unusual bridge crossed the Housatonic River in the New Hartford area, known as Satan's Kingdom prior to 1912. Later, this was the site of the first steel bridge in Connecticut, which was subsequently destroyed by the Flood of 1955.

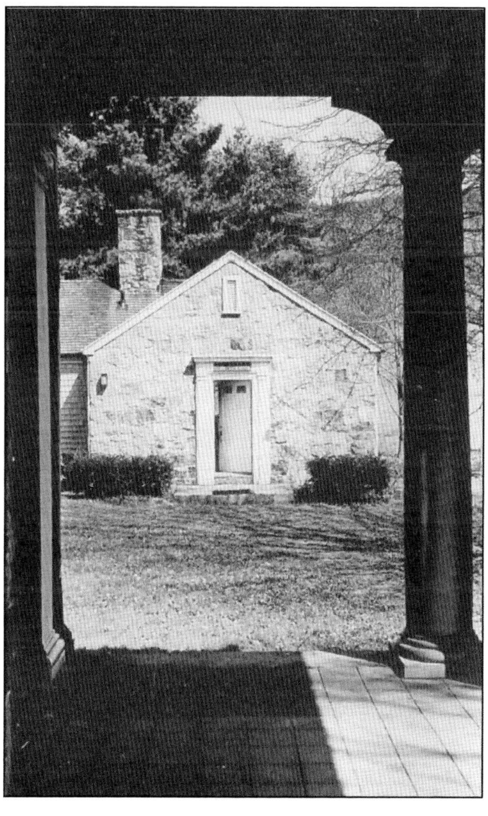

This is the town clerk's office in Cornwall. Cornwall is well known for Mohawk Mountain, which now boasts a ski area as well as a state forest.

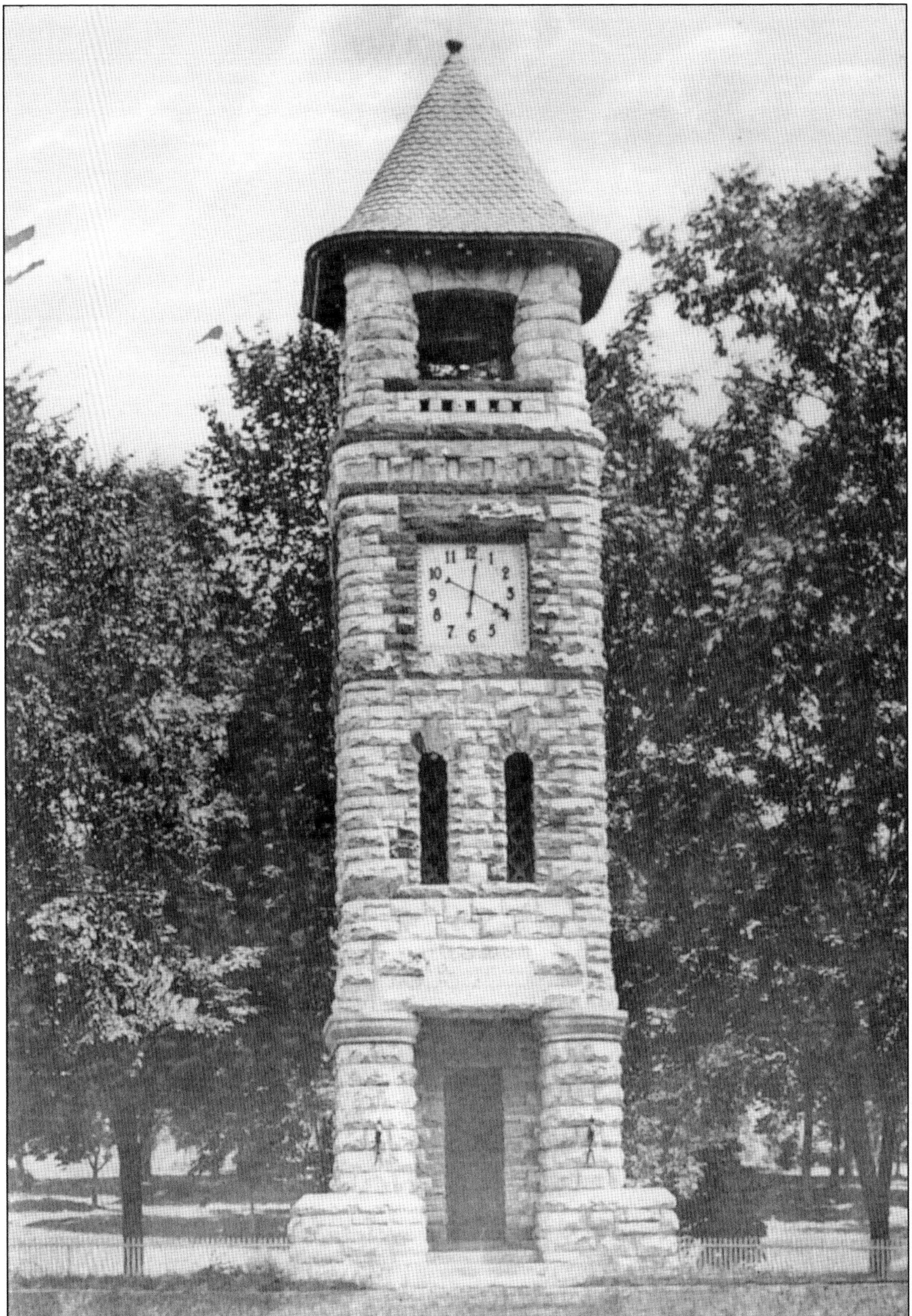

The Sharon town clock sits in this picturesque park. Sharon once flourished during the eighteenth century as a manufacturing town, with stoves, tools, cigars, and wooden mousetraps being made here in abundance.

Nine

A Time to Cast Stones, A Time to Gather Stones

Burton and Silas Patterson were both surveyors
in the Litchfield Hills during the early 1900s.
One of the family deeds spoke of surveying
the area around what was once known as Dudleytown.
The following entries from the journal of Burton Patterson
exemplify farming as a way of life at that time:

"July 9, 1908.
A beautifully clear day—I was home all day.
Worked some in the garden.
A fine hay day.

July 2, 1908.
Home all day. Heavy thunder showers in afternoon—man struck
with lightning at house of Horace Williams of Puffingham and killed.
Peck in West Woods, Sharon had 10 or 11 cows struck and killed."

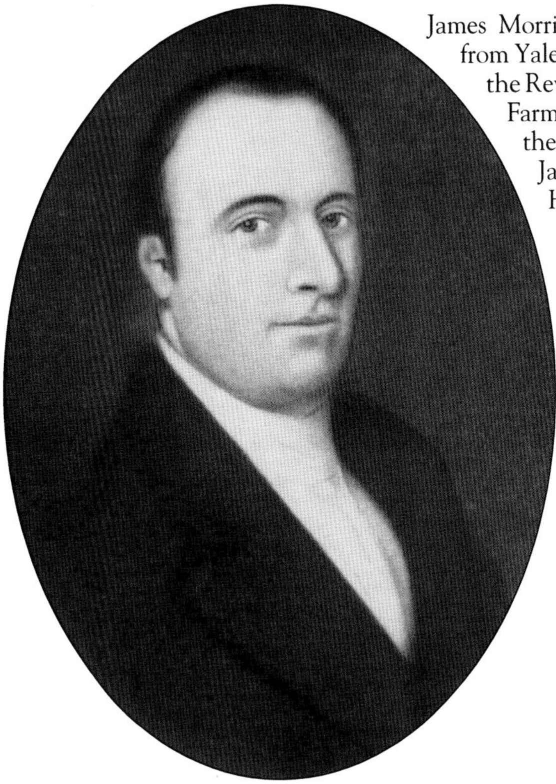

James Morris was born in Litchfield and graduated from Yale University. He served as a captain during the Revolutionary War and later settled in South Farms, acting as both a justice of the peace and the principal of the famed Morris Academy. James Morris died on September 9, 1814. He was the son of Deacon James Morris.

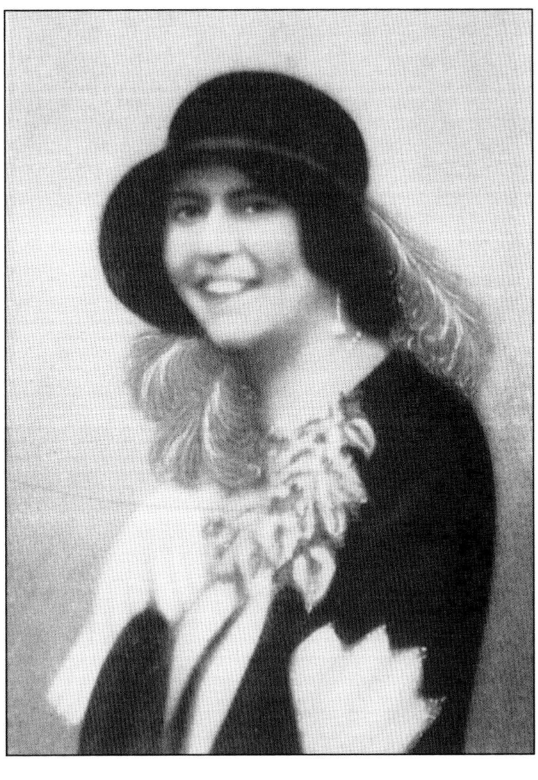

Aline Morris was born in France and emigrated to the U.S. in 1918. She quickly became interested in performing public work and gathered together a group of women with similar interests and concerns. They performed tasks to support war efforts. Aline eventually became an American citizen.

Dwight Morris was born in South Farms in November 1817. He was admitted to the Bar Association in Litchfield in 1839.

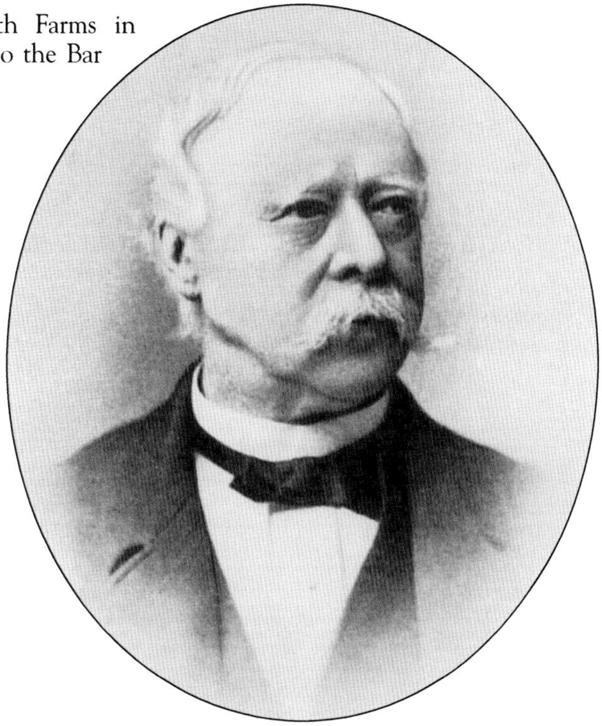

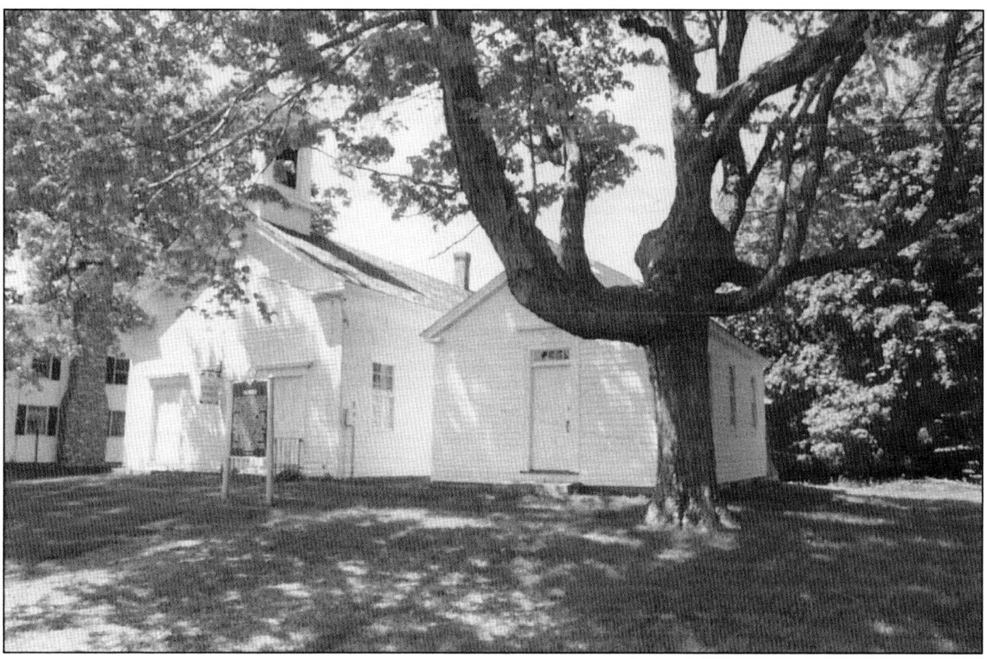

The old Town Hall and Mill School in Morris were built in 1861, after Morris separated from Litchfield in 1853. The school operated from 1772 until 1914, and then stood vacant until 1939. Charles Kirchberger bought the building and used it as part of a cider mill. It was later donated back to the Town of Morris by Ethel Kirchberger as a historical landmark. (Courtesy of the Morris Historical Society.)

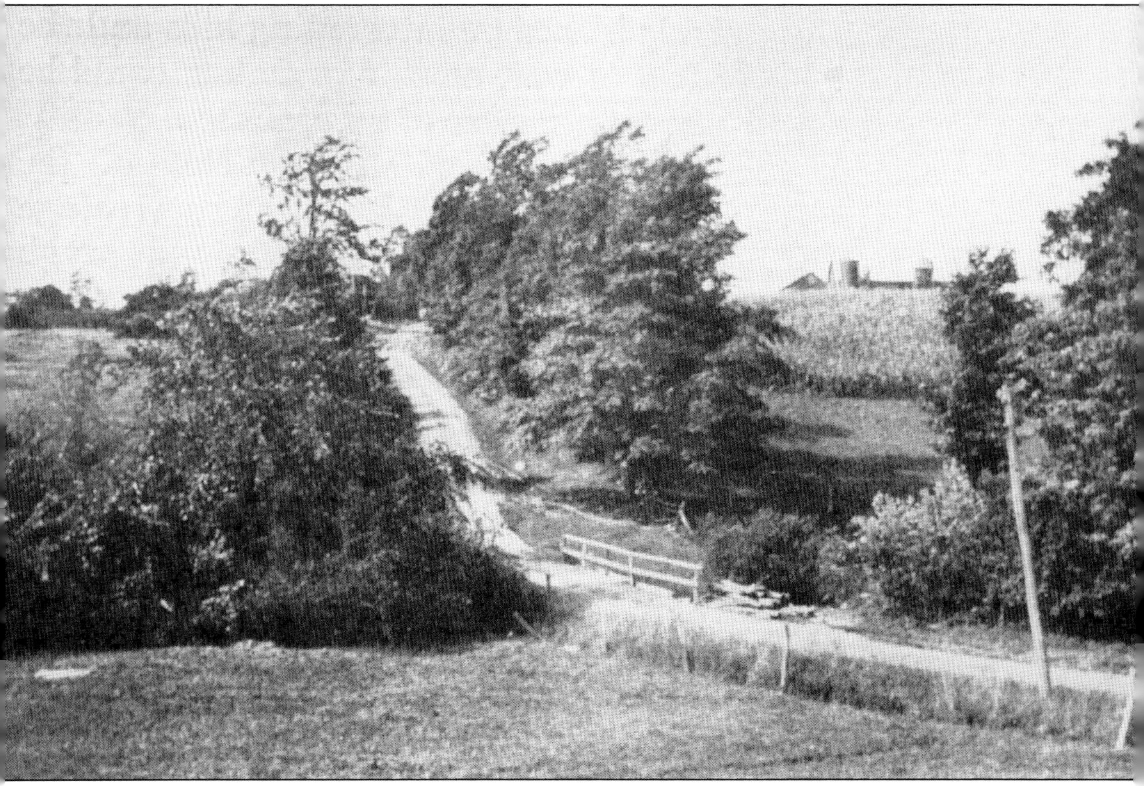

Ebenezer Lyman Jr. was the first settler of Torrington in 1737. One of the settler's first needs was for protection from hostile Indians. Other settlers voted to build a fort near Lyman's home at the top of this hill in West Torrington to protect them from anticipated "attacks." The fort stood 75-by-100 feet and was 8 feet tall. Warnings were given by the lighting of small fires at various high points stretching to Albany, New York. One night a fire was spotted and settlers shut themselves into the crowded fort for three days awaiting attack from the fierce, warlike Mohawk tribe. The attack did not occur and it was later found that the fire was incidental and not one meant to warn settlers.

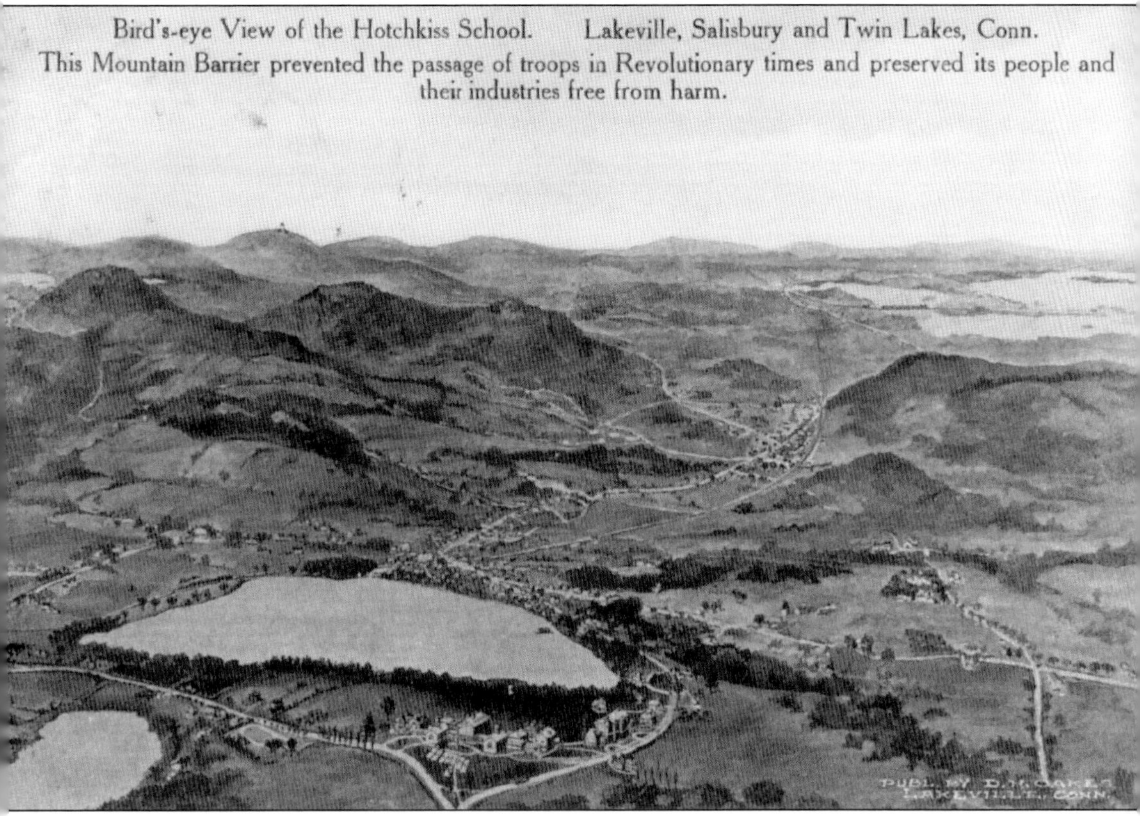

Although this is an aerial view of the Hotchkiss School in the Lakeville/Salisbury area, it also denotes how the mountains acted as a barrier for the passage of troops during the Revolutionary War, thus protecting the people and industries of the area.

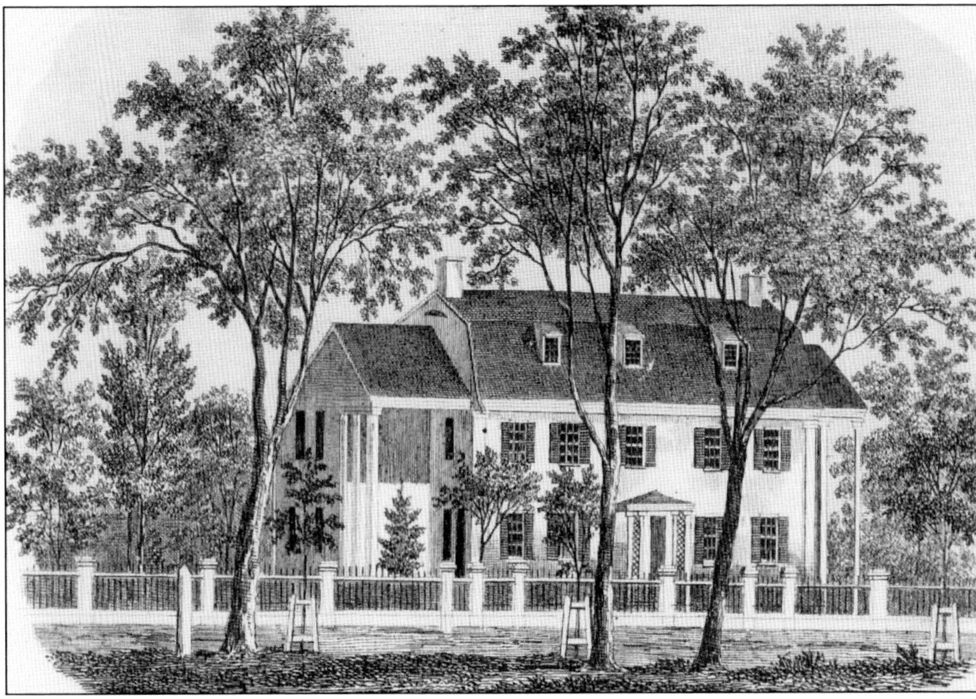

The Tallmadge House was originally a tavern when it was built in 1775. Benjamin Tallmadge bought the home and he and his brothers, John and Miles Beach, established B. Tallmadge and Co. in 1783. John left the business to establish a branch in Warren. Benjamin retired in 1808.

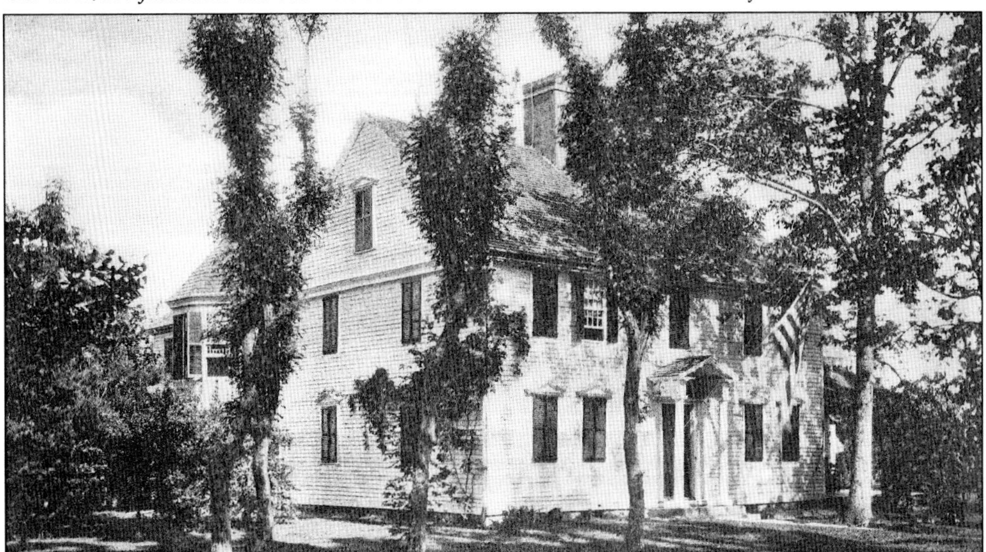

The homestead of the Honorable Oliver Wolcott and his family was built in 1754 in Litchfield. It is the oldest house built in the borough of Litchfield. George Washington and Lafayette were entertained there. Three generations of Connecticut governors came from the Wolcott family: Roger Wolcott Jr., Oliver Wolcott Sr., and Oliver Wolcott Jr. Oliver Wolcott Sr.'s daughter married Matthew Griswold, who was a governor, and their son was later a governor. Oliver Wolcott Sr. signed the Declaration of Independence.

Oliver Wolcott served as the sheriff of Litchfield County from 1751 to 1771. It has been said that Judge Wolcott performed clandestine wedding ceremonies from his porch at the Wolcott Mansion on South Street in Litchfield at odd hours of the night. The couple to be wed would stand outside the window and he would perform the ceremony, many times clad in his night clothes.

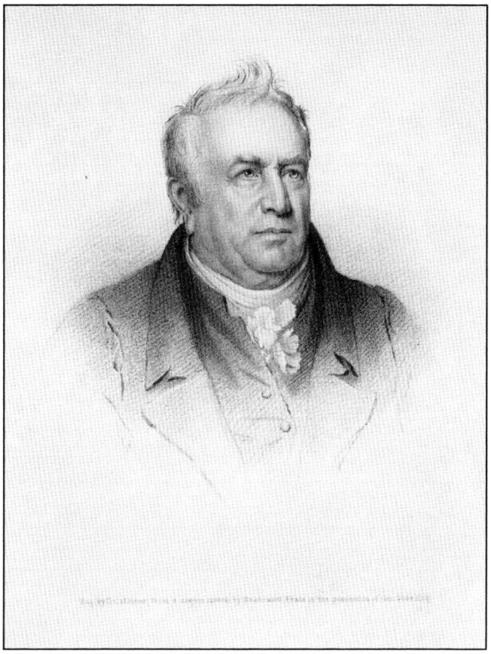

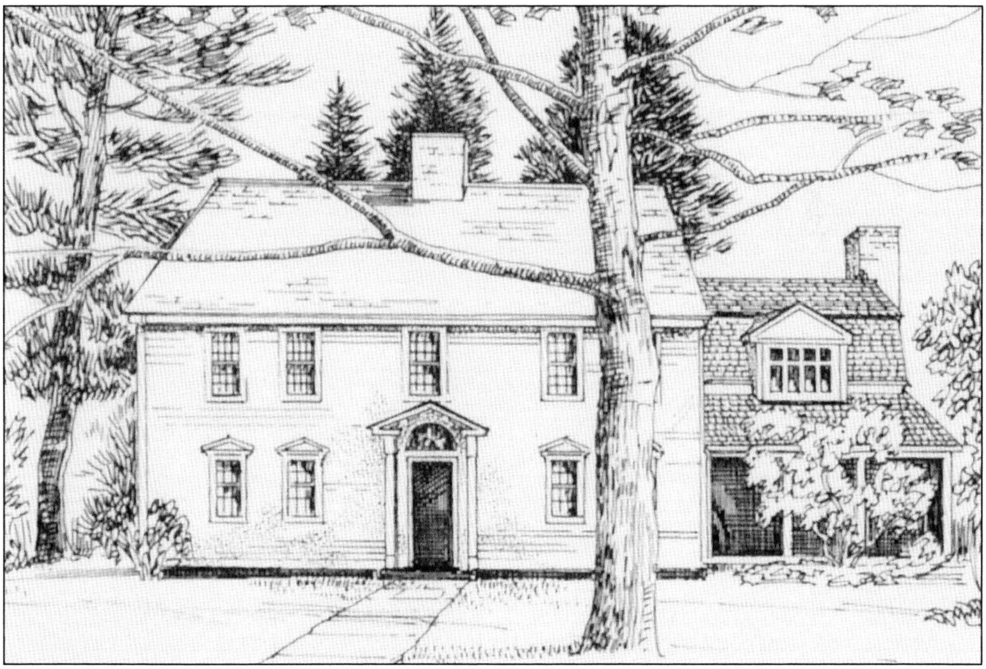

This view of the Wolcott Mansion shows the porch from which Judge Wolcott performed wedding ceremonies. His daughter, Mariann, and some of her young friends made a significant contribution to history following the reading of the Declaration of Independence to Washington's troops. After the "Sons of Liberty" captured a lead statue of George III weighing 4,000 pounds, Mariann, her sister Laura, her brother Frederick, and three neighbors used the lead to produce 42,008 bullets.

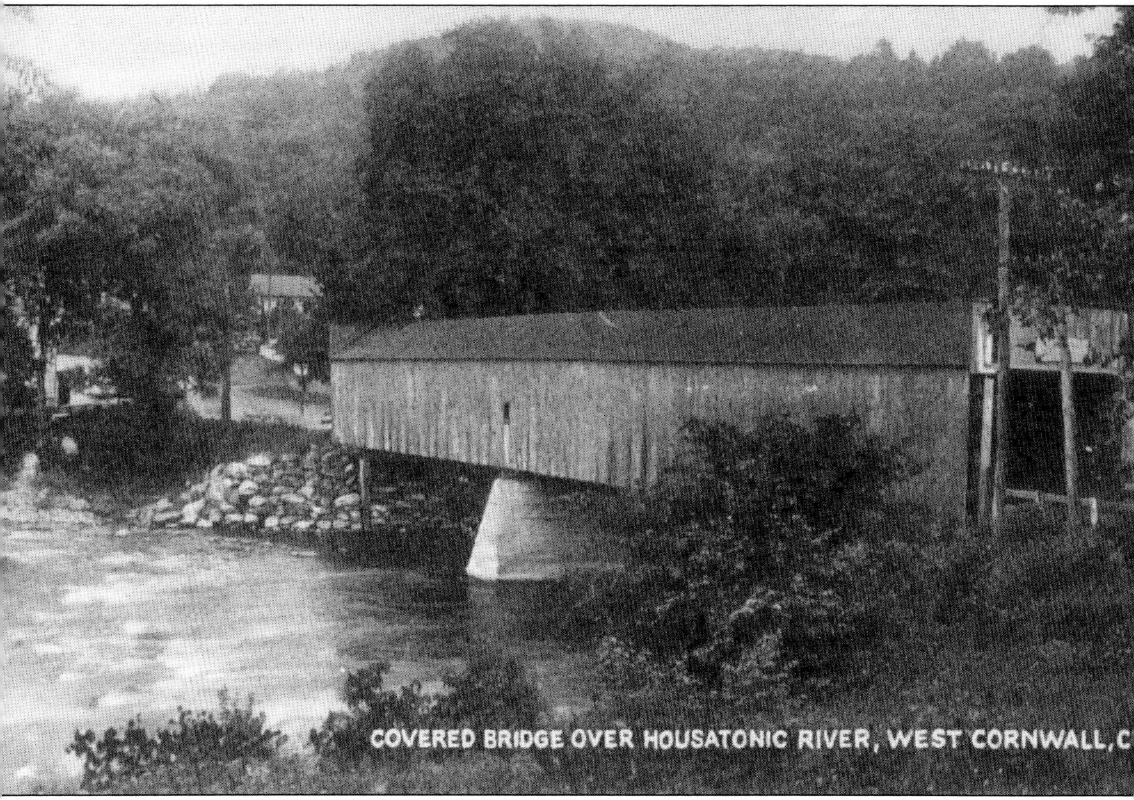

This covered bridge in Cornwall was typical of the five other covered bridges found in the northwest corner of Connecticut.

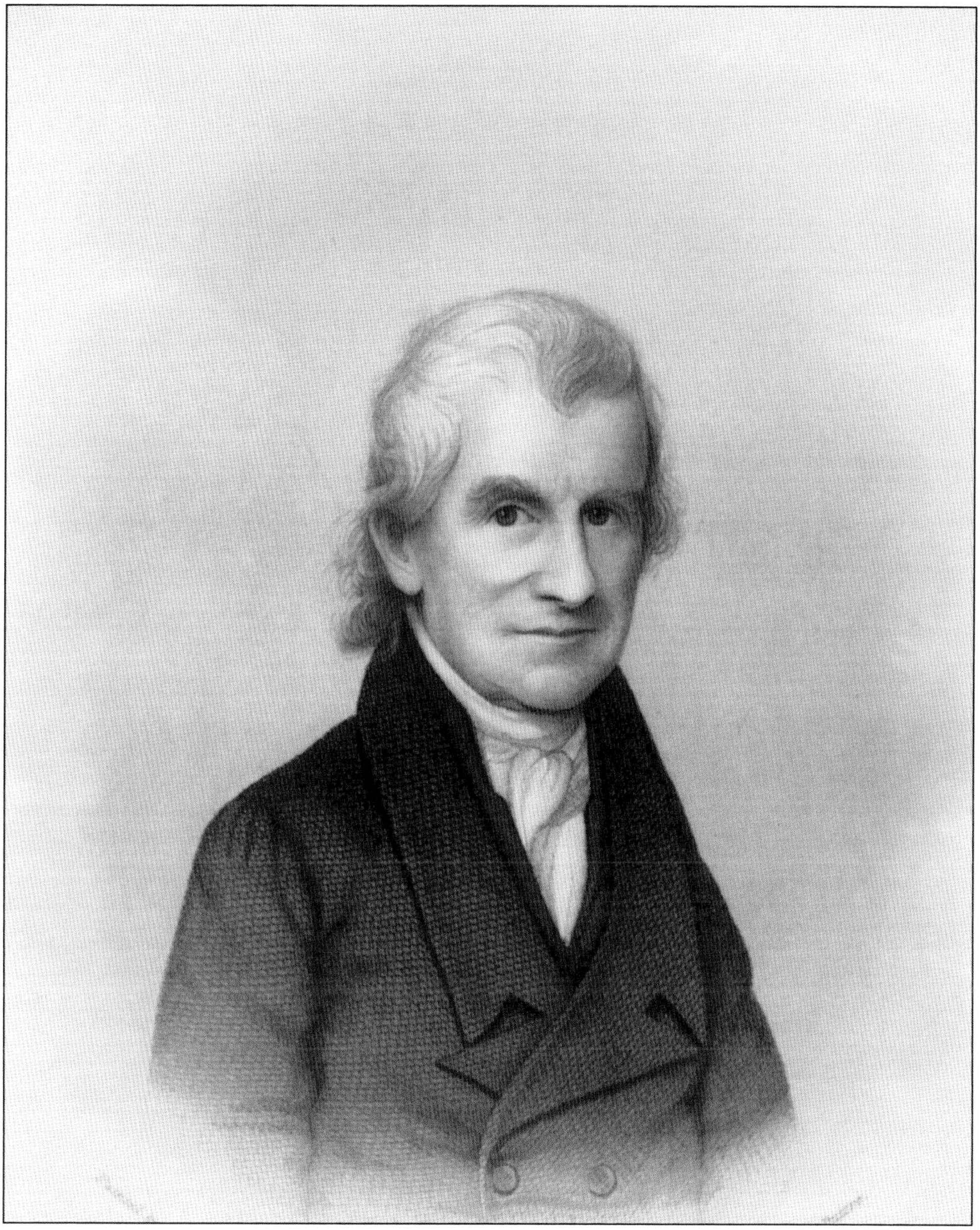

Major Moses Seymour lived in Litchfield with his wife, Molly Marsh (the daughter of Colonel Ebenezer Marsh). They had one daughter and five sons. Major Seymour acted as the town clerk for thirty-seven consecutive years, which was unprecedented in Litchfield's history. During the Revolutionary War, Seymour was stationed in Litchfield by Washington as a commissary of supplies to the armies. He was also expected to guard and make purchases of artillery. Major Seymour died at the age of eighty-four and is buried in Litchfield's East Cemetery.

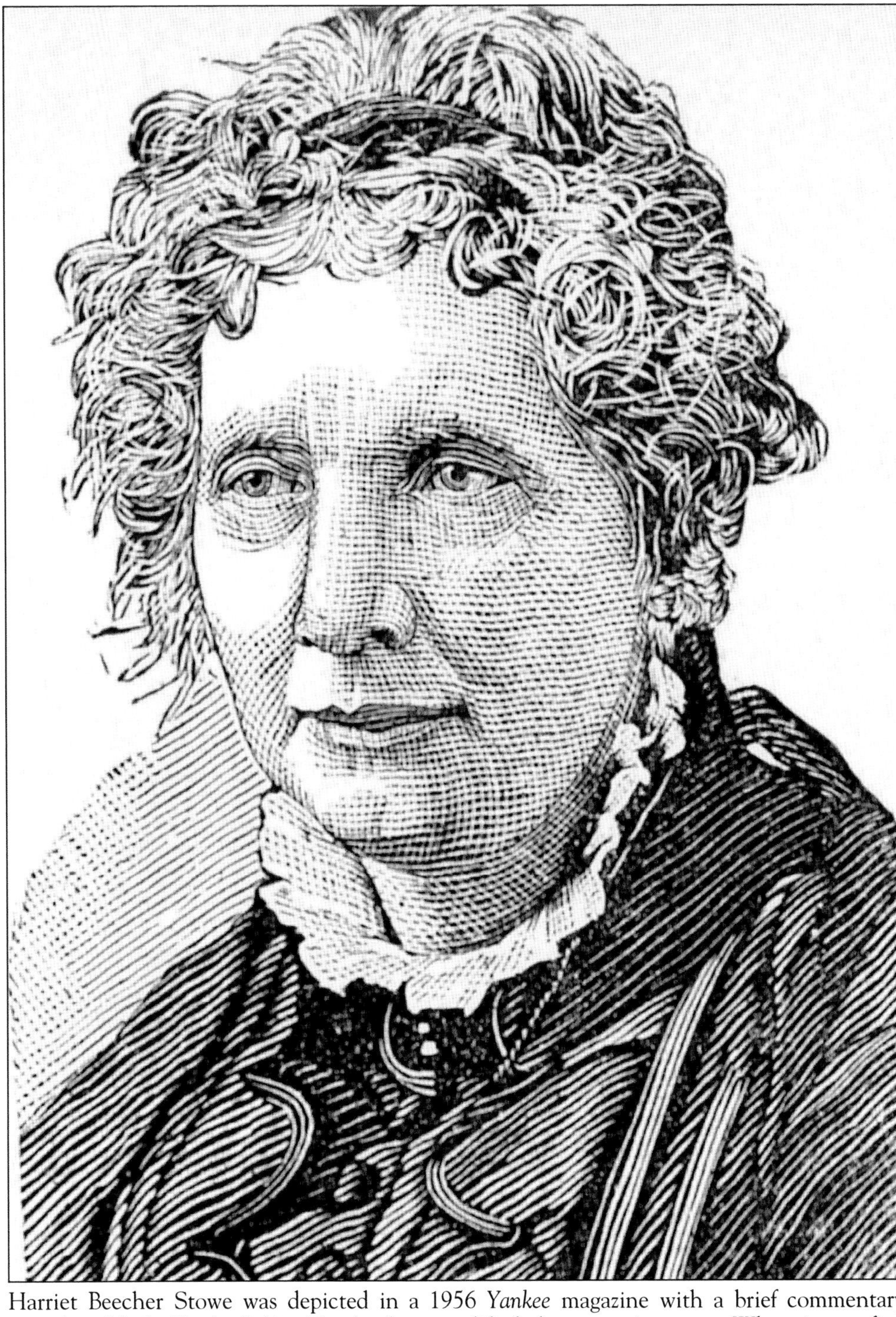

Harriet Beecher Stowe was depicted in a 1956 *Yankee* magazine with a brief commentary regarding *Uncle Tom's Cabin*. Her book exemplified slavery at its worst. When it was first released in 1852, 300,000 copies were sold. Many Northerners joined the abolitionist movement because of it, while Southerners were enraged by Stowe's depiction of the treatment of slaves.

The first local Temperance Society was formed in Litchfield in 1789 and was led by a group of farmers. Their pledge read, in part: "We do hereby associate and mutually agree that hereafter we will carry on our business without the use of distilled spirits as an article of refreshment, either for ourselves or for those whom we employ."

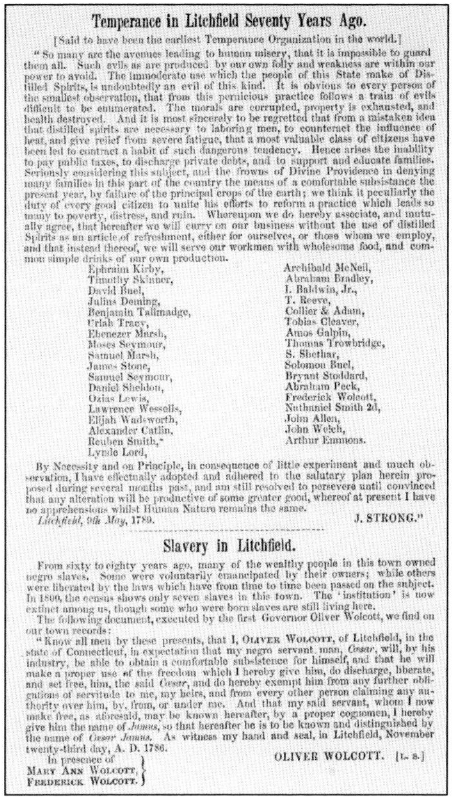

Temperance in Litchfield Seventy Years Ago.

[Said to have been the earliest Temperance Organization in the world.]

"So many are the avenues leading to human misery, that it is impossible to guard them all. Such evils as are produced by our own folly and weakness are within our power to avoid. The immoderate use which the people of this State make of Distilled Spirits, is undoubtedly an evil of this kind. It is obvious to every person of the smallest observation, that from this pernicious practice follows a train of evils difficult to be enumerated. The morals are corrupted, property is exhausted, and health destroyed. And it is most sincerely to be regretted that from a mistaken idea that distilled spirits are necessary to laboring men, to counteract the influence of heat, and give relief from severe fatigue, that a most valuable class of citizens have been led to contract a habit of such dangerous tendency. Hence arises the inability to pay public taxes, to discharge private debts, and to support and educate families. Seriously considering this subject, and the frowns of Divine Providence in denying many families in this part of the country the means of a comfortable subsistance the present year, by failure of the principal crops of the earth; we think it peculiarly the duty of every good citizen to unite his efforts to reform a practice which leads so many to poverty, distress, and ruin. Whereupon we do hereby associate, and mutually agree, that hereafter we will carry on our business without the use of distilled Spirits as an article of refreshment, either for ourselves, or those whom we employ, and that instead thereof, we will serve our workmen with wholesome food, and common simple drinks of our own production.

Ephraim Kirby,
Timothy Skinner,
David Buel,
Julius Deming,
Benjamin Tallmadge,
Uriah Tracy,
Ebenezer Marsh,
Moses Seymour,
Samuel Marsh,
James Stone,
Samuel Seymour,
Daniel Sheldon,
Ozias Lewis,
Lawrence Wessells,
Elijah Wadsworth,
Alexander Catlin,
Reuben Smith,*
Lynde Lord,
Archibald McNeil,
Abraham Bradley,
I. Baldwin, Jr.,
T. Reeve,
Collier & Adam,
Tobias Cleaver,
Amos Galpin,
Thomas Trowbridge,
S. Shethar,
Solomon Buel,
Bryant Stoddard,
Abraham Peck,
Frederick Wolcott,
Nathaniel Smith 2d,
John Allen,
John Welch,
Arthur Emmons.

By Necessity and on Principle, in consequence of little experiment and much observation, I have effectually adopted and adhered to the salutary plan herein proposed during several months past, and am still resolved to persevere until convinced that any alteration will be productive of some greater good, whereof at present I have no apprehensions whilst Human Nature remains the same.

Litchfield, 9th May, 1789. J. STRONG."

Slavery in Litchfield.

From sixty to eighty years ago, many of the wealthy people in this town owned negro slaves. Some were voluntarily emancipated by their owners; while others were liberated by the laws which have from time to time been passed on the subject. In 1800, the census shows only seven slaves in this town. The 'institution' is now extinct among us, though some who were born slaves are still living here.

The following document, executed by the first Governor Oliver Wolcott, we find on our town records:

"Know all men by these presents, that I, OLIVER WOLCOTT, of Litchfield, in the state of Connecticut, in expectation that my negro servant man, *Cesar*, will, by his industry, be able to obtain a comfortable subsistence for himself, and that he will make a proper use of the freedom which I hereby give him, do discharge, liberate, and set free, him, the said *Cesar*, and do hereby exempt him from any further obligations of servitude to me, my heirs, and from every other person claiming any authority over him, by, from, or under me. And that my said servant, whom I now make free, as aforesaid, may be known hereafter, by a proper cognomen, I hereby give him the name of *Jamus*, so that hereafter he is to be known and distinguished by the name of *Cesar Jamus*. As witness my hand and seal, in Litchfield, November twenty-third day, A. D. 1786.

In presence of
MARY ANN WOLCOTT,
FREDERICK WOLCOTT.

OLIVER WOLCOTT. [L. S.]

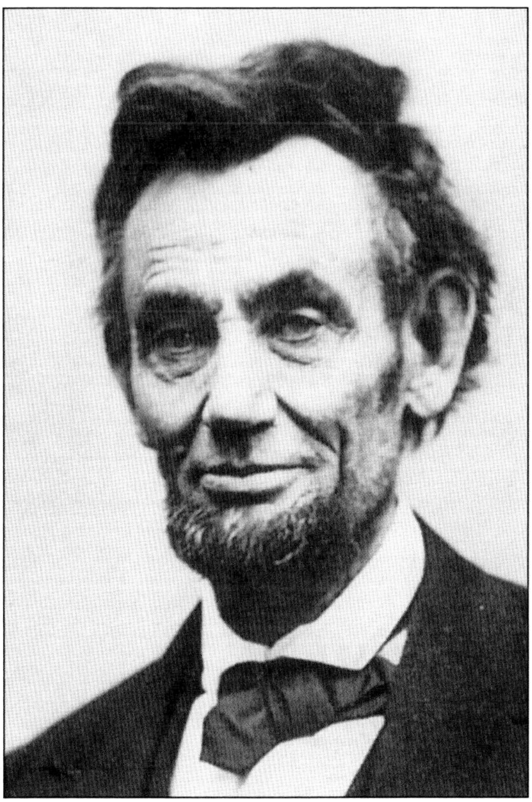

President Abraham Lincoln stated: "As I would not be a slave, so I would not be a master." Lincoln viewed slavery as a monstrous injustice, and wanted the new states joining the Union to be free of slavery. Between 1607 and 1800, hundreds of African slaves were brought to the early colonies. Men, women, and children were kidnapped, chained, and loaded onto cargo ships for passage to the U.S. Many died along the way—the survivors were sold at auctions.

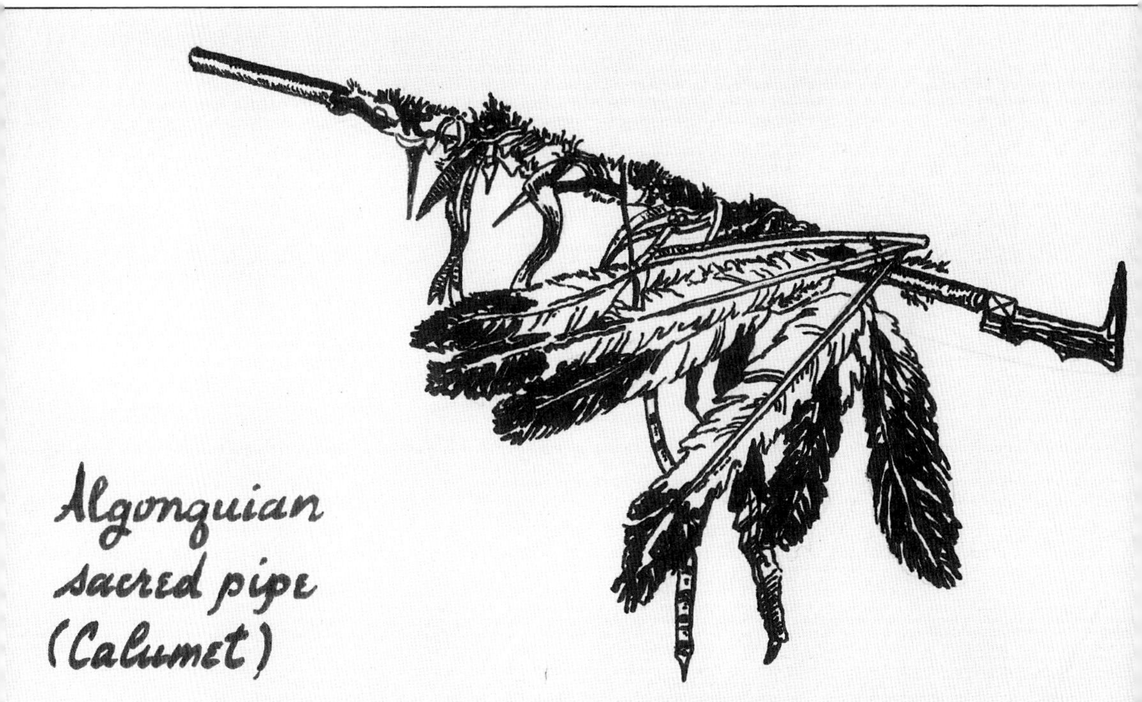

George Catlin (of Litchfield) lived among various Indian tribes and was well known for his art, which depicted life on Indian reservations. This style of pipe, made of the red, pink, or gray stone, is found in the Great Lakes country and can be carved with a knife when it is first quarried. It turns hard when exposed to air. The stems were made of light wood or reeds carved with beautiful designs. White feathers meant peace, and red meant war. The Alogonquians grew tobacco to smoke as well as kinnikinnik, a mixture of dried plant matter, such as willow bark, and the leaves of a tobacco plant. Catlin studied law in Litchfield and became intrigued by Indians. He produced hundreds of Indian scenes in the western wilderness, and wrote books about the Indian lifestyle with his own illustrations. This illustration of one of the pipes drawn by Catlin was reproduced by illustrator and poet Aino Boszik of Kennebunk, Maine.

Ten

A Time For War, A Time For Peace

*An Indian once wandered into a Litchfield Inn requesting sustenance
but was refused. A patron graciously offered to pay
for the famished young Indian's meal and drink
and the hostess reluctantly acquiesced. The Indian promised his
benefactor that he would one day recompense the favor.
Years later, while traveling through the wilderness,
the benevolent resident of Litchfield was taken prisoner
by an Indian who carried him far to the north.
Life was hard, but while working alone in a field,
the prisoner was furtively approached by a tribesman
who arranged to meet him at a certain place and time.
When the prisoner arrived, he found the Indian plus two muskets,
ammunition, and knapsacks. The Indian signaled the man
to follow him. For many days and nights they wandered south,
the Indian strangely quiet. Alas, they arrived at the top of an eminence,
presenting cultivated country with a few houses.
The Indian asked his companion "Do you know this place?"
The response was "It is Litchfield." His guide reminded him
of the night he had paid for the supper of a weary Indian.
The man nodded. The Indian then extended his arms before him
in a sweeping gesture stating "Now I pay you, go home."*

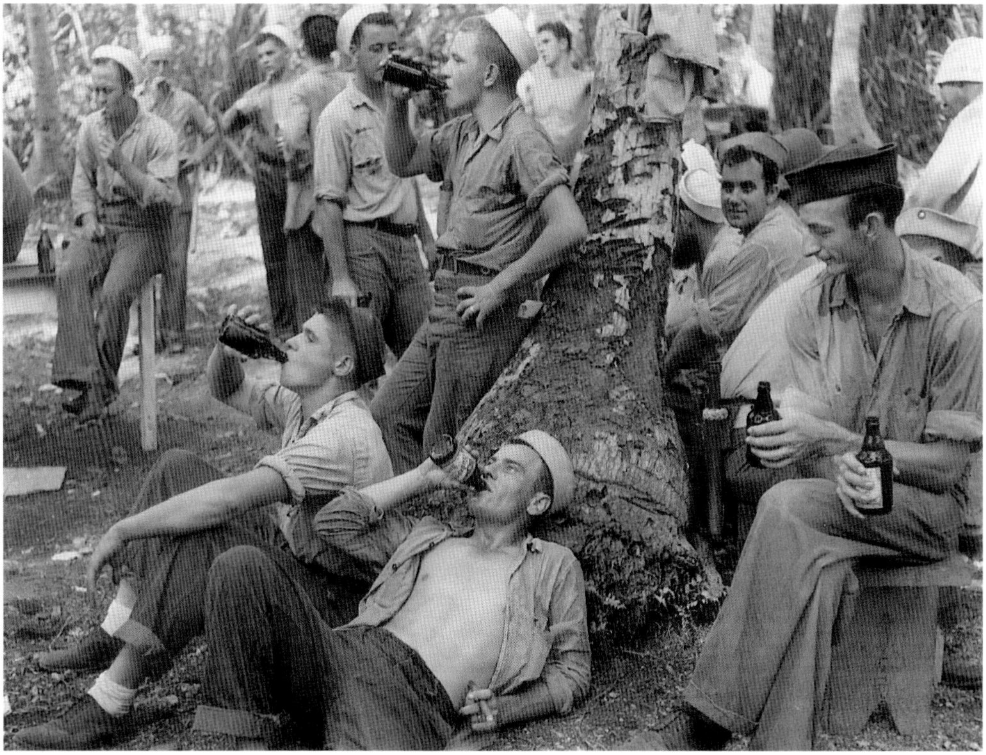

This crew of World War II navy men take a well-deserved break in the Phillipines. Pete Radocy can be seen leaning against the base of the tree, holding a beer.

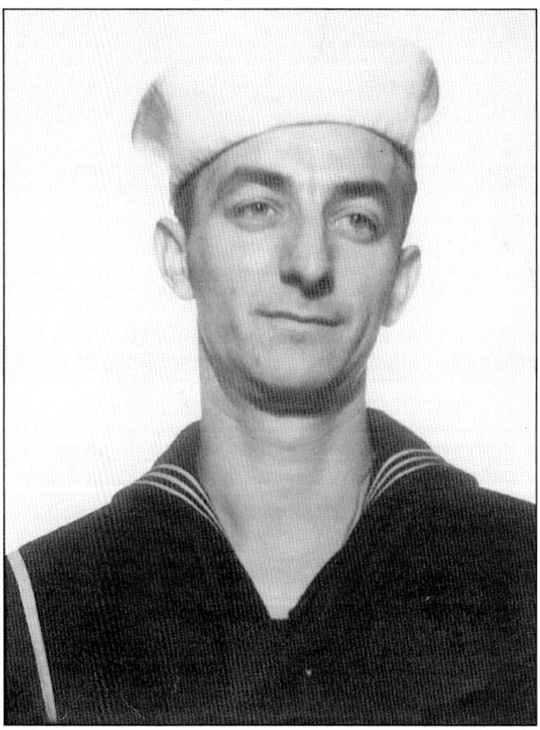

"Pete" Radocy of Torrington was a first-class seaman aboard the USS *Hilbert* during World War II. In December 1944, Radocy's ship was loaded with holiday mail for the troops. With shock, Radocy recalls that at one point a giant wave "came out of nowhere," sweeping a young sailor out to sea. Radocy was involved in two actions during which he saved his ship and its crew of 240. The USS *Hilbert* logged 125,000 miles. Radocy was commended for his actions and just recently received a Philippines Liberation Medal.

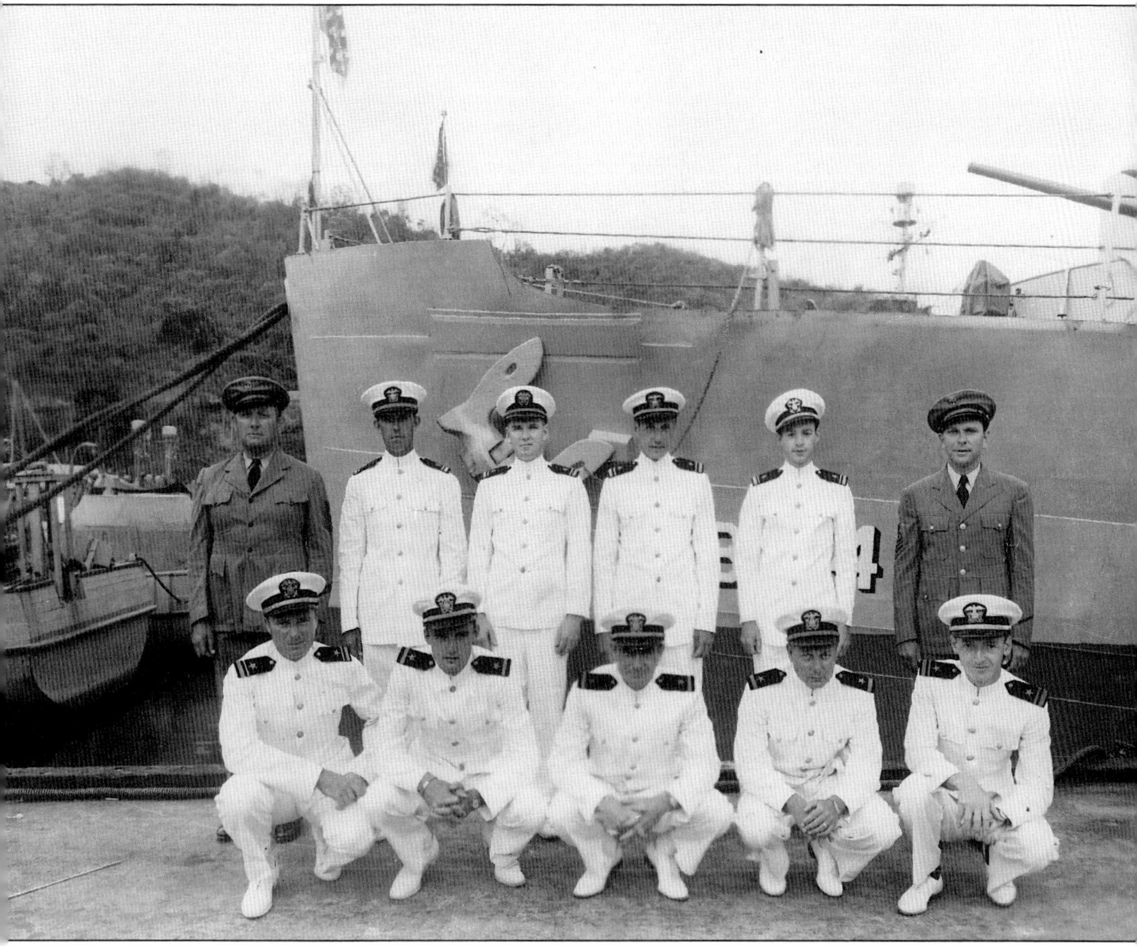

Edward Lancaster Jr. of Litchfield served alongside "Pete" Radocy during World War II. Lancaster was a lieutenant in the Navy and a gunnery officer in the Leyte Gulf when the *Indianapolis* sank. His sub chaser was dispatched but the search was futile and the rescue unsuccessful. The search lasted ten days but nothing was found. In a recent letter to the author, Lancaster stated that his ship was shot at only once but it was luckily just out of range. The part that he found scary was the number of times that they knew they were being watched and tracked but were not shot at for some reason. Lancaster's subchaser was one of about one thousand U.S. warships in the Leyte Gulf when news of the surrender broke. Lancaster described the reaction of the American troops: "the pyrotechnic display from a thousand jubilant ships was fantastic—the best fireworks display ever."

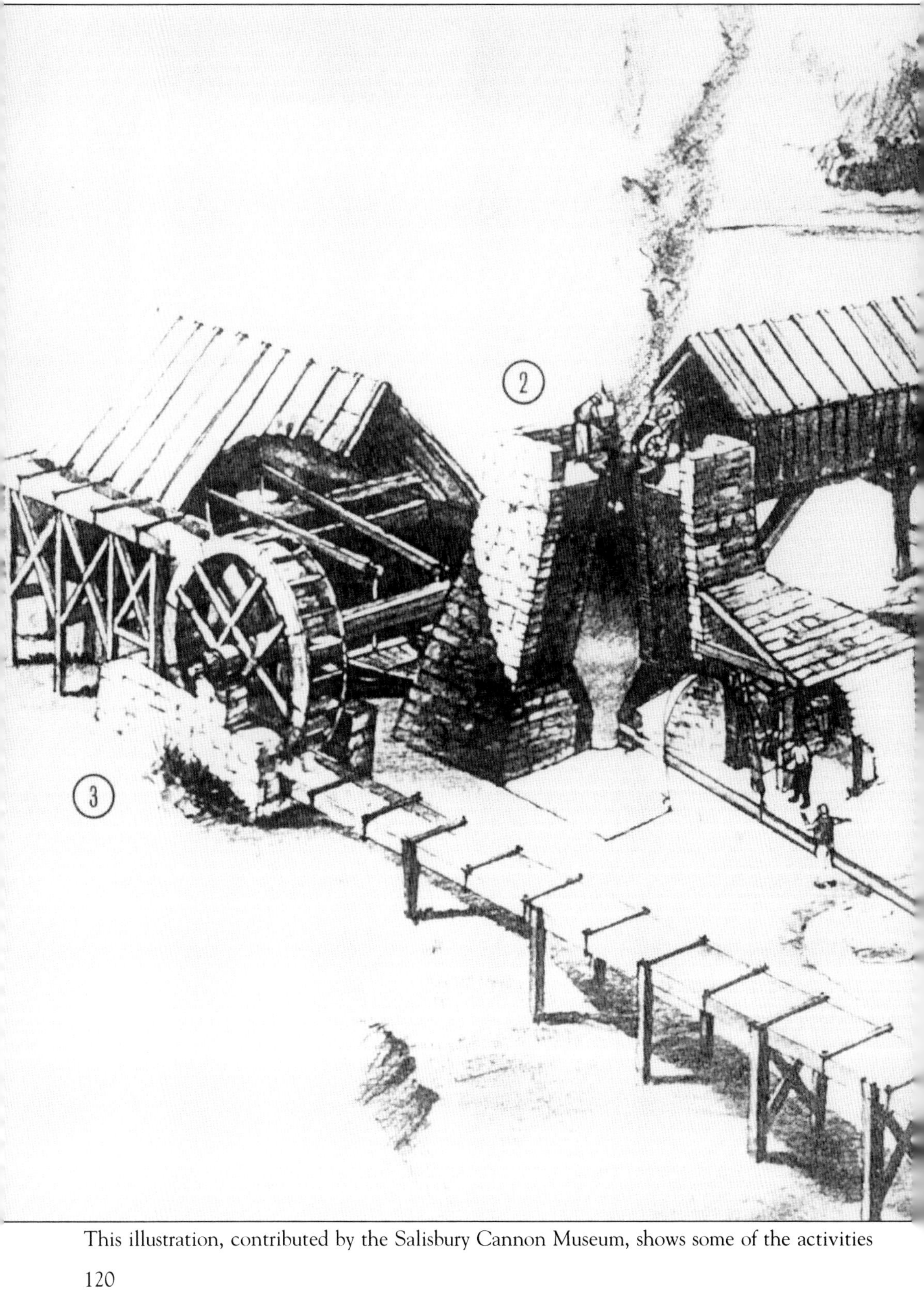

This illustration, contributed by the Salisbury Cannon Museum, shows some of the activities

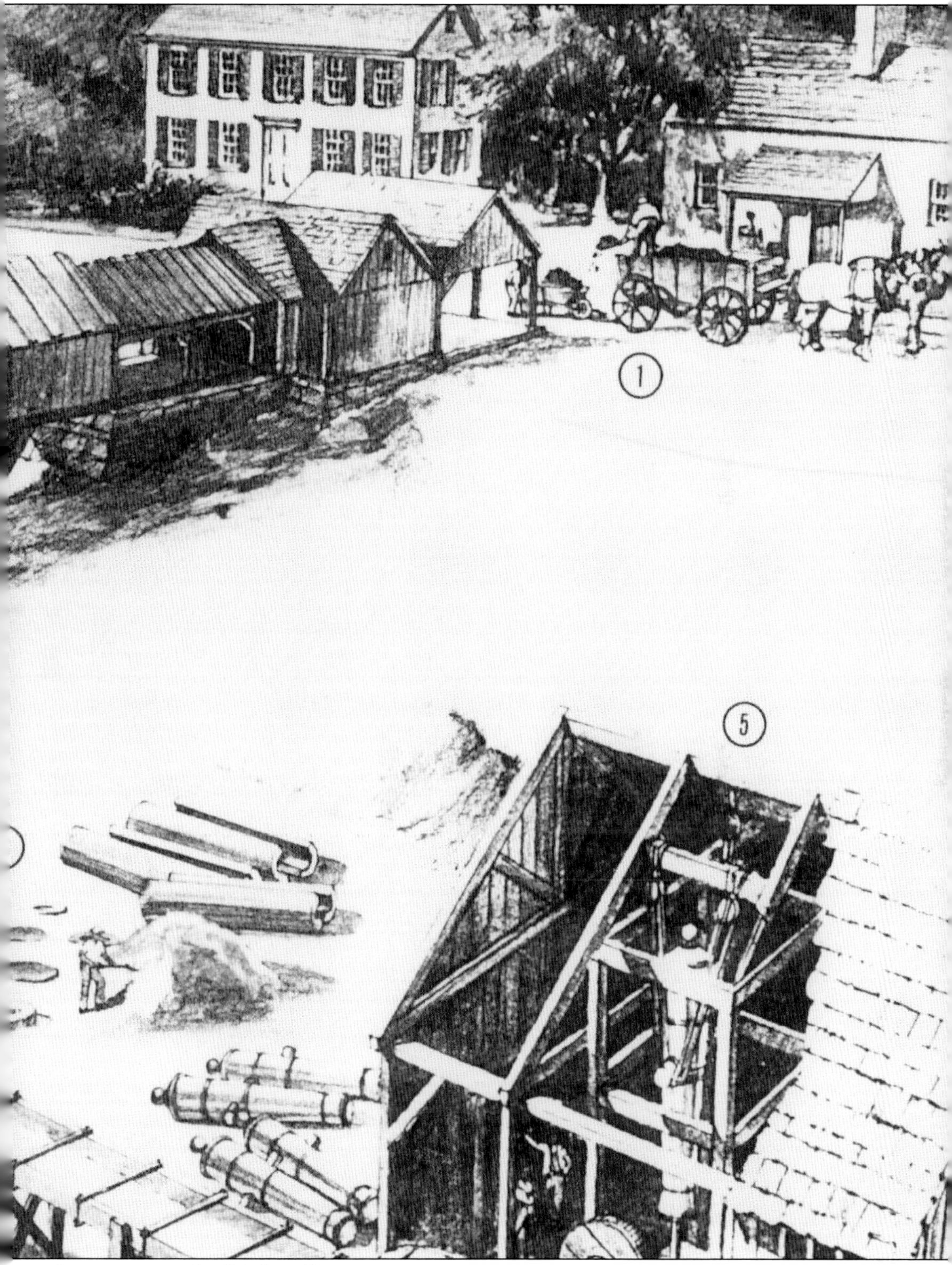

that went on at the Salisbury Furnace.

THE MAKING OF A CANNON

STEP ONE

Delivery of Raw Materials

The making of iron requires three raw materials: iron ore, charcoal and limestone .

STEP TWO

Loading the Furnace

The raw materials were carted by wheelbarrow through the bridge house and fron the top of the furnace stack were dumped into the blazing fire below.

STEP THREE

Compressed Air

The bellows pumped air into the furnace. The compressed air is what created the blast necessary to make the charcoal burn hot enough to melt the iron ore.

STEP FOUR

Filling the Molds

Twice daily, white-hot liquid iron was run off the furnace into molds set muzzle up in the ground. After cooling, the molds were lifted and broken open.

STEP FIVE

The boring mill

The cannon was then placed in a rig and was carefully bore with a drill.

During the eighteenth century, American troops needed cannons desperately, and Salisbury was the place chosen to produce them. Salisbury had large quantities of both limestone and iron ore as well as forests for wood. These were the three most necessary ingredients needed for iron production. Thus, in 1748, the first iron forge was built on the site. Ethan Allen and two partners purchased the site and constructed a blast furnace in 1762. (Printed by permission of the Salisbury Cannon Museum.)

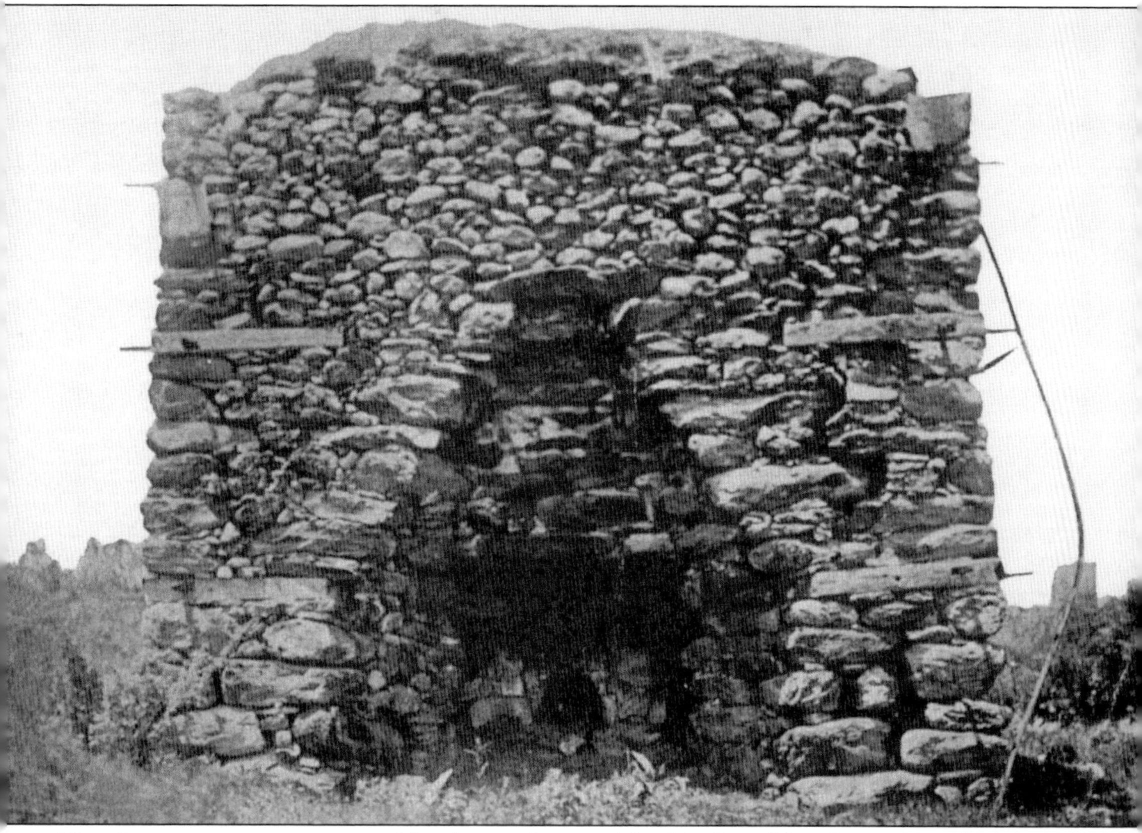

Blast furnaces were a common sight during this era. The Mt. Rega blast furnace was built in 1810 and stood 1,000 feet tall. It was located near a lake (where it got its water power) and a forest (from which timber was cut to make charcoal). These furnaces reached their peak during the War of 1812, when they manufactured the anchors for "Old Ironsides" and the USS *Constitution*. In 1847 the bellows failed and the furnace cooled—every ironmaster's nightmare.

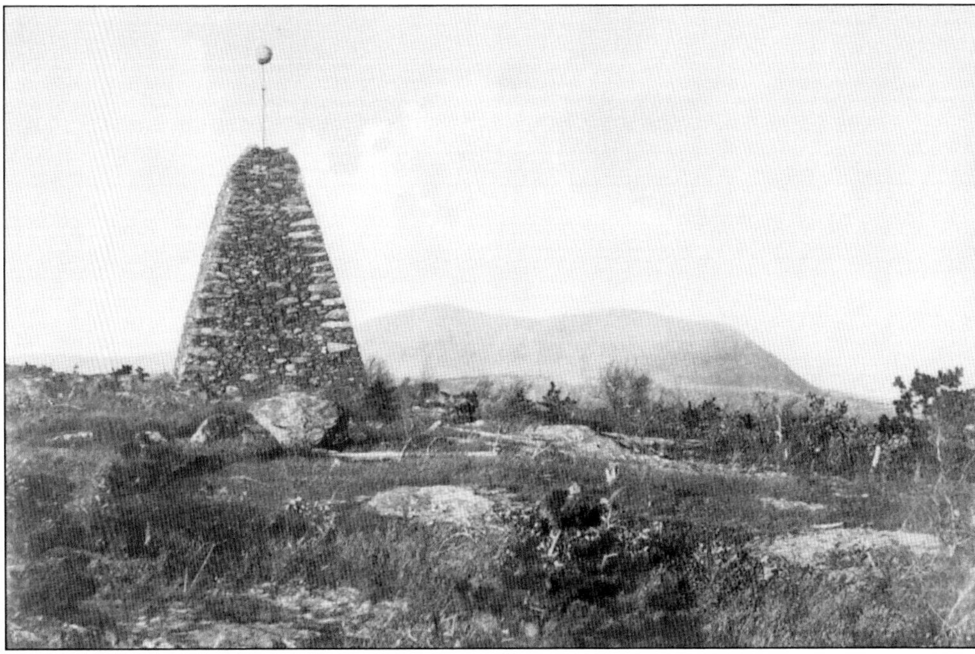

This monument on Bear Mountain marks the highest point of point of land in Connecticut. It is located in Lakeville.

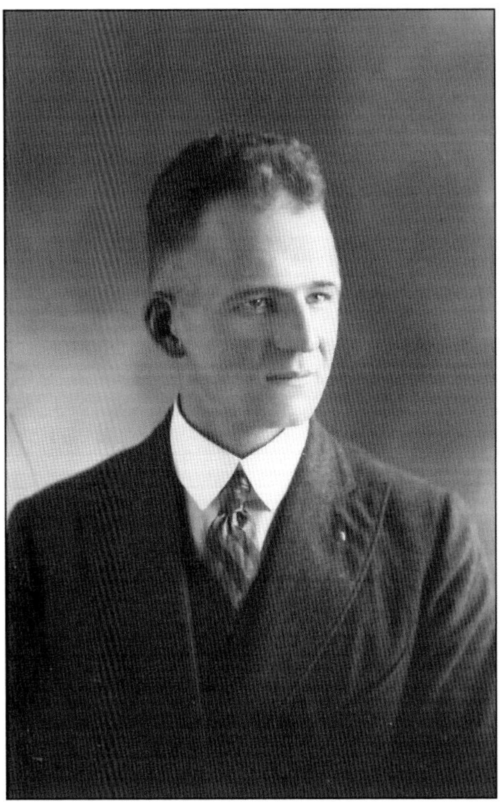

Nathan Hale Strong was named after the Nathan Hale whose parents had married into the Strong line. Nathan Strong served in World War II as a medic in North Africa for the U.S. Army. Nathan Hale was a revolutionary war hero who was captured by the British and condemned to hang as a spy. His last words were "I only regret that I have but one life to lose for my country." Today, his words stand as a lasting testimony to patriotism and courage.

Donald Strong, the brother of Andrew and Nathan Hale Strong, also served in World War II.

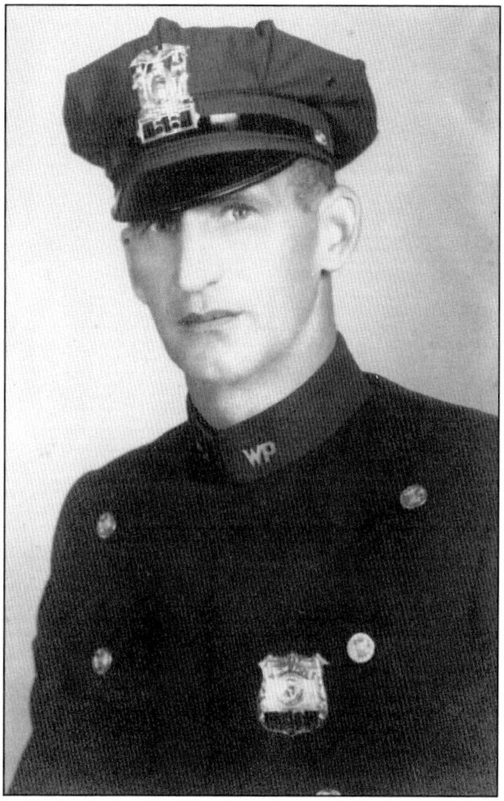

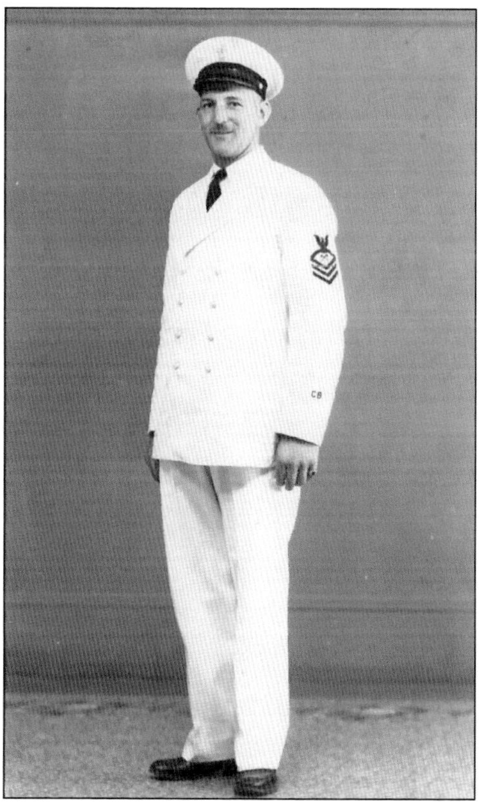

Andrew Strong is the son of David and Alice. He served his nation in World War II along with his brother, Nathan Hale Strong.

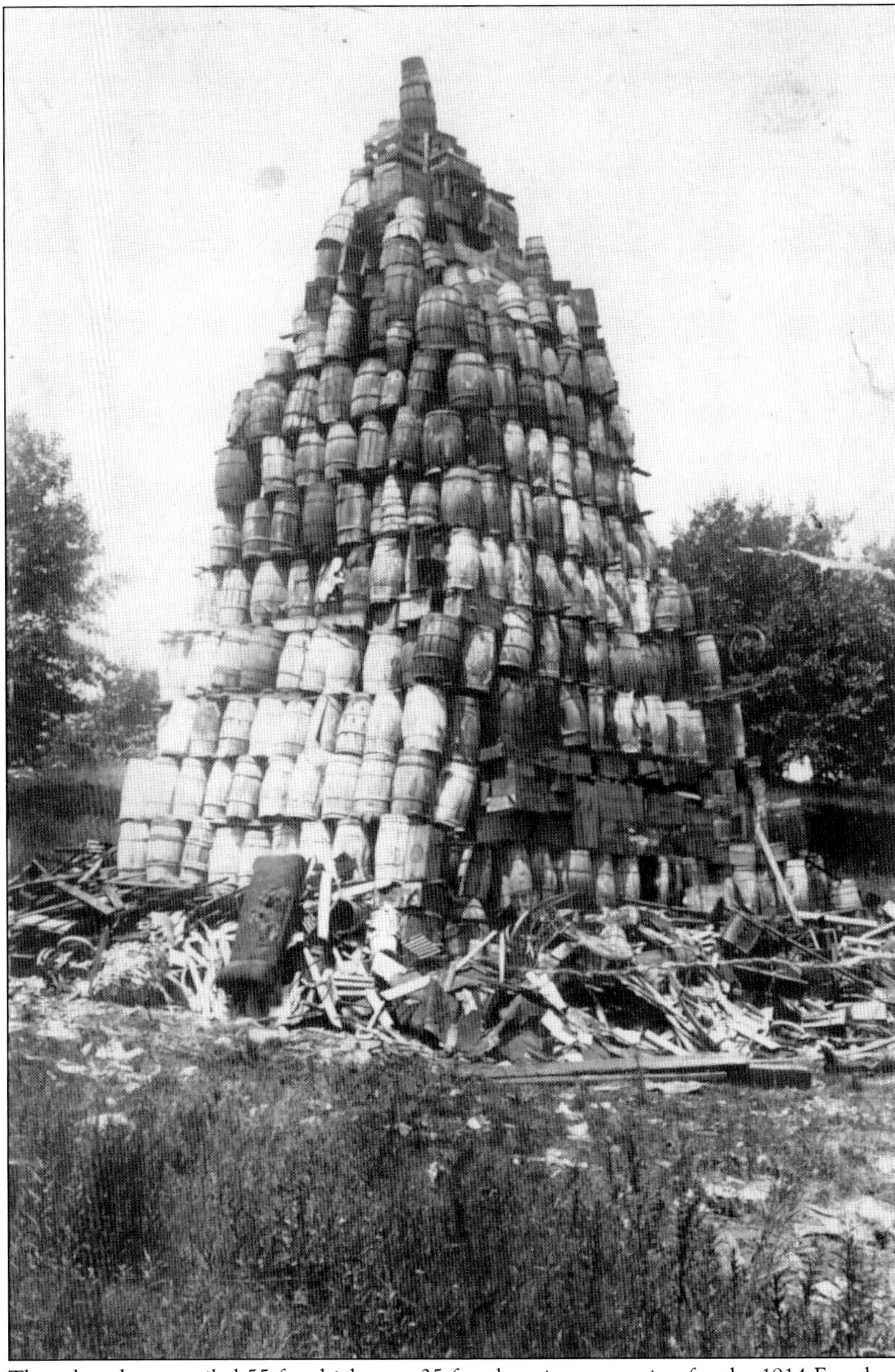

These barrels were piled 55 feet high on a 35-foot base in preparation for the 1914 Fourth of July Celebration.

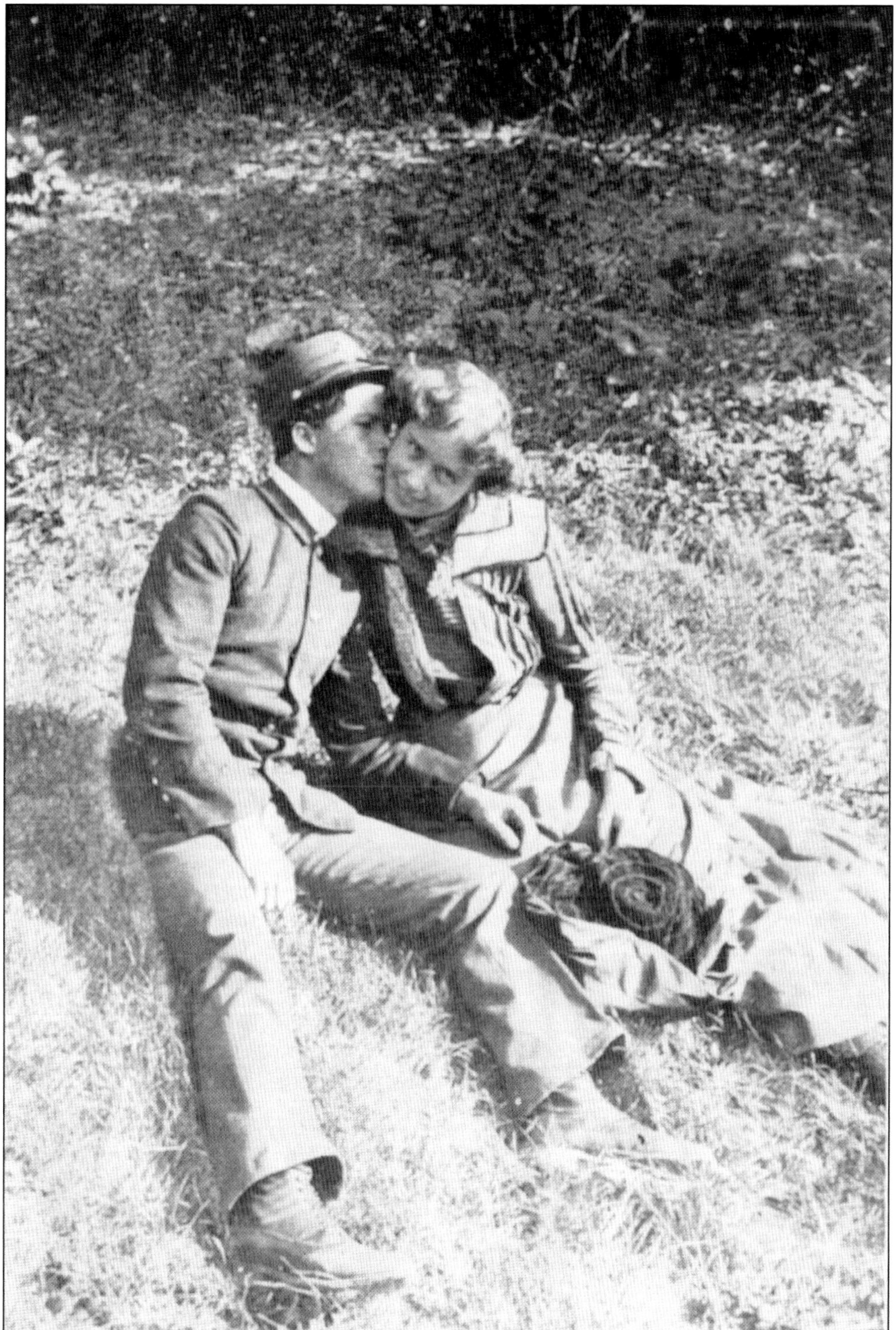

Both peace and war have their victories.

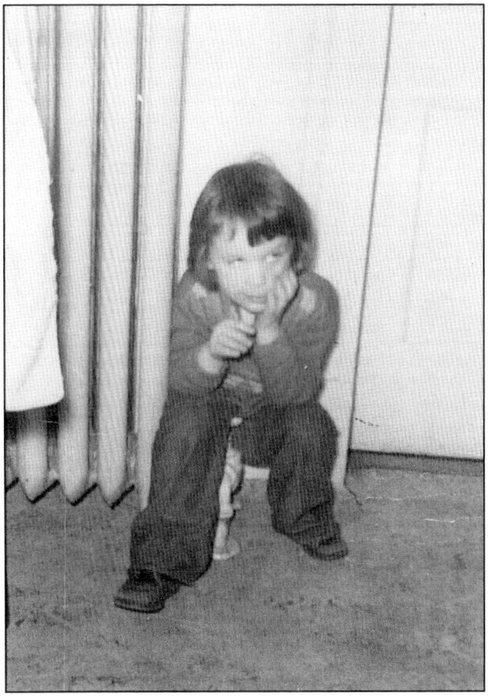

This is a photograph of the author, upon moving to Litchfield, Connecticut, in 1958. Little did I know I would remain in the Litchfield Hills for the next thirty years.

Acknowledgments

While compiling the photographs and historical information for this book, I felt much like the early settlers of colonial New England must have felt, walking through a new frontier. There were challenges to be met, barriers to be crossed, bartering, a building of trust, and eventually a "product" was produced. Such products are rarely the result of the efforts of a single individual, and this one is no exception. There are so many who have helped in this endeavor to capture history in this somewhat unique manner. It required the cooperation and support of friends, family, and strangers as well. It would not have been possible without the individuals who contributed photographs and personal stories (both joyful and tragic), the organizations and historical societies throughout northwestern Connecticut who shared their knowledge and expertise, and those, such as Louise Zubrod, who never doubted a successful ending.

To name those individuals and organizations would require another book but every effort has been made to credit images and textual materials to those who offered them as resources. Special thanks to my sister, Vina McDermott, who also acted as my "local" research assistant, and to Christopher Osborn Jr. (a descendant of the many Osborns who settled and continue to inhabit the Litchfield Hills area), who acted as my personal attendant during my visits to Litchfield. Area newspapers and radio stations supported the effort by helping to "spread the word." The response was at times overwhelming, as people came forth offering photographs, journals, deeds, stories, opinions, and leads to other valuable resources. These individuals have been credited throughout the pages of *The Northern Litchfield Hills*. To those who helped me to "manage" my load and still be my friends, I thank David Clark Jr. and Claudette Lefebvre. To any that I have forgotten to mention or failed in some way to acknowledge, I apologize. I know you are aware of the deep level of my appreciation.